Unpackir

Marcus B. Weaver-Hightower

Unpacking School Lunch

Understanding the Hidden Politics of School Food

Marcus B. Weaver-Hightower
Foundations of Education
Virginia Tech
Blacksburg, VA, USA

ISBN 978-3-030-97287-5   ISBN 978-3-030-97288-2   (eBook)
https://doi.org/10.1007/978-3-030-97288-2

Cover illustration: © William Andrew/gettyimages

This Palgrave Macmillan imprint is published by the registered company Springer Nature Switzerland AG
The registered company address is: Gewerbestrasse 11, 6330 Cham, Switzerland

In memory of my father, O'Neal, and my mother, Faye, who both shared a birth year with the National School Lunch Act and who taught me to love and respect food.

Acknowledgments

I owe a great debt of gratitude to the many people that made this book not only possible but a reality.

Some research for this book I completed during a sabbatical from the University of North Dakota, during which I received support from Rhodes University in South Africa, particularly the Department of English, and from the University of South Carolina. At Rhodes, I thank Dirk Klopper and the Rhodes University Library staff. At the University of South Carolina, I especially owe thanks to Doyle Stevick, Kara Brown, Craig Kridel, and the staff at the Thomas Cooper Library.

Numerous people helped in getting me information and arranging contacts. Jorí Thordarson was a superb teacher on the workings of Canadian policy. Becky Francis and, even more, Nicola Tilt got me access to schools in England. Bekisizwe Ndimande, my (non-genetic) brother, was a source of support and encouragement, and he was my guide at a South African township school. Thank you, representatives at the School Nutrition Association, Healthy Kids Canteen Association, and the Physician's Committee for Responsible Medicine, for speaking with me. Thanks to the staff at the Library of Congress in Washington, DC, and the staff at the British Library for their assistance in finding me some rather obscure materials. Perhaps most especially, thank you to Janet Spaeth and the interlibrary loan specialists at the Chester Fritz Library at the University of North Dakota; I bugged these wonderful professionals more than any others to help me access materials, and they always got what I needed.

I have great admiration for and owe thanks to Michael Nelson and the staff at the School Food Trust (later the Children's Food Trust) in England. They were generous and superb teachers. Thanks to Gurpinder Lalli for helping me understand England's school dinners better, as well.

Faculty and student friends at the University of North Dakota were instrumental to this project. Jacqueline Nyenhuis was a particularly excellent thought partner on nutrition and politics. Hamzat Koriko was a tireless research assistant on this project for several semesters; thanks for making all those calls! So many of my advisees and students in seminars have been subjected to my school food rants, too, so I can't name them all, but I thank them for bearing it! And thanks for the many forwarded stories! Particular thanks to my deans and departmental colleagues there for supporting and advising about my work on school meals for many years.

I thank, also, my new colleagues and students at Virginia Tech, including those in the School of Education, in the Food Studies program (particularly Anna Zeide), and the Center for Food Systems and Community Transformation (especially Kim Niewolny). I've not met Garland Mason in person yet, but her five articles worth reading each week netted me so many insights; thanks for that work on all our behalves.

I have learned a great deal from many scholars working on food studies, but I give special thanks to Sarah Robert and contributors to the collection *School Food Politics*. Sarah was a patient collaborator, and that experience was formative in so many ways.

Naturally I owe special gratitude to my editor, Milana Vernikova, and the others at Palgrave who handled this project with dedication and care.

To my family—my wife, Becky, and my living children, Harrison and Evie—thank you for your patience while I grumpily typed away. Harrison and Evie, thanks for letting your lives in the cafeteria provide fodder for my research. Becky, you were amazing in making the work of this book possible. I always know you love me—and right back at you—but your generosity still floors me. I'll keep trying to make myself deserving of it.

Contents

About the Author

Marcus B. Weaver-Hightower is Professor in Foundations of Education and affiliate in the Food Studies program at Virginia Tech, where he teaches gender and education, sociology of education, and qualitative research. He was awarded a Fulbright fellowship to Australia, where he conducted a year-long study of the development and implementation of the world's first federal-level policy on the education of boys. Before this, he taught high school English and coached girls' soccer in Goose Creek, South Carolina. His research interests include the politics of food, the politics surrounding boys' education, masculinity studies, and the use of comics and graphic novels in qualitative research and classrooms. He has authored *How to Write Qualitative Research* (Routledge, 2019) and *The Politics of Policy in Boys' Education: Getting Boys "Right"* (Palgrave Macmillan, 2008), and he co-edited *The Problem with Boys' Education: Beyond the Backlash* (Routledge, 2009), *School Food Politics: The Complex Ecologies of Hunger and Feeding in Schools Around the World* (Peter Lang, 2011), *Leaders in Gender and Education: Intellectual Self-Portraits* (Sense Publishers, 2013), and *The Wiley Handbook of Gender Equity in Higher Education* (Wiley, 2020). His scholarly articles have appeared in

Educational Researcher, Review of Educational Research, Teachers College Record, Gender and Education, The Journal of Mixed Methods Research, and *Journal of Contemporary Ethnography,* among others. His work was awarded the 2013 Anselm Strauss Award for Qualitative Family Research from the National Council on Family Relations and a 2012 Critics Choice Book Award from the American Educational Studies Association.

Abbreviations

AMS	The USDA Agricultural Marketing Service
CBO	Congressional Budget Office
CEP	Community Eligibility Provision for Universally Free School Meals
CSA	Community Supported Agriculture
ERP	Eliminate Reduced Price
FDA	US Food and Drug Administration
HHFKA	The Healthy Hunger-Free Kids Act of 2010
LACA	Local Area Caterers' Association
LEAs	Local Education Authorities
LFTB	Lean Finely Textured Beef ("pink slime")
NSBP	National School Breakfast Program
NSLA	National School Lunch Act of 1946
NSLP	National School Lunch Program
Ofsted	Office for Standards in Education, Children's Services and Skills
SNA	School Nutrition Association
SNAP	Supplemental Nutrition Assistance Program (formerly known as "food stamps")
STAR	Service to All Relations School
USDA	United States Department of Agriculture
USSGA	United States School Garden Army

List of Figures

List of Tables

1

In School Food, the Political Is Personal

My son Harrison turned five during the research for this book. You know what that means: kindergarten. Suddenly my family was thrown into a world of waking at 6:30 a.m., navigating the confusing parking lot during drop off, getting vaccination records, doing daily homework, turning in school picture money, attending parent-teacher conferences, chaperoning field trips, attending school fairs and parent-teacher organization meetings, and guiding our son in his increasingly complex social relationships. And, of course, I came face to face with the realities of school food in a way more personal than simply studying it. My beautiful, precious son would go elsewhere for nearly ten hours most days, so he would have to eat. Now *other* adults would control what he consumed.

First, and what some think of as all of school food, was Harrison's lunch. Choice was apparently the guiding principle of lunch. Each day, first thing after putting away his Justice League backpack, he chose his lunch by putting a clothespin bearing his name onto the appropriate card. The most basic choice had been made before arriving: school lunch

© The Author(s), under exclusive license to Springer Nature
Switzerland AG 2022
M. B. Weaver-Hightower, *Unpacking School Lunch*,
https://doi.org/10.1007/978-3-030-97288-2_1

or a lunch from home? For a host of reasons—like food quality, cultural eating preferences, lack of vegetarian or vegan options, price, food safety concerns, class anxieties about eating meals "meant for poor kids," and more—parents may choose to pack a lunch rather than having their children eat school lunch. We decided Harrison would eat school food, though. At $2.15 a meal at the time (40¢ for reduced price meals or even free, depending on family income), it was an unbeatable bargain. It meant one less thing to cram into the hectic mornings before school (and who has the energy the night before?!). School lunch was nutritionally balanced, at least when it arrived in front of him; whether he ate it was a different question. And, of course, while perhaps ethically questionable, it gave me a chance to collect valuable data about school food. So he ate school-made lunch.

This seemingly simple first choice, school lunch or packed lunch, actually holds numerous complexities. Perhaps most importantly, it presented a socially important choice to Harrison. He learned quickly that who one was as a person, his identity, was somehow connected to whether one packed lunch or got it from the cafeteria. He wasn't clear on exactly what that entailed, but somehow the message got through: in that school, you're "better" if you pack lunch. The kids with packed meals got to line up for lunch first, and often their parents included highly coveted junk foods, like Twinkies, chocolate bars, and Lunchables—and often sweet notes. We tried to explain to Harrison that packed lunch was not "better," nor did it make the person "better," and we gave him a litany of reasons why. In the end, though, I know—as a sociologist and someone who went to school myself—such social distinctions function as truth (on a bodily, material level) if those around you *act as if* they are true. Metaphysical truth doesn't keep you from envying your friends or from getting looked down on, teased, or bullied.

Back to the kindergartners choosing in the morning, more choices confronted those eating school lunch. Every day they faced at least four lunch options, and they chose first thing so the cafeteria staff would know exactly how much of each to make. This cut down on waste (*before* the kids got it, anyway) and helped ensure more profit for the multinational management company running the cafeteria. (Yes, huge numbers of cafeterias aren't just locally operated but rather contracted

Table 1.1 Actual school menus from Harrison's school

Day	October 1–5	October 8–12
Monday	Chicken Nuggets BBQ [barbeque] Sandwich	Chicken Nuggets Sloppy Joe
Tuesday	Broccoli Chicken Alfredo Cheeseburger	Chili Macaroni Chicken Sandwich
Wednesday	Beef Tacos Hot Ham and Cheese [Sandwich]	Soft Chicken Taco Hot Dog
Thursday	Roast Turkey with Rice Chicken Sandwich	BBQ Chicken with Rice Hot Turkey and Cheese [Sandwich]
Friday	Cheese Pizza Corn Dog	Cheese Pizza Hamburger

with catering corporations like Sodexo or Aramark.) Two of the four daily choices were constants. One was a sun butter sandwich (made from sunflower seed butter, not peanut butter because of allergies), with jelly and without on alternating days. Kids with debt on their lunch account could only have the sun butter sandwich. The other daily choice was a salad, either "Popeye" (after the cartoon character because it included spinach), chef, taco, "peppie" (I think because it featured pepperoni), or "Minnie Mouse" (perhaps because the cucumbers looked like the eponymous rodent's ears).

The other two daily choices varied, but most were what's known as "carnival fare" among some school food reformers (Poppendieck, 2010, p. 1). Think pizza, corn dogs, burgers, fries. Consider, for example, the randomly selected two-week stretch in Table 1.1. Only 4 of 20 selections for a fortnight weren't fast food lookalikes! And remember that students have free choice, with no easy way for parents to monitor, so we had no way to predict or know if Harrison would even choose the four non-carnival entrees. If he or anyone else wanted to, they could eat nothing but sun butter sandwiches for lunch. Or, he could have a two-week diet comprising chicken nuggets twice, cheese pizza twice, a cheeseburger, chicken sandwiches twice, a beef taco, a hot dog, and a turkey and cheese sandwich.

Choice sounds like a great thing. Indeed it underpins our neoliberal sensibilities in modern America, which I discuss further in Chapter 3, and it makes it more likely that students will actually eat the food rather than waste it. Another perspective, however, sees choice as an abrogation of adult responsibilities. Harrison was five years old. Was he choosing lunch based on his long-term growth and his physical and cognitive development needs? Or did he choose what his peers most valued, what made him fit in? Was he choosing what was healthiest or what was most satisfying to his biological cravings for salt, fat, and sugar? After all, what information did he have, as a five-year-old, to make an informed choice? If I had entrusted him with his share of our family budget, he surely wouldn't have necessities like food, shelter, and clothing. No, you would have found him naked and hungry in a field somewhere, surrounded by superhero toys and comic books.

Leaving food choices to kids represents a choice by adults. What does it say about adult priorities? Are we privileging health or momentary pleasure? Are we privileging students' and society's long-term health or the short-term profit (for most, just solvency) of districts and food service providers? Are we privileging difficult nutrition education or the quiescence that comes from giving kids the junk food for which they clamor? We adults make those choices for children when we hand over choices about their food to them. As with all school food decisions, it comes down to Jen Sandler's critical heuristic: "Who feeds whom what, how, and for what purpose?" (Sandler, 2011). Each *who, how,* and *what* in that question represents a political choice we make as a community and society.

The story of school food does not end with lunch, of course. Children and adults encounter and enact school food through myriad practices and events. We overlook food issues often, yet they are numerous and rarely regulated.

For one, other meals happen at school, too. For Harrison, the school day always started with breakfast. His school, like a growing number in the United States, created a "breakfast in the classroom" program, free for all students regardless of income (Food Research & Action Center, 2019). The school could afford this free-to-all system by, first, creatively using the federal subsidies allotted to free and reduced students to buy cheaper food for everyone, and second by having students and teachers do the preparing and distributing. Thus, each day, the lunch-room walls were ringed by big blue, wheeled coolers filled with milk and packaged, processed breakfast products heated or thawed by a skeleton cafeteria crew. A student would wheel the cooler to the classroom where classmates would eat the contents.

Here was October's breakfast menu for Harrison, as written:

MONDAY—Apple Frudel, Orange Juice and Milk

TUESDAY—Snack n Waffle, Fresh Banana and Milk

WEDNESDAY—Breakfast Pizza, Apple Juice and Milk

THURSDAY—Cereal w/Graham Crackers, Fresh Apple and Milk

FRIDAY—Ham and Cheese Biscuit, Orange Juice and Milk

The non-perishable products the cafeteria generally bought as a month's supply to save money and because the highly processed, packaged fare can be stored for long periods without spoiling, thus making waste minimal. And, of course, one cannot help but applaud a system that makes sure every kid gets breakfast, regardless of parental income, late buses, and myriad other reasons kids don't eat in the morning. But one does pause at this menu. Milk, while not uncontroversial (e.g., Coles, 2000; Severson, 2010), is overall a healthy food in my view. An apple and banana are fantastic. The entrees, though, leave much to be desired. Like the lunch choices, most smack of fast-food fare. All are highly processed and mostly full of sugar (Siegel, 2019), and this menu suggests to kids that these are not only *appropriate* choices for breakfast, but they are the *only* choices. Harrison might have seen a different breakfast at home on the weekends, but would the other children?

In addition to meals, schools serve snacks to young children, too. For Harrison and his classmates, snacks proved a crucial part of the day, particularly since they ate "lunch" at 10:30 a.m.! Snack choices seemed similarly suspect. Check out October's snack menu, which they repeated, just like breakfast, week to week:

MONDAY—Animal Crackers, Milk

TUESDAY—Goldfish, Juice

WEDNESDAY—Doritos, Juice

THURSDAY—Bug Bites [Keebler-branded cookies], Milk

FRIDAY—Kids Mix [a Quaker-branded mixture of Cap'n Crunch Cereal; Mini Rold Gold pretzels; Mini Doritos; Smartfood cheese-flavored popcorn; Cheetos; and candy-coated chocolate pieces.], Juice

Milk seems OK. But Doritos? Juice *seems* better than soda, but juice often contains as much or more sugar, ounce for ounce, as soda. While often promoted as if a one-to-one substitute for fruit, juice has few of the whole fruit's benefits, particularly the fiber (Chaykin, 2012, Episode 3; O'Neil & Nicklas, 2008). Animal crackers are better than some snacks, but they are still cookies. Name brands abound in this list, and I know that the kids actually got those name brands, not just a generic. Many schools can get branded items more cheaply than their retail versions because they buy in bulk. Also the companies more than willingly shave off some profit for the brand loyalty built by having their logos and formulations in kids' hands often (Institute of Medicine, 2006; Ludvigsen & Scott, 2009; Molnar & Boninger, 2015; Schlosser, 2001).

My son also went to an after-school program from 2:25 p.m., when school let out, until 5 p.m. or so, when the working day ended for his mother and me. That program gave him a snack, too. They didn't post a menu, but when I picked him up during snack time, he always was eating either a Pop Tart or Doritos (both name branded) and drinking a juice box.

If we add it up, in one week (October 1–5), my son, rapidly growing his body on whatever he ate, *could* well have had the menu in Table 1.2 based entirely on his own choices, and this just at school.

Table 1.2 The worst-case scenario menu

Monday, Oct. 1	Tuesday, Oct. 2	Wednesday, Oct. 3	Thursday, Oct. 4	Friday, Oct. 5
Apple Frudel	Snack'n Waffle	Breakfast Pizza	Cereal w/ Graham Crackers	Ham and Cheese Biscuit
Orange Juice	Fresh Banana	Apple Juice	Fresh Apple	Orange Juice
Milk	Milk	Milk	Milk	Milk
Chicken Nuggets	Cheeseburger	Beef Tacos	Chicken Sandwich	Cheese Pizza
Milk	Milk	Milk	Milk	Milk
Animal Crackers	Goldfish	Doritos	Bug Bites	Kids Mix
Milk	Juice	Juice	Milk	Juice
Pop Tart or Doritos	Pop Tart or Doritos	Pop Tart or Doritos	Pop Tart or Doritos	Pop Tart or Doritos
Juice box	Juice box	Juice box	Juice box	Juice box

Often, too, a well-meaning after-school teacher would surprise students with candy slipped into their backpacks, something Harrison always eagerly looked for when leaving. And as I said, this doesn't include the snacks and treats my wife and I or his grandparents, uncles, and aunts gave him during a week. While we tried to feed him healthy, balanced meals at home, few families can avoid the quick meal out during errands, before or after practices, or for special celebrations. But given this menu from school—the institution we trust to teach him the best, evidence-based way to treat his body—we would be hard pressed to correct his path toward a quick-serve, highly processed, name-branded food lifestyle.

Of course Harrison also got more healthy side dishes served to him each day at lunch. The cafeteria served a highly varied selection of nutritious fruits and vegetables, like (for the same week as above) steamed cabbage, diced pears, apples, sweet peas, celery sticks, applesauce, bananas, pinto beans, baby carrots, diced peaches, candied yams, collard greens, pineapple tidbits, orange wedges, corn niblets, and fruit cocktail. Yet we can't know whether he ate the healthier foods. They must, by law, have been served to him; his tray had to have two servings of fruits and/or vegetables to count as a "reimbursable" meal, making the school eligible to get repaid by the federal government. Yet school cafeterias generate tremendous waste (Buzby & Guthrie, 2002), particularly for fruits and vegetables, and without my wife or me there pestering him to finish his pinto beans, did he actually consume them?

Some will argue, of course, that solely examining foods' names deceives the casual viewer. After all, food service professionals and manufacturers, particularly in schools, have grown adept at making their carnival fare conform to dietary guidelines. Some of this has been done with policy manipulation, of course, like the lobbying efforts to keep "pizza as a vegetable" or to keep unlimited servings of potatoes (see Snack Two). Most changes, though, have come via food technology like vitamin and mineral fortification, fat reduction, whole grain processing, and so on. Thus food manufacturers now engineer their food to make what the menu calls "corn dog" into a vitamin-fortified, whole-grain battered, reduced-fat turkey corn dog that staff bake rather than fry. These products meet the letter of the law on a test tube level, but do they function as healthily in the body (Pollan, 2008)? And what happens to a child's idea of food acceptability when, after they leave school, such highly (but almost invisibly) engineered foods aren't available in the grocery store or local drive-through restaurant? Outside school, the snacks are "real." Inside they are "copycat" snacks, and that plays into the hands of food marketers (Siegel, 2019; Wilking, 2014).

Believe it or not, despite all the children have consumed so far in this chapter, kids still eat more at school than meals and snacks. Some schools, including Harrison's, also regularly have parties; many schools have stopped allowing parties, though. For the Halloween party—called the "Fall Party"—nearly every family of the 27 children sent food. From this massive store of victuals, each student got

- a Little Debbie cake
- potato chips
- popcorn
- carrots
- celery sticks
- ranch dressing

- pretzels
- a cheese stick, and
- a Capri-Sun juice pouch.

Remember, these were five-year-old kids, with stomachs that couldn't possibly accommodate that much food. They had snacks left over that the children ate the next day; basically they had back-to-back party food days! Luckily, Harrison's teacher billed herself as concerned about nutrition; otherwise the carrots and celery might not have been there. "Extras," like parties, students usually celebrated with sweets and other junk foods, which only adds to the pleasure food culture lavished on children.

Food Curricula

Perhaps you're already overwhelmed from the amount of food in schools just from lunch, breakfast, snacks, and parties. Yet the role of Harrison's school in teaching him and his classmates about food does not stop there. Food, as a hugely important facet of human life, appears frequently in the curriculum. He learned how pumpkins grow. There was a whole week with an apples theme. A field trip to the local colonial village included learning to hoe rows and plant corn, to shell the dried corn, and to identify which animals live and get eaten on farms. Harrison learned sight words using a book on barbecuing ("Look at the steaks. Look at the potatoes. ..."). On and on, the quest for food, the science of food, and the cultural meaning of food inhabits the explicit curriculum students experience every day. Yet schools teach myriad implicit lessons about food, too—what education researchers call the "hidden curriculum" (Apple, 1995; Jackson, 1968).

Take as a prime example of the hidden curriculum on food the spring semester unit on "goods and services." The teacher wanted them to learn the basics of business, of work, and about products made and sold locally. The capstone event was a field trip to Krispy Kreme Doughnuts and a Piggly Wiggly grocery store. When asked, the teacher's aide said they didn't intentionally pick food-oriented venues, but "food is always a winner" in getting the kids excited. And the kids were indeed excited. At Krispy Kreme, the manager regaled them with the company founder's rags-to-riches story while the kids stared, awestruck, at a river (literally) of doughnuts and glaze flowing by on a conveyor. After the lecture, the kids sat down for free small pink lemonades and a still-warm "Original Glazed" doughnut. They also left with paper hats emblazoned with Krispy Kreme logos. For the kids it was joyful and exciting and delicious—all the things parents hope for their children. Yet it was not the soundest snack, nutritionally. Look at what each child ingested, based on Krispy Kreme's nutritional information at the time, in Table 1.3.

For a child this age, 380 calories represent between 23 and 31 percent of their day's total, depending on activity level (USDA, 2020, p. 141)— basically a meal's worth of calories. Someone invested in redeeming this snack could say "Well, at least it has some vitamin C, calcium, and iron." Only the vitamin C appears in a proportion befitting the calorie load, though, and children rarely have vitamin C deficiency except in extreme cases of neglect or poverty (Popovich et al., 2009; D. Smith, 2011). (Or maybe long seafaring voyages?!) Balance those few positive nutrients against the other nutritional properties: This snack contains 14% of daily sodium limits, 53% of the doughnut's calories come from fat (the Dietary Guidelines recommend 25–35% maximum), and it had a high sugar content. Because this load of calories comes with little nutritional value (the classic definition of "empty" calories), the kids' bodies have

Table 1.3 Nutrition information for field trip menu

	Doughnut	Lemonade	Total
Calories	190	190	380
Fat (g)	11	0	11
Sodium (mg)	90	80	170
Carbohydrates (g)	21	47	68
Dietary Fiber (g)	0	0	0
Sugars (g)	10	47	57
Protein (g)	2	0	2
Vitamin C (% of daily value)	2	200	202
Calcium (% of daily value)	4	0	4
Iron (% of daily value)	4	0	4
Other labeled vitamins and minerals	0	0	0

two choices: eat more calories to make up the nutrients or eat the right calorie amount but forgo the nutrients. Over the long term, this biological choice creates a recipe for obesity or malnutrition (an imbalance, not necessarily the common meaning of lack)—or even both in cases where seeking out nutrients simply gets met by more empty calories.

I anticipate some readers screaming, either in their heads or aloud, "It's a treat! They're kids! They can't just live on broccoli! Let them have some fun! Haven't you ever had a doughnut? One doughnut won't hurt you!" All true. Harrison ate this snack while I watched. I had a doughnut, too, though not the lemonade; I'm no ascetic. No, the trouble arises from such food not being a "treat" (Siegel, 2019)—meaning just an occasional splurge within an otherwise fruit, veggie, and whole grain-filled diet. As shown throughout this chapter, children attend schools full of carnival fare, and many adults have lost perspective on how often children *really* eat such food. Trouble looms, too, from the messages children get about such food's acceptability and role in their diets. I'll return to that below.

Back to the "goods and services" field trip, the next stop was a Piggly Wiggly grocery store. Perhaps most familiar in the US Southeast (and Wisconsin for some reason), Piggly Wiggly was the first-ever fully self-service grocery store. Before that, grocers retrieved things for consumers from behind a counter; consumers relied on the grocer's knowledge to inform them about their food. Today, grocery stores provide a largely anonymous space where most consumers must make choices relying on the information manufacturers print on boxes and labels (Vileisis, 2008). At Piggly Wiggly, unlike at Krispy Kreme, this history wasn't given. Instead, the manager gave a store tour.

First stop, the bakery. A young bespectacled woman assembled a cake shaped like a clown car while the children looked on, oohing and ahhing. She fashioned Oreo wheels onto a cream horn—"Who likes Oreos?!"—gluing them down with neon icing, and she topped an icing body with a plastic clown head. The resulting dessert was boxed for the class to consume later. The kids also toured the storage area, chorally reading a sign on the cardboard box bailer. They asked questions about where the food came from before it got on the truck bound for Piggly Wiggly. They visited the lobster tank, where all got a chance—those who weren't too squeamish anyway—to touch a live lobster. While it was a great opportunity to learn some science (the manager explained why lobsters have differently sized claws), imagine the poor lobster's distress!

The tour highlighted the cash registers, as well. There the children met "Mr. Pig" himself—a person in a giant costume. Between bouts of hugging Mr. Pig, they got the chance to scan a bottle of "Coca-Cola Classic" at the cash register. Then, a group photo was taken with Mr. Pig; "Let's do it in front of the Coca-Cola display," the manager suggested—a massive wall of boxed Coke 12-packs with an NCAA Final Four basketball theme. We then walked into the produce cooler, where the manager explained that Piggly Wiggly gets lots of vegetables and fruits from all over ("Here's one from Washington. This one is from California"). Even so, consistent with their current advertising slogan, "Local Since Forever"—appealing to foodies and neoconservative protectionists alike—much purportedly came from nearby farms. The manager couldn't actually find any local products right then, though.

Each child was given a photocopied and stapled coloring book, featuring two pages of fruits and vegetables to color and two pages featuring Mr. Pig. The manager also grabbed a big plastic bowl of fresh pineapple wedges for the kids to sample alongside the bagged lunches the school had sent with the kids. The teacher announced that she was passing out pineapple (some of the juiciest, sweetest I've ever sampled); "If you don't want any, just say 'No thank you.'" Many kids did say "No thank you"—a nice lesson in manners—but many kids ate it gladly. Perhaps because he felt bad that some kids weren't sampling the pineapple, the manager soon returned with a huge plastic tub of 4″ sugar cookies covered in sprinkles. The kids were not given the option to say "No thank you" to the cookies later, though I heard that bus misbehavers didn't get one.

This field trip featured much explicit curriculum. The kids learned about businesses and what they do. Sure, they probably already knew about grocery stores and fast-food outlets, but they got to see behind-the-scenes work usually invisible to them. The store managers tried to give age-appropriate lessons; the Piggly Wiggly manager asked them to tell him the starting letter of words they encountered ("What letter does 'palettes' start with?"). Yet much of what the kids also learned was an unspoken, "hidden" curriculum. Brand names were everywhere, from the stores themselves to the products in them ("Who makes the best doughnuts in the world? Krispy Kreme!"). The stores gave away product samples, a sort of taste test for hopefully new customers. The kids went home with logos that their parents would see, on a paper hat and a coloring book. They were met with smiles and hugs and enthusiasm, all building pro-social feelings about those businesses. They learned to distance the terrified lobster in front of them from something they would actually have killed so they could eat it (Stewart & Cole, 2009).

Importantly, the school sanctioned these lessons. Parents tell their children to listen to their teachers and do what they say, so of course students come to believe that if their teacher takes them somewhere, it's good. If a teacher tells you something, it's supposed to be true. What was the teacher's message? Something like, I know you won't want pineapple, but I know you will want cookies. Because she didn't try to disrupt this notion—and there weren't lessons beforehand about how to fit a doughnut into an otherwise healthy, balanced diet—the kids were given no other message than approval for eating this way.

Again, I'm not saying treats are bad or that one should never eat fast food. And I don't expect Piggly Wiggly to make a clown car from broccoli, tofu, and hummus (though I suppose that might get kids to eat those!). I'm not saying the teacher was derelict or a food company shill; most teachers would do the same. I'm also not trying to be a buzzkill. Yet we must recognize limits. When we don't, we produce what we have now: soaring rates of childhood obesity and problems like diabetes, heart disease, high blood pressure, liver disorders, colon blockages, and joint pain—things almost unheard of afflicting children just a few decades ago. Adults often limit children's diets in particularly unhealthy ways by *assuming* that children will only eat certain things—burgers, fries, sweets, and so on. Adults show our own biases about childhood when we only offer them doughnuts, cakes, cookies, corn dogs, pizza, hamburgers, and sugary juice—often to "catch their interest" or motivate behaviors—and when we shy away from offering fruits and vegetables. The message is "sweets = fun and produce = not fun." And kids accept this assumption themselves; researchers Ludvigsen and Scott (2009) found that many kids have come to believe that only certain foods are for kids; if you eat "adult food," you're not a "real" kid. Such messages and practices may literally kill our kids. We are killing them with what we consider kindness: unrestricted, even encouraged access to the supposedly joyful tastes of childhood.

The Hidden Ubiquity of Food Lessons

Clearly, food is everywhere in schools. Alongside the breakfasts and lunches, snacks, parties and field trips, food also makes for learning *material*, a supply with which to work or decorate. It might be used as a positive reinforcement: Get a question right and you get a candy. Harrison's main teacher didn't use food this way, but his literacy tutor did. Food might be used as a manipulative for math: How many M&Ms do you have left if you give three away (or eat them)? Perhaps more unfortunately, food features in some lessons where eating is never the goal, like learning about textures by sticking everyone's hands in it, using it as a seasonal decoration (gingerbread houses and jack-o-lanterns), or making art like macaroni necklaces and corn-roller paintings. Such uses of food painfully disrespect children for whom food is not so abundant that it can be "played with" and for people holding cultural, religious, moral, and political beliefs against wasting food (Hannon, 2006).

The school, of course, also teaches Harrison and his classmates *how* to eat. First, as I mentioned, they eat lunch at 10:30 a.m. The message? Eat when it suits a schedule, the adults' schedule, not the regular rhythms of your body. The students have 30 minutes for lunch, including the time spent getting to the cafeteria, standing in line to get their lunch, and checking out with the cashier. By the time they sit down, they have about 15 minutes to eat. This conveys to them, "Hurry! The food and context hold no importance, so swallow it down and go. Don't think of lunch as a social time where you can discuss the food and learn the social conventions of meals. It's a time to service the body, and only efficiency counts." I saw this myself one day when I joined Harrison for lunch. Most kids had to hurry to eat, with no discussion from teachers about the food and no suggestions that kids try this or that vegetable; the teachers had to cram their lunches in during that short time, too.

Yet the school's reach into the food beliefs of students doesn't stop even after students leave the school's campus. One Friday about 9 p.m., a recorded call from the school informed us that a school fundraiser would occur at the local Sonic drive-in restaurant. Bring the kids and help the school raise some much-needed funds! Teachers would be there working, taking orders, and serving food. Who wouldn't want to boss their teacher around?! Such fundraising efforts go on around the country, with kids and teachers selling candy, gift-wrap, car washes, and on and on. Nationwide, 80% of schools sell food as part of fundraising efforts (Center for Science in the Public Interest, 2007). For the Sonic fundraiser, Harrison's school would get 10% of sales between 5 and 8 p.m. on that Monday night, and any tips the teacher-carhops earned would go to the school. So, for the $24 my family spent, the school got $2.40 plus the $3 tip we gave to my son's physical education teacher for skating the food over to us.

For the school, this fundraiser was obviously a chance to earn money for supplies, equipment, and field trips. Given the constant economic crisis schools endure, they find any such opportunity to involve parents and raise money hard to pass up (Apple, 1995). Yet the lucrativeness of such deals seems suspect at best; the school may get 10% of sales, but Sonic keeps 90%. Even the average vending machine makes more for a school, usually around 33% of sales (Center for Science in the Public Interest & Public Health Advocacy Institute, 2006). It's better than some, though. Campbell's Labels for Education requires families to bring in labels from more than $33,000 worth of soup just to get a $300 video camera (Center for Science in the Public Interest, 2007, p. x)—a measly 1% return.

Sonic, though, reaps a tremendous payoff from a school fundraiser. They got, as I said, 90% of the sales ($21.60 of my $24), and the fundraiser likely brought families who otherwise probably wouldn't have gone to Sonic on a traditionally slow Monday night; Sonic won't hold fundraisers on busy weekend nights. Even more, though, Sonic benefits from the extra advertising. Each household was called twice *by the school* about the fundraiser, prominently repeating the name Sonic. The guidelines Sonic gave (retrieved November 2, 2012, from http://sonicb oomsc.com/documents/FundraisingInformation.pdf) suggested putting out their branded signage the day of the event so that every parent dropping their children off would see the name. And all the school's nearly 600 students came home wearing a sticker emblazoned with the Sonic logo, reminding parents to "Take Me to Sonic Tonight!" (Fig. 1.1). For a company with a modest $22.5 million annual national advertising budget at the time (according to their 2011 Annual Report), advertising to 600 families for the price of a couple of yard signs and stickers yields a high return. Yet this kind of promotion isn't just any advertising, with the commercialism explicit. No, this kind of advertising makes Sonic appear as a benefactor of public education, selflessly "giving up" its profits to benefit children (M. L. Smith, 2004). Perhaps even worse—and ethically questionable—the school does the advertising for Sonic, giving

Fig. 1.1 Harrison's "Take Me to Sonic Tonight!" sticker (3″ circumference)

Sonic's products the tacit endorsement of trusted community authorities. Extra customers, cheap advertising, school endorsements, free labor from teachers (after an already long day), and 90% of the sales: What's *not* to love from Sonic's vantage point?

Parents and the children, though, reap meager benefits from this fundraising arrangement. Many parents likely think, as Sonic says in its advice to schools on the fundraiser, "Everyone has to eat," so why not eat at Sonic *and* get the school some money? The few hundred dollars the school likely made from the fundraiser can buy things to help the children learn and develop. The families can have a fun night at Sonic eating tasty food and socializing with teachers in a different context. Those are positives.

But what about the costs of those benefits? Parents spend lots of money for a relatively small educational return; the $24 we spent would have been much more useful and lucrative as a cash donation to the school. Also, Sonic's food is not the more nutritious versions served at school or advocated in health lessons, making for a difficult mixed message for a five-year-old to resolve. Sonic serves full-fat, fried versions of the engineered carnival fare served in schools; the Sonic we visited didn't even have a salad option on the menu. And while, as critics might argue, the occasional fast-food meal may not harm children's health, fast-food meals are anything but "occasional" for many children. In 2007–2008, a third of children ages 2–11 and 41% aged 14–19 ate fast food *each day* (Powell et al., 2012), similar to 2015–2018 when an average of 36.3% of 2- to 19-year-olds ate fast food on any given day (Fryar et al., 2020). The school endorses such behavior when it invites students to fast-food restaurants and even has teachers sell them the food as "guest" carhops. Even more, though, the school has sold its students as a "captive audience" for corporate advertising, an act both ethically questionable and potentially harmful to students by contradicting curricular messages, displacing other educational activities and healthier meals, and discouraging critical thinking (Jhally, 2003; Molnar et al., 2011).

Naturally many other companies beyond Sonic seek to make money from schools. A huge industry surrounds school food, both in and out of school. Inside schools, food manufacturers and distributors make billions of dollars each year from selling food to districts. According to the

School Nutrition Association (2008), the professional organization for school nutrition professionals, in 2008 pre-K–12 schools accounted for $15.9 billion (with a *b*) in retail-equivalent sales, about 2.5% of *all* US food service and restaurant sales. Districts spend hundreds of millions on the ancillaries of school food, too—things like ovens, refrigeration, trays, cutlery, napkins, uniforms, and software to run the operation. For Harrison's lunch, for just one small example, PayPams, the company that collects lunch money for the school online, charged $1.95 each time I topped up his account. The more times parents fund kids' accounts—as when less economically advantaged parents must put in smaller amounts at a time—the more money PayPams makes. If even just *half* the kids at that one school eat school lunch and topped up accounts once a month (both conservative stipulations), that's nearly $5400 a year. Do the same math for the entire district's 8800 students and PayPams would have made more than $77,000 from a single district (and they contract with "thousands" of schools), just from fees for adding lunch money. And PayPams is not the only lunch account service.

Outside the formal meal programs, because of concerns about rising food allergies and food safety issues, administrators insist parents purchase treats for parties or bake sales at a store so they have a nutrition label and ingredient list. Thus grocery stores and other commercial food vendors get more of a cut, being able to charge for "value-added" (more processed or prepared) goods rather than the raw ingredients that parents can prepare at home.

Restaurants get in on this gravy train, too, not only sponsoring events, incentive programs, and fundraising like Sonic, but also sometimes directly selling their name-branded food right in the cafeteria. In 2009 more than 35% of all US school districts sold fast food brands in their lunchrooms (School Nutrition Association, 2009). Domino's Pizza was the most prevalent brand, showing up in 26.6% of districts nationwide; local pizza restaurants have the same percentage, and they receive the same branding effect. A study of changes from 2007 to 2012 (Terry-McElrath et al., 2014) showed that 10.2% of elementary students, 18.3% of middle school students, and 30.1% of high school students' schools had branded fast food available at least once weekly; 1.3% of elementary, 9.0% of middle, and 19.3% of high school students had it available *every day*. And, of course, farmers and producers benefit from the roughly $1.3 billion annual federal purchases of commodity foods, called "USDA Foods" (U. S. Department of Agriculture, 2021). The feds spend millions more annually to prevent surpluses on commodities like meats, fruits, vegetables, and dairy products—surpluses that would otherwise be wasted or sink the prices. Clearly, school food represents big business for the private sector, no matter its reputation for being a cheap government welfare program (Weaver-Hightower, 2011).

The Politics of School Food

The "realities" of school food—and these are not always like those in Harrison's school, but vary greatly—are tense and complicated. Food's production, distribution, and consumption touches on the emotional, physical, intellectual, cultural, religious, moral, political, economic, and personal beliefs of everyone involved. That includes the students and teachers who eat it, the parents who purchase it, the administrators who manage it, the nutrition staff who prepare it, the distributors who sell it, the manufacturers who process it, and the farmers who grow it. All have a deeply *personal* stake in that food.

Even so, as the old feminist motto rightly taught us, "the personal is political." I use the story of my son Harrison as a jumping off point, a way to illuminate the shadowy parts of school food, what it means, and how we might think about and, perhaps, change it. *Unpacking School Lunch: Understanding the Hidden Politics of School Food* examines the political side of school food, but I always keep in mind the personal connections the actors involved bring to the table.

By *politics* I don't mean the simple division of Democrats and Republicans in the US political system. Certainly these political parties have differences of philosophy, opinion, and policy, but I mean something slightly more nuanced when I say "politics." As a start, consider how Robert Paarlberg (2010) defines food politics:

The struggle over how the losses and gains from state action are allo-
cated in the food and farming sector is what we shall call *food politics*.
The distinctive feature is not simply social contestation about food but
the potential engagement of state authority. If you and I disagree over
the wisdom of eating junk food, that is not food politics. If you and
your allies organize and take political action to impose (or block) new
government regulations on junk food...that is food politics. (p. 2)

Of course, the state (at whatever level) involves itself in *school* food politics, as well. And it's not just the contestation that's important; the state
being on one side of the contest makes the politics higher stakes.

Paarlberg's definition does not go deep enough, in my estimation. Any
serious analysis of school food politics must go beyond nation-states.
As I have previously written, with my colleague Sarah Robert, school
food politics have *transnational* aspects and *local, interactional* levels,
too (Weaver-Hightower & Robert, 2011). As for transnational politics,
we increasingly have our food choices made for us by nongovernmental
organizations (like the United Nations' Food and Agriculture Organ-
isation) and huge multinational corporations (like Unilever, ADM,
Monsanto, Coca-Cola, McDonald's) that don't answer to nation states
in any traditional sense.

If Monsanto succeeds in eliminating all but its own genetically modified
seeds from the market (Patel, 2007), for example, it hardly matters what
any one country's government has to say, much less what a neighborhood
school food reform group wants. Yet this is still food politics. (p. 3)

Regarding the local interactional politics, we must remember that
individuals act outside the state's control, as well. The power to act
relies on many types of capital—economic, social, rhetorical, cultural
(Bourdieu, 1977)—not just the state's traditional powers, so certain
actors' priorities sometimes supersede what the state or the public want.
We see this frequently in education, for example, when Bill Gates'
educational reform wish list shapes policy more (and more quickly)
than the grassroots efforts of hundreds, regardless of what an individual
government wants (Kumashiro, 2012).

Yet, even beyond the transnational and local, politics happens at the *individual* level, as well. We, each of us, live our lives within multiple arenas of politics (Weaver-Hightower, 2008). From the "simple" decisions we make (what we wear, eat, or watch) to the "more complicated" (what political party to work for or against, what to tell our political representatives about how to govern us, what sacrifices we will make for the common good), nearly everything we do has a political consequence. As education scholar Michael Apple (2000) notes, simply turning on a light bulb puts one in a social relationship to the miners who dig the coal that powers that light. That many of these miners die, get maimed, or become ill from this work makes this relationship inherently political. Paarlberg's definition gets it wrong on this point, I think: It *does* involve food politics if you and I disagree, because society has an inequitably distributed capacity to act on a person-to-person level, not just between people and the state. If you and I disagree about junk food but, say, you know the local school district's nutrition director, you can more easily practice politics.

So, food is political at multiple levels, along multiple dimensions of identity, all simultaneously. Individual vegans may practice politics by avoiding meat because of cruelty to animals. Entire countries may wage fiscal or physical battles over subsidizing farming. When a place has not enough to go around, food can provoke uprisings, bitter conflicts, and criminal assaults. Food defines us by gender, too, separating us by who cooks, when, using what implements (e.g., Belasco, 2008; Inness, 2001). Women do most everyday cooking, and this constrains their lives through the "second shift" (Hochschild, 2003) of full-time employment and full-time house- and childcare. Food defines us by social class, as well (Bourdieu, 1984). What you serve guests, where you go out to eat, what beverages you consume, indeed all the food choices you make, reflect the socioeconomic class position in which you grew up or to which you aspire. The politics of food involves what you eat, where you eat, how you eat, when you eat, with whom you eat, and sometimes, sadly, whether you eat.

So it is with school lunches, too. No matter who you are, you have a particular relationship to the lunch served in a school cafeteria today. You may, as a taxpayer, fund that lunch. You may serve it or eat it. You may make policy regarding it. You may teach your children about it. You may care for someone who became ill because of it. Wherever you sit in the complex ecology that school food inhabits, you participate in the *politics* of food.

In this book, then, I treat "politics" as a broad term, meaning the ways ideas, people, and institutions are given or denied legitimacy, power, and resources. In this way, poor kids who may stand in a different lunch line for their free or reduced meal are embroiled in a politics of food. The anorexic girl who denies herself lunch at school in favor of wresting back control of her body from the world around her is immersed in food politics. The vegan teacher who demands his students think critically about what the school serves is entangled in food politics. The principal who accepts a Coca-Cola sign in exchange for the money to buy textbooks is struggling to survive food politics. I, too, have a place within that politics.

About Me

I am not an expert in every topic that touches school food; too many of them exist, as I show in my next chapter's ecological analysis. I am not a nutritionist. I am not a farmer or a food scientist. I am not a doctor (not a medical one, anyway). I am not an agricultural economist. What I am is an educator and researcher of the politics and sociology of schools. Oh, and I worked numerous fast food and restaurant jobs in my younger years, so I know some about producing food at scale.

I am also not a holier-than-thou food saint. In a book like this, some might fear they will have to sit through a food snob's jeremiad. Those worried that these will be the moralistic rantings of a vegan, organic-only gourmand on a high horse about the disgusting over-processed foods served in schools, you can rest easy. Those who were hoping for that might be disappointed. As the comedian Jim Gaffigan (2014, Ch. 3) says, I'm more an "eatie, not a foodie."

My own eating reflects that of most Americans. I eat fast food. I eat processed foods. I eat meat. I don't always pick the organic, fair-trade option, though I have begun to do so more after having researched this book. I eat in the car sometimes. I often eat too many calories, too much fat and sugar, and not nearly enough vegetables and fruit. And I generally *like* school lunches.

In fact, I have always been fascinated by food. Many of my child-hood memories have food as a central element. My earliest memory is my second birthday cake. I remember a conversation with my mother that first showed me the power of words: She told me we were having Stove Top brand stuffing for dinner, and, in my characteristic sarcasm, I asked "Instead of potatoes?!" (playing off Stovetop's 1970s advertising). Later, for dinner, we had potatoes. Obviously my mom didn't get the joke. I remember also the "kitchen sink" sandwiches I made to gross my older brother out, composed of whatever I cobbled together from the kitchen cabinets, including molasses, wheat bread, ketchup, marmalade, and other vile things rolled into an oozing ball. What can I say? I was six and we were latchkey children.

Food has been a continuing object of desire and source of either control or lack thereof throughout my life. I have struggled with weight, gaining 30 pounds, then losing 50, then gaining more. I binge. I find it impossible to leave two cookies in the package (Wansink, 2007). I obsess over particular foods. I crave greasy hamburgers but also appreciate fine cuisine. I take every opportunity to have pad thai, but savor moments with a huge cardboard sleeve of french fries steaming from the fryer. And I still eat peanut butter and honey sandwiches, just like they made in my elementary school; honey was a USDA commodity given free to our cafeteria, so I developed a taste for that combination over the more traditional jelly.

No matter my own views and practices, however, I know that my choices are not entirely my own. I am a member of the first generation of children to come through the US's obesogenic spike in the 1980s. I am shaped, figuratively and literally, by the times I have lived in and the social world I have inhabited. It's an important point to keep in mind—an old sociological debate—that individuals' lives take shape from their own choices (their "agency") and from the constraints of the world as they find it ("structure").

Overview of the Book

In the pages that follow, I delve into the world of food anew, a world both dangerous and comforting for me and for many. In particular, I explore the world and role of school food. What children eat and drink has much to say about society generally and how we value our and others' children. School feeding has been among the largest and most successful social welfare programs in America's history—perhaps the world's most successful (World Food Programme, 2020)—and this speaks to our continuing understandings of food as both material necessity and powerful symbol of human rights. Most importantly, and a central thesis of this book, school food politics essentially involve a competition over who will define the basic terms we use. What counts as "need"? What counts as an educational or human "right"? Or, in splashier debates, what counts as a "vegetable" or "water"? Who ultimately decides who eats what, and who decides how core concepts around school feeding ultimately get defined, makes a huge difference in the lives of millions. That realization drives this book.

To give you the global view, let me outline upcoming chapters. Before you get to Chapter 2, you'll run into the first of five "Snacks" between the large meals that are the main chapters. These five interstitial vignettes dig more deeply into various recent controversies that have arisen in US school food, all of which illuminate, I argue, the priorities and beliefs that guide US child nutrition. The controversies place food at the nexus of almost everything important about human life (culture, religion, economy, health, labor, pleasure, sustenance, safety, identity), not to mention everything important about schools (the care of children, the teaching of culture and skills, health and nourishment, safety). We fight hard over food in schools because the outcome is crucially important. The results of most fights over how we feed people in schools show that some meanings and ideologies ultimately prove more important than others. Just as Michael Apple (1990) reoriented education scholars' thinking about curriculum by asking "Whose knowledge is of most worth?", we might reorient our thinking about school food (itself a kind of curriculum, of course) by asking "Whose values about food are of most worth?" (to paraphrase Sandler, 2011). Who wins when fights break out over food?

In Chapter 2, then, I give the whys and hows of school food in the United States—my focal country, though not the only one I consider. To help grasp the US school food system, I lay out an ecological view of the school meal system, with its diverse actors, in diverse relationships, within diverse environments and structures, undergoing diverse processes. I provide a brief history of the current school food programs, especially the National School Lunch Program and National School Breakfast Program, because this history still structures and constrains the programs today. The chapter also does some theorizing about how policy works—or doesn't—within the US school food domain. Three dynamics, especially, create impediments to reform: diffuse policy responsibilities, multiple competing stakeholders, and internal tensions within the major ideologies. These impediments have created what I term a *palimpsest policy* that holds onto original but outdated purposes for school feeding while layering moderate changes on top. The chapter ends with a tour of some impacts of school food both in and out of schools, for students as well as the economy, agriculture, and the environment. It's a lengthy chapter with lots of facets, but that's emblematic of school food's complexity.

In Chapter 3, I present a central thesis of this book: US school food (and other countries) has been characterized by conservative resistance to food provision and regulation in tension with progressive incrementalism toward healthier, more accessible food provision. Both resistance and incrementalism have prevented major reform. Even so, I focus on conservatives in the chapter, showing how four major conservative ideological groupings identified by Apple (2006)—neoliberals, neoconservatives, authoritarian populists, and the technical/managerial new middle class—all participate in resisting the provision, expansion, and regulation of school meals.

Chapter 4 takes a deeper dive into these four conservative ideologies' rhetoric and specific arguments. I give numerous examples from public debates, thematically arranged into each ideology and into rhetorical tactics, that demonstrate how US conservatives have sought to undermine public faith in the value of school food and its reform.

Chapter 5 shifts the focus to England and the fifteen-year journey of school meals reform there. Starting with Jamie Oliver's high-profile documentary series (Gilbert & Walker, 2005), the UK's school food has gone on remarkable ups and now downs of government attention, policy, and support. The English example provides important lessons to anyone wishing to reform food practices, both supporting my thesis about conservative resistance and examining new neoliberal governance techniques with which reformers must contend.

Chapter 6, then, closes out the main part of *Unpacking School Lunch* with a progressive vision of school meals. It's not enough to simply complain about conservatives resisting any change or, in some cases, attempting to backslide toward less access and fewer nutritional standards. Rather, progressives must proclaim what they stand for, and they must demonstrate how programs can work and the impact those programs can make. To thus put my "money where my mouth is," I present case studies of several schools and districts (among hundreds, maybe thousands out there) doing wonderful things with school food and nutrition education. Not incremental tweaks, but radical things. I end by drawing out some tenets that show what progressives want from school eating and learning.

I include a short coda, finally, to assess the future, particularly coming at the tail end of a global coronavirus pandemic that has disrupted the world but also highlighted the importance of school feeding. If anything, the pandemic showed the wisdom of school food programs, not just for poor children but all children, and it demonstrates the workability of universal free feeding.

This book represents the culmination of nearly 15 years of researching and thinking about school food politics. What you read in these pages comes from my reading of policies and academic studies from around the world. It represents the results of traveling around the United States, to England, to Australia, and to South Africa, where I have interviewed numerous people involved with school food provision. I have been to conferences for school food personnel (what I with utmost affection call the "Lunch Lady Conference," described in Snack Three), to organizations fighting to accomplish various progressive reforms to school food, and to school cafeterias in England and the United States. I have spoken with and read about numerous progressive activists. I have consulted with and written with scholars and practitioners from around the world.

It has taken a long time for me to wrap my head around the complexity of school food and its politics. Yet I have much left to learn. In fact, I originally intended to title this book *Mystery Meat* because school food often seems like a riddle to solve. The metaphor of "mystery meat" feels apt. Nearly every third grader uses this famous phrase for something that kind of looks or tastes like meat, but you can't decide which kind. What animal(s?) does it come from? Sometimes the day's lunch menu helps, but it doesn't always. As I will explore further in the first "Snack" below, sometimes mystery meat has a literal meaning in school lunches, not just a vague aspersion tossed around by insensitive children. The politics around school meals metaphorically seem like mystery meat, too. School food and its processes can seem inchoate, mysterious, complicated. Tracing from what's on the plate back to the ten thousand decisions that produced it can prove difficult. Some people want it kept mysterious because that's how they can make or save money. That fits the nature of school meals as a topic, with connections to so many aspects of schooling, so many people, so many industries, and so many policies. I hope the remainder of *Unpacking School Lunch* removes some mystery, helping show how politics shapes what my kids, your kids, and everybody's kids eat at school. Strategizing how to make what kids eat better starts there.

Snack One: "Pink Slime"

I originally called this book *Mystery Meat*, as I said in the main chapter, in part because it recalls the past decade's most controversial US school food controversy: "pink slime." Pink slime truly represents—or did, given the exposure it got in the US media—a mystery meat. Its technical name is "boneless lean beef trimmings," or at the USDA "lean finely textured beef" (LFTB), but if you've ever seen a picture, you might think "pink slime" fits better. Meat producers use LFTB as a filler in ground beef, to bulk up the product and increase its leanness. It consists of parts and trimmings that might otherwise go to waste, tissue and scraps from near the cow's hide that are especially prone to fecal matter contamination. These bits get pulled off by a centrifuge, ground finely, and then treated with ammonia—yes, ammonia, though a "food grade" kind—to raise the pH level and kill most bacteria (Greene, 2012). What comes out at the end "kind of looks like play dough" (Cox, 2012). Yum.

Though not the first time the product had been criticized, the biggest controversy over LFTB erupted in early March of 2012 when ABC News reported that "pink slime" was used in most retail beef (Avila, 2012). While certainly not the most appetizing looking product by itself, much public uproar more concerned the ammonia treatment and the lack of labeling for products including LFTB. And not coincidentally, people were concerned that LFTB was widespread in school food. As much as 7 million pounds of LFTB had been mixed into the USDA's 2011 supply of ground beef—about 117 million pounds altogether. Experts estimated that "pink slime" was in roughly 60% of US schools' ground beef (Greene, 2012).

Congresspeople called for the banning of LFTB in school lunches. Retail grocery stores halted the use of ground beef containing it—at least temporarily. Major fast-food outlets like McDonald's and Burger King had already stopped using such fillers after Jamie Oliver's US *Food Revolution* television series (Smith, 2010). A petition was circulated by blogger Bettina Elias Siegel (https://thelunchtray.substack.com), which garnered more than 250,000 signers on change.org, asking the USDA to stop serving "pink slime" in the National School Lunch Program.

The USDA's response to pink slime panic? During the controversy's height in 2012, their concession was to make it *optional* whether schools wanted to buy LFTB-enhanced ground beef (Cox, 2012). It was a devil's bargain for schools, because despite the outcry, hamburger cut with LFTB costs less. By the time the agribusiness-friendly Trump Administration USDA got to weigh in on the issue, in 2018, they agreed that LFTB should just be called "ground beef"—no labeling required (Fassler, 2019). You might have had it for lunch today. A lot of US students surely did.

Most food industry experts regard LFTB as perfectly safe. Some suggested that Americans just want to have it all, cheap meat and the "luxury" of not having to worry about its unpleasant production (Ogle, 2013, Conclusion). I'm convinced that people were angry and shocked about this for other reasons, though. Most Americans don't know what's in our food—whether from ignorance or deception (Wilson, 2008)—but sometimes when we find out, we rationally decide we want it out, no matter how safe it supposedly is. Sure, ammonia gets used in other things we eat, like some puddings, but tell me which ones and I won't want to eat those, either. I think many critics of LFTB were responding to adulteration without choice. Some critics, like the USDA microbiologist that coined the term *pink slime*, also thought of it as "cheating. It's economic fraud" (Gillam, 2012). Really, industry wants to have it all, too: as much profit as they can get with the "luxury" of not having to inform consumers about how they make our food.

When it comes to school food, furthermore, the public does have a higher bar—at least in some respects. We don't want to think that children, even those receiving "welfare food," get fed something that many don't see as natural. And we don't want parents cut out of decisions about what public institutions serve their children, because children, developmentally, aren't capable of deciding whether they want ammonia-puffed, centrifuge-cut trimmings and connective tissue included in their burgers and meatballs.

2

The Whys and Hows of School Food in America

Why school food? Why concern ourselves with what many view as a small portion of the school day, a distraction from schools' "real" mission—learning to read, write, do math and arts, and think? Perhaps anyone who has invested in reading this book already has an interest in or concern about what kids eat. Many worry that kids aren't eating healthy food at school and that they aren't learning good eating habits. Some parents want their kids to eat more vegetables, more organic food, more local food, more whole grains, less sugar, less salt, and on and on. These are definitively important concerns—ones I have myself, you'll remember from Chapter 1. Still, while usually the most immediate and the ultimate issue, *what* kids eat is only one reason to consider school food. The public, educators, researchers, and policymakers need to understand and address school food issues for many other reasons, as well.

As I argued in an article about a decade ago entitled "Why Education Researchers Should Take School Food Seriously" (Weaver-Hightower, 2011), people like me who research and practice education must think more about what happens in the cafeteria. Yet education researchers are

© The Author(s), under exclusive license to Springer Nature Switzerland AG 2022
M. B. Weaver-Hightower, *Unpacking School Lunch*,
https://doi.org/10.1007/978-3-030-97288-2_2

not enough; school food broadly touches society in ways few other policy realms do, so school food should ideally enjoy wide civil debate. The reasons for needed public interest match what I said for researchers: School food (a) affects students' health, (b) affects student attainment and achievement, (c) affects teaching and administration, (d) teaches children about food, (e) implicates identity and culture, (f) affects the environment and animals, (g) represents big business, (h) provides a window into educational politics and policy, and (i) impacts social justice.

In this book, I focus mainly on the last three—the economics, policy apparatus, and differential impacts of school food—because we often overlook these in debates about what kids eat. Yet *what* and *how* kids eat get determined more by money and politics than any other factors. Because of that, school food represents a social justice issue *par excellence*.

Moreover, examining school food provides insight into education issues *other than* food. Put simply, school food politics have much to teach us about the ways that conservative politics, particularly, operate across areas of education. Almost no matter the educational policy arena—curriculum, standards, vouchers, homeschooling, privatization, masking during pandemics, and on and on—understanding the conservative techniques and discourses mobilized over school food prove similar and illuminating. The rest of this book lays out this case.

In this chapter, I offer a way of thinking about school nutrition's structure and politics. My conceptualization challenges typical lay perspectives about school feeding. Rather than a direct line from federal mandate to cafeteria to child's stomach, school food politics involves a vast and complicated ecology of tense and competing interests. These interests operate in a US policy arena complexly layered with numerous policies and rules based on oppositional, sometimes outdated priorities. Untangling these, though, aids our understanding of how to make progressive reforms to the system (discussed in Chapter 6).

The Policy Ecology of School Food

Food, perhaps more than any other area of US educational provision, gets directly controlled by policy. While teachers can often close their classroom doors and do what they like with their curriculum and pedagogy, school nutrition programs operate under highly specific federal guidelines, and the government wields multiple means of inspecting and incentivizing compliance. Don't offer enough vegetables? No reimbursement. Want commodities? Most come prepackaged as "CN labeled" food that already meets the guidelines. Too much fat on the menu over the week, violated multiple times? No reimbursement. Keep the vending machines on during lunch? Pay a fine. Provide too many children with free or reduced meals that don't qualify? Pay a fine. In the technical parlance of policy studies, I would characterize US school food policy as distributive, regulatory, redistributive, material, rational, procedural, and regulatory (Anderson, 2014). In simpler terms, school nutrition policy exerts strict control from the top down. Because of this we cannot understand school food without also understanding policies that have shaped it.

One can best grasp school nutrition policy (or any policy), I argue, using an ecological metaphor (Robert & Weaver-Hightower, 2011; Weaver-Hightower, 2008). An ecological viewpoint requires one to consider the vast complexity of creating and implementing a policy. Think of it like the diagrams you might have seen in your elementary school science textbooks. Trees and caterpillars and birds and plants and microbes in the earth, all connected with arrows to show how each feeds off the other. They are all interdependent. So it goes with policy: kids eating at school depends on cafeteria staff, farmers, policymakers, bureaucrats, and more working together to supply the food.

Political science has not always conceived of policy this way. In the mid-twentieth century, for instance, they generally viewed the policy process as a straight line from social need, to finding a rational solution, to policy implementation (Sabatier, 2007, Chapter 1). Many people still think of policymaking in this rather sanitized way. Policymaking reality proves far messier, though. As Stephen Ball (1998) aptly puts it,

National policy making is inevitably a process of *bricolage:* a matter of borrowing and copying bits and pieces of ideas from elsewhere, drawing upon and amending locally tried and tested approaches, cannibalising theories, research, trends and fashions and not infrequently flailing around for anything at all that looks as though it might work. Most policies are ramshackle, compromise, hit and miss affairs, that are reworked, tinkered with, nuanced and inflected through complex processes of influence, text production, dissemination and, ultimately, re-creation in contexts of practice. (p. 126)

Genuinely understanding school food policies requires thinking more complexly about how it comes to be—how this policy "bricolage" gets "reworked, tinkered with, nuanced and inflected"—and an ecology metaphor suits this nicely.

Using my ecological metaphor (Weaver-Hightower, 2008), any policy ecology includes (a) all *actors* involved, (b) in all their complex *relationships*, (c) existing in particular *environments and structures*, and (d) which undergo various *processes*. The *actors* fill the varied roles necessary to maintain the ecology, and many actors perform multiple roles (a cafeteria worker can also be a parent and a reform activist, for example). An ecology's *relationships* fall into four basic types: competition, cooperation, predation, and symbiosis. In other words, actors can, respectively, work against one another, with one another, for the other's destruction, or off one another.

The ecology's *environments and structures* similarly define the resources and barriers for actors and their relationships. These include boundaries, or limits within which actors work and policies apply; extant conditions, or the natural and human sociocultural environments at the time of analysis; pressures toward change; inputs like money, time, human labor, materials, and technology; rates and amounts of resource consumption; niches and roles that actors take up; adaptive decentralization, or the relative lack of centralized control—whether the state or otherwise—over the ecology; and agency, the ability to act within and potentially change the ecology. These environments and structures shape both what already exists—the status quo—and possibilities for reforms. Finally, the ecology's *processes* include dynamics that occur as time unfolds and conditions change. These include the emergence of new policy areas (and their ecologies), the entropy or breakdown of extant policy ecologies, adaptation to altered conditions, conversion of the policy system to a dramatically different form, fragmentation or splitting into multiple ecologies, the succession or replacement of a policy ecology by a new one, conservation of resources, anticipation of changes, and the creation of role redundancy. Because policy ecologies are never stable or fixed, but instead remain in flux, analysts must track such processes to understand why some actors succeed and others do not.

For those not familiar with it, the US's school food ecology, described simply, centers on the National School Lunch Program (NSLP) and the National School Breakfast Program (NSBP), both federal programs implemented by individual states and territories. The federal government supplies most of the money and establishes minimum requirements, but states can set their own standards (if higher) and take responsibility for inspection and training. Any school, even nonprofit private schools, can participate in the NSLP and NSBP. If a school doesn't want to participate, they can opt out. The *vast* majority of US schools—"nearly 100,000" public and nonprofit private schools combined (Economic Research Service, 2021)—participate in the lunch program—around 94% of public schools. A slightly smaller percentage—94% of those serving lunch—also serve breakfast (Ralston et al., 2008; U.S. Department of Agriculture, 2012; U.S. Department of Agriculture, Food and Nutrition Service, Office of Policy Support, 2019). When they participate schools get cash reimbursement for every meal served, the amount of which depends on whether the meal was full-priced, free, or reduced-price. Importantly, schools *must* offer subsidized meals, based on family income. The meal itself must meet certain food- and nutrition-based requirements to get reimbursed. Schools that participate also get surplus agricultural commodities—called USDA Foods—to use in meals, paid for with federal dollars.

So, walk into almost any US school around noon and you'll find kids—no matter their gender, sexuality, family income, race, disability, or other difference—eating some kind of hot meal. It remains perhaps the most universal US schooling experience.

Yet the United States stands as only one among many countries around the world that provide food to students at school. Only 34 countries, in fact, have no national school meals program (Rutledge, 2016, p. 140), and it has little to do with the country's development level, for numerous prosperous European and Oceania countries are among those without programs. Still, to focus on those who *do* have school feeding, the scale of this undertaking is impressive. As the World Food Programme (2020, p. 16) puts it, "At the beginning of 2020, national school feeding programmes delivered school meals to more children than at any time in human history, making school feeding the most extensive social safety net in the world." About 388 million children, they say—half of all children around the world—receive meals every school day. It might be fair to say that eating school meals is the most universal schooling experience around the world, not just in the United States.

Other countries' differences highlight the US system's individuality. In Canada no national feeding program exists, but rather the policies are province-level and thus diffuse. This results in a "patchwork of provincial subsidies, corporate donations, parental volunteer efforts, and non-profit pilot projects," though some pan-Canadian agreements have installed uniform but largely voluntary nutritional requirements (Fawcett-Atkinson, 2020; Kimmett, 2011; Ruetz & McKenna, 2021). Australian schools, similarly, have no expectation for feeding except as a moneymaking volunteer effort; school canteens have historically served as fundraisers for the school council, they don't typically open every day, and recent efforts to improve nutrition are state-level and voluntary (DeLeon, 2011). England, though, has a structure much like the United States', with national reimbursement schemes historically run through local education authorities, but the New Right's conservative reforms in the 1980s damaged the program in ways that Reagan's attempts in the United States never did (see Chapter 5). In the West African country of Ghana, school feeding campaigns began relatively recently, and they focus on poverty amelioration and farmer assistance, but its distribution has been uneven across regions; it also largely gets funded from outside, nongovernmental entities (Morgan & Sonnino, 2008). In Italy, conversely, reforms have largely focused on progressive intentions to inculcate nationalistic ways of eating, with a more seasonal, organic, and local focus (Morgan & Sonnino, 2008). In South Africa, the province-based feeding schemes focus on Black-majority township schools, and generally participation does not depend on whether pupils can pay. In South Korea, politics roiled for years in the late 2000s over whether to give free meals to every student regardless of income—a policy that ultimately passed (Kang, 2011).

What a school meal entails can look different across these countries. In the United States and England, schools generally offer a full meal, often including fast food-like entrees like pizza and burgers. In Italy and South Korea, lunches better resemble balanced meals, with a small protein and vegetables alongside pasta or rice. In Canada and Australia, schools often sell canteen fare, like packaged sandwiches, salads, and snacks. In India, with the world's largest school feeding effort, the Mid Day Meal Scheme (http://mdm.nic.in/), the lunch usually consists of cooked grain with some soup or chapatis and usually vegetables, often eaten with bare hands while kneeling lined up on the floor. In Ghana and South Africa, the schools serve basic foods, generally some kind of maize porridge, supplemented sometimes with vegetables. In many countries, school food consists only of a vitamin-fortified biscuit, but this provides crucial nutrition and sustenance (Drake et al., 2016; World Food Programme, 2013). Seeing these various ways schools provide meals (or don't [Rutledge, 2016]) illuminates the complex determiners within any school food ecology.

The United States has a highly complex school food policy ecology, and multiple competing interests operate within institutional structures dense with varied, overlapping policies. Take the example of just one district from North Dakota, depicted in Fig. 2.1. It underscores the complexities, showing the many actors, each with their own interests, and selected ways they relate to each other.

Figure 2.1 depicts a way to trace where a meal came from and what influenced its specific composition. The particular meal, pictured in the lower left, includes a ham and cheese sandwich on a bun, tortilla chips, a salad with ranch dressing, chocolate pudding, and chocolate milk. (For full disclosure, this meal was served before the Healthy Hunger-Free Kids Act of 2010 requirements, discussed later, went into effect.) Though I paid full price for it (just over $2), this was at that time a "reimbursable"

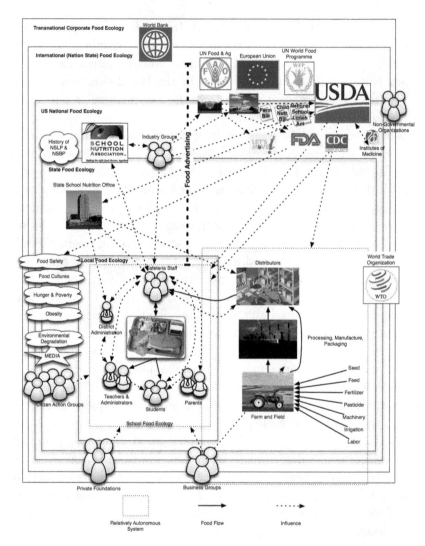

Fig. 2.1 The school food ecology of a single North Dakota school. Update of figure in Weaver-Hightower and Robert (2011), "School Food Politics"

meal, meaning it had the components necessary for the school to get paid back.

The ecology's *actors* bringing me that meal included not only the "lunch ladies" who served it and the janitorial staff who cleaned up after, but also, as the figure shows, thousands of others, including the farmers who grew it and the suppliers of the many components that went into the agricultural enterprise; the food engineers, cooks, and other laborers who manufactured and processed the various component foods; the transportation workers that got the food everywhere it needed to go; the brokers who sold the food to the cafeteria; the district nutrition director who planned the meal, bought the stock, and managed the kitchen staff; the superintendent who supervised the nutrition director's work; the trainers and inspectors at the state nutrition office; policymakers and state education department administrators; USDA officials who oversee the states, the program, and the billions of dollars that fund it; Congress members and their staffs who create and tinker with the legislation; and various agencies that inform Congress or implement their wishes. And, of course, that happens amidst pressures and influence from individuals and groups from the business sector, civil society, the media, transnational corporations, nongovernmental organizations, and more. Given these many actors, each with agendas, interests, and ideologies, no wonder school nutrition policy has been a volatile and impassioned topic since its inception.

Relationships in so complex a system run the gamut of cooperation, competition, predation, and symbiosis. Food manufacturers, for instance, have competitive relationships among one another, but many have a symbiotic relationship with governments because their profits depend on federal money, and they take direction from federal mandates in formulating their products. Yet they also make it possible for the government to incrementally change nutritional guidelines. If, for example, the government wants sodium reduced in school foods, manufacturers accomplish this by changing their recipes and processes. Perhaps the most important aspects of relationships between ecological actors, though, are lines of influence and power. In the United States, the federal government wields much power over school nutrition policy—with mostly only administrative control residing at the state level—and a few influential groups help shape policy directions. These include agriculture groups, perhaps most prominently groups for commodities like beef, dairy, and potatoes; media conceived broadly, for school food has been a hot topic for news, documentaries, reality shows, and more; and the School Nutrition Association, which represents nutrition directors, cafeteria staff, and manufacturers. These groups don't always get their way, but they wield the most relational power to influence school food.

Despite the volatile and passionate debates about it, which I explain later, the US National School Lunch Program's (NSLP) *environments and structure* have been remarkably—and for many, frustratingly—stable over its history. The powerful relationships of certain actors noted above explain much of this stability. Given the NSLP's genesis as an agricultural price support program, explained below, agricultural groups and their Congressional allies have been powerful players in shaping US school lunches (Levine, 2008). Attempts to limit potatoes or eliminate flavored milk in recent years, for example, have been defeated by industry pressure, not by public outcry. And so it has gone throughout the NSLP's existence; its basic structure as an agriculture program first and child nutrition-cum-poverty program second has changed little. Pressure groups have been able to tinker around the edges, especially during some marked periods of instability for the program, but the status quo—a shorthand we might give to history, tradition, and the inertia of social relations—has held its ground (see also Baumgartner et al., 2009).

Every social system, including policy, undergoes changes as times and circumstances change. For school food these *processes* can include, among others, ever-shifting resource conditions (an overabundance of commodity cranberries, say, "encouraging" schools to put them on the menu often); budgetary constraints; changing demographics, like more worldly, sophisticated palettes among students, or growing poverty creating more need; and political demands, such as for more sustainable, healthier food or for cheaper, more efficient service. As we've seen in recent years, this can also include shocks like pandemics and economic recessions. Though US school food continues to experience numerous processes that shape it (the cloud shapes in Fig. 2.1), many important tensions originate in the program's history, starting in the 1940s.

A Brief History of US School Food

Few policies spring fully formed from the ether, without pressure and without antecedent. The US's school feeding program proves no exception. Indeed, several charitable initiatives paved the way for a national school lunch system, providing both infrastructure and logistical information for further growth. Firstly, there were the local charitable programs that operated, usually in major cities, to provide basic nutrition for the poor. The Children's Aid Society of New York was among the first, starting in 1853, but other major cities followed, albeit strikingly slowly. Philadelphia, Boston, Cleveland, and Milwaukee did not start their programs until after the turn of the twentieth century; Chicago and Los Angeles began providing school meals by the early 1920s. Driven by significant public concern over poverty and its learning impacts, these programs arose rather suddenly and underwent intense development over the next few years, many moving from the responsibility of charities to school boards as they proceeded (Gunderson, 2013; Ruis, 2017). Such programs illustrated, through their trials and errors, that school feeding could be done, it could be done economically, and it improved the health and education of children.

Such health and education goals were particularly salient in the run-up to the National School Lunch Act (NSLA) of 1946, which eventually enshrined the current model for school lunches. The United States was exiting the 1930s' Great Depression and finally easing some rationing begun during World War II. Hunger and deprivation were not distant memories, and food scarcity and poverty were taking their toll on public health. Of course, public health has importance itself, but only when poor public health weakened the military's recruiting pool did *federal*-level action become more pressing. When, during World War II, Lewis B. Hershey, head of the Draft Board, estimated one-third to two-fifths of recruits got rejected by the military for "disabilities directly or indirectly connected with nutrition," feeding school children became a military priority, too (quoted in Levine, 2008). Nowhere was this as evident as the 1941 White House National Nutrition Conference for Defense, convened by President Franklin Roosevelt in late May—months before the attacks on Pearl Harbor. Federal officials turned to the quickly developing nutrition sciences for guidance in transforming the American diet, and school lunches were a major, longstanding goal for these scientist-reformers. Indeed, from this conference focused on war preparations came the United States' first national nutritional recommendations, including the now iconic notions of "recommended daily allowances" (RDAs) and "food groups" (Levine, 2008, Chapter 1). Thus began a longstanding connection between the NSLP and the nation's military and democratic goals. Indeed, the preamble to the National School Lunch Act, at its origin in 1946 and to the present day, begins

> It is hereby declared to be the policy of Congress, as a measure of national security, to safeguard the health and well-being of the Nation's children and to encourage the domestic consumption of nutritious agricultural commodities and other food, by assisting the States, through grants-in-aid and other means, in providing an adequate supply of foods and other facilities for the establishment, maintenance, operation, and expansion of nonprofit school lunch programs. (PL 79-396, 60 Stat. 230, § 2)

"National security" purposes appear first, even before "health and well-being." That priority persists to this day, with groups of ex-military leaders like the organization Mission: Readiness (2010) gaining national headlines for decrying the poor health of present-day recruits, now due to obesity rather than malnutrition, and school lunches were their top concern.

Also evident in the Act's policy declaration, school feeding posed an ideal solution for another major problem: volatility in agricultural prices. The 1920s had seen huge nationwide accumulations of agriculture surpluses as farmers tried to compensate for falling prices by producing more and more. Once the Great Depression was in full swing, and starvation and tremendous unemployment became visible problems, the federal government endured tremendous criticism for allowing such surpluses to simply go to waste. How could such waste exist amidst so much want (Poppendieck, 2010, pp. 48–54)? To address this, Section 32 of the Agricultural Adjustment Act (1933) gave the US Secretary of Agriculture the ability to purchase surplus foods and donate them to schools and state welfare offices. Thus, giving commodities to school lunch programs became the first federal foray into school feeding. Later, to also address massive unemployment, the federal government added Works Progress Administration workers to help prepare school food. It's the agricultural support, though—paying farmers for their surplus to avoid commodity prices going down—that has remained a major component of the National School Lunch Program.

This origin, crucially, contradicts what many believe about the school lunch program; school feeding did not begin as a citizens welfare or educational program, though those were certainly benefits. Understanding the program *then and now* requires recognizing that it mainly operates to serve the economic and social interests of powerful groups and institutions—the military, economic interests, and agriculture. I'm absolutely not saying that individual and social benefits derived from the school lunch program are unintended or cynical. Yet children's nutritional benefit nearly always comes second to other concerns, and the historical record bears that out.

The interwar and Depression-era policy rationales noted above—military, agriculture, and welfare support, combined with existing school feeding and commodities programs' knowledge and experience—presented a compelling case for a national school food program. Much work still lay ahead, though. In formulating the program's final structure, legislators had to navigate another vexing US social issue of the 1940s: race. The lunch program's biggest proponents, in fact—Georgia senator Richard Russell, whose name the law now bears, and Louisiana senator Allen Ellender—explicitly supported segregated schooling and white supremacy (Levine, 2008, pp. 76–87; Ruis, 2017, Chapter 6). In creating the law's final form, these Southern politicians held off all suggestions and amendments that included direct federal control over the program. They insisted from the start that passage would depend on funding being distributed by the states. A state-based system, they argued, would ensure that federal officials could not interfere with "local custom"—a euphemism for segregation, Jim Crow laws, and institutionalized white supremacy. Many others saw this states' rights discourse for the racism it was, including Adam Clayton Powell, a New York congressman, who fought for an amendment to deny funds to any state that discriminated based on race. While Powell's amendment eventually passed, it did not challenge "segregation"—only "discrimination," which segregationists denied on semantic grounds—so no funds were ever withheld from states, even those who maintained unequal, segregated school systems for another twenty years (Levine, 2008, pp. 82–87).

The National School Lunch Act

After all the wrangling over the Act's formulation, the resulting National School Lunch Act signed into law by President Truman in June 1946 was a remarkably short policy document given its contested origins and current complexity. The original Act takes up about five pages—succinct compared to the 84-page Healthy Hunger-Free Kids Act of 2010—and consisted of eight divisions. I explain each division below because this original formulation still defines the program's operations today.

The aforementioned "Declaration of Policy" set out the intention to provide military, welfare, and agricultural supports through a program of "assisting the States, through grants-in-aid and other means." This phrase proves crucial, for it puts the onus of implementation on states, which was key to maintaining white racial dominance in Southern states and deeply segregated Northern cities. States would decide how to distribute money and resources.

The Act's second division, "Appropriations Authorized," also proved crucial to the program's shape and politics, for it gives control to the US Secretary of Agriculture. This responsibility allocation has been a major point of contention, with many wondering why the Secretary of Education does not run it and thus avoid apparent conflicts of interest between child health and agribusiness profit. The US Department of Education didn't exist at the time, of course; education was not even a cabinet-level issue until the Department of Health, Education, and Welfare in 1953, though there was an advisory Office of Education within the administration when the NSLA was signed. The Office of Education had nowhere near the USDA's clout or capacity, though. And because the clear intent of NSLP's framers—particularly Richard Russell—was to have the program provide economic development to poor, rural agricultural areas, not having the program under the USDA's auspices was a deal-breaker (Levine, 2008, pp. 73–75). That did not settle the issue, though, as some still call for transferring the program to the Department of Education, the Department of Health and Human Services, or even the Centers for Disease Control and Prevention (e.g., Cooper & Holmes, 2006).

The NSLA's third division, "Apportionment to States," set out the first means testing used to distribute the funding to states. The agricultural intent—again, a key requirement for agriculture-heavy Southern and Midwestern states' congresspersons—shows in the allocation of 75% of the funds for commodities and food purchases. Those funds, and another $10 million in non-food aid, were to be distributed by multiplying each state's children by the state's proportion of per capita income compared to the national average. Despite whatever charges of self-interest we might bring against the law's framers, this provision clearly shows their intent did include poverty alleviation.

The Act's fourth division, "Direct Federal Expenditures," allowed the Secretary of Agriculture to spend up to 3.5% on administration, and the remainder was to be used "for direct expenditure by him for agricultural commodities and other foods." This finally codified the commodities program that started in 1935. Here was the authority to, say, buy up surplus pork or peaches and send them to schools to figure out how to use them (pork with peach sauce, anyone?!), all the while preventing drops in pork and peach prices for farmers.

In division five, "Payments to the States," the legacy of states' rights discourses and racial segregation becomes clear. This division established the disbursement of federal funds "by the State educational agency," rather than to individual districts and schools, as was the case with federal assistance previously. Southern states insisted on this provision to avoid challenges to segregated schooling from having payments made to individual districts and Black schools. State-level politics, they perhaps realized, would form a bulwark against any big cities' challenges to segregation policies held dear in more suburban and rural areas. Importantly, this division's other requirements provide the only major difference between the program as intended and as it survives today. Originally the Act called for states to make a one-dollar match for every federal dollar, increasing over time until the states paid $3 for every federal dollar, with a percentage reduction for states with per capita incomes below the national average. States do still put funds into the provision of school lunch, but it has never come close to the rather hopeful $3 match the original Act anticipated. Rather than short-term aid for getting programs off the ground, the National School Lunch Act has become a (thus far) permanent program supplying the majority of the funding for meals.

The Act's sixth division, titled "State Disbursement to Schools" was largely logistical, outlining what schools could and couldn't pay for. It also laid out the basis for per-meal reimbursement, which has become a program hallmark. In this provision lies the route that the NSLP took toward becoming largely a welfare program with a strong technical/accounting ethos.

Division seven addresses "Nutritional and Other Program Requirements." The first part, packed with several important provisions, first commands that the Secretary of Agriculture set nutritional requirements "on the basis of tested nutritional research." It does not spell out, however, who would provide such research, which has spurred modern conflicts over nonprofit versus industry-funded research (Nestle, 2007). This first section of division seven begins a battle over just *whose* definition of nutrition will win the day.

The same division creates the blunt split between free and reduced-price lunches, which on its face looks like a progressive social welfare tool, but the resulting means testing creates tremendous difficulties of under-enrollment, charges of fraud, paperwork nightmares, stigma, and deep concerns about fairness (Poppendieck, 2010, Chapter 7). Nevertheless, the initial tripartite cost structure—free, reduced-price, and full price—has remained remarkably stable across the program's history; it answers conservative moral concerns that those who *can* pay something *should*. This three-level price structure also, somewhat accidentally, created one of the most often used (and often problematic) measures of social class in US education research (Gorard, 2012; Harwell & LeBeau, 2010). Presciently, the Act's framers also mandated in this section that schools could make "No physical segregation of or other discrimination against any child … because of his inability to pay." Still, the struggle against stigmatizing the program and its child-beneficiaries continues, as examples of subtle and not subtle differentiation between free and paid lunches still crop up (see Snack Five), resulting in many students and parents feeling stigmatized (e.g., Abdouramane, 2016; Bailey-Davis et al., 2013).

The seventh division of the Act, finally, established that NSLP participants be nonprofit entities. While still most programs operate as nonprofit, being run internally by school districts, the impressive growth in contracting school lunch provision to corporations and other private enterprise (now at 20% of schools)—not to mention marketing and selling brand-name food—marks another aspect of the program that has not always lived up to its original ideals (U.S. Department of Agriculture, Food and Nutrition Service, Office of Policy Support, 2019, p. xvi). Many organizations profit from program funds.

While the Act's seventh division established the NSLP as a nonprofit feeding program, this does not preclude private schools from participating. The division's second section provides that private schools can participate, even in states that prohibit giving funds to such schools, but private schools in those states must deal directly with the federal government and schools would still pay matching funds. Today, however, most states administer private school participation in the program, and thousands of private schools participate. Thus, much like the ability to provide state funds for textbooks and transportation to private, even religious, schools, from the beginning food provision has crossed the public–private school divide.

The NSLA's eighth and final division, "Miscellaneous Provisions and Definitions," as its name implies, contains a hodgepodge of requirements and policy prescriptions. The first two seem innocuous enough: schools and states must keep records and make them available for audit, and the Agriculture Secretary can make any reasonable demands on those running the program. Other requirements in this last division, though, provide a window into the Act's aforementioned racial politics and its historical moment. Paragraph C says:

> In carrying out the provisions of this Act, neither the Secretary nor the State shall impose any requirement with respect to teaching personnel, curriculum, instruction, methods of instruction, and materials of instruction in any school. If a State maintains separate schools for minority and

for majority races, no funds made available pursuant to this Act shall be paid or disbursed to it unless a just and equitable distribution is made within the State, for the benefit of such minority races, of funds paid to it under this Act.

The "just and equitable distribution" mentioned was left to the states themselves. Not surprisingly, in segregated states this distribution followed the existing "separate but equal" doctrine that kept Black schools anything but equal. Thus we see embedded in school lunch, perhaps the most successful social programs in US history, a struggle to continue policies of white supremacy, fought primarily using federalism's divisions between state and federal authority to maintain that racist system. We might, then, also view the continuing fights over school food as an extension of a racial politics, a fight deeply connected to other programs seen as welfare. In the United States, welfare politics *are* race politics (e.g., Schram et al., 2003). This has profound implications for anyone who would theorize school food. As Jen Sandler (2011) deftly argued, race politics provide a key to understanding the answers we might ask about "*who feeds whom what, how, and for what purpose?*," and that has been true from the policy's beginning.

Since the NSLA

Formulation of the National School Lunch Act did not stop with its original signing, of course. It has evolved, now encompassing three major bills rather than just one—the Richard B. Russell National School Lunch Act, the Child Nutrition Act of 1966, and the Healthy Hunger-Free Kids Act of 2010. This evolution in the program's history proves important, for it can be difficult from today's vantage to see the NSLP's historical intent. The average citizen now sees it solely as a program for poor kids. As I detail above, though, that overlooks perhaps more important impulses for the program, particularly the economy, the military, and—despicably—as a tool in the racist project of segregation. Indeed, the program's noticeably slow expansion in its early years strongly suggests that poverty amelioration was a low priority.

It wasn't until the mid to late 1960s that attention was paid to the program's hunger relief effects—really, the lack thereof. Widely publicized reports and images of impoverished peoples created concern that vast swaths of the United States were living in poverty, and that the lunch program was doing little in those areas. Subsequently the 1970s saw dramatic expansion of both funding and programs, including the National School Breakfast Program (perhaps inspired in large part by the Black Panther Party's free breakfast program [Blakemore, 2021]) and other school-based nutrition programs (Levine, 2008). Though President Nixon (1969) noted upon election that "the moment is at hand to put an end to hunger in America itself. For all time," his administration was more hindrance than help during the largest expansion in the program's history (Poppendieck, 2010, p. 63). It was Congress that pushed for expansion; Nixon's accomplishments lie mainly in creating the infrastructure within the USDA for administering the growing list of nutrition programs and, less helpfully, in opening the NSLP to private businesses. Despite Nixon's obstructions, the 1970s saw Congresses expand nutrition programs—including the newly created Special Supplemental Feeding Program for Women, Infants, and Children (WIC), elderly programs, summer meals for children, and more—by tenfold, from $1.25 billion to $12.5 billion (Poppendieck, p. 73). While these expansions helped much-needed food reach hungry and impoverished children, they also not-so-helpfully focused public attention on school lunch as a "welfare" program.

Connection to welfare nearly proved fatal for the program in the 1980s, when worldwide conservative political resurgences threatened to slash all but the most rudimentary social safety nets. Margaret Thatcher was wildly successful in destroying the meals program in England (detailed in Chapter 5), and Ronald Reagan—riding into the presidency on widespread anger over taxation, food price hikes, gas shortages, and a flagging economy—nearly did the same in the United States. Reagan and other conservatives blamed the nation's economic problems on federal spending on social programs, constantly painting them as wasteful, prone to fraud (the "welfare queen" image), and encouraging of sloth and dependency. Reagan's administration thus quickly targeted

the NSLP and other domestic social spending. They annually but unsuccessfully pushed to end federal oversight for school food by converting
direct funding (reimbursing per meal) to block grants (lump sums) to the
states. Through the 1981 Omnibus Budget Reconciliation Act, though,
they successfully reduced the subsidies for all meals, hiked reduced-price
meal charges, ended equipment grants, and increased the paperwork
requirements for free and reduced-price meals. The result was a devastating dropout of nearly one-fourth of the programs' participants—in
real terms, millions and millions of children were forced to stop eating
meals at school. For those trying to provide the meals, Reagan's neoconservative, neoliberal reforms resulted in what Poppendieck (2010, p. 73)
called "a very concrete quadruple whammy: fewer lunches sold, smaller
reimbursements for each meal provided, a smaller commodity entitle-
ment, and expensive new accounting requirements." Rather than take
the politically unpopular step of killing school meals with one stroke,
Reagan's administration simply tried to slowly defund them to death.

Reagan's attacks might have been just as successful as England's conservatives were but for the administration's strategic mistakes that were
lampooned mercilessly in the press and by Democrats. Here I'm referring to the infamous "ketchup as a vegetable" rule. In attempting to help
struggling foodservice directors find ways to eliminate around 25% of
their operating budgets after the 1981 reforms, the USDA developed
several suggestions and rule changes that could save money while still
trying to meet nutritional standards. One of their suggestions, alongside
cutting portions and using meat substitutes, was counting pickle relish
and other condiments as vegetable servings (Sinclair, 1981). Democrats
had a field day, taking to the Capitol steps to demonstrate the meager
fare that students would get if the new rules were enacted, including
ten french fries with ketchup counting as two vegetables. The public
backlash was swift, and though the administration pulled the recommendation days later, the whole affair tainted all future cuts Reagan proposed.
Indeed, it remained a lasting image of his presidency, even mentioned in
prominent obituaries when Reagan died in 2004 (Berger, 2004). Nevertheless, conservative attacks on school meals continued throughout the
1980s and into the 1990s. They focused at various times on cutting
funding, making the program a block grant, reducing waste, eliminating

fraud, cutting subsidies for full-price meals, and increasing the private sector's role. Perhaps tainted by the backlash against Reagan, however, few major cuts have been made to the program since. It has, instead, remained perhaps the most popular US social programs ever created, and funding has increased.

School nutrition's popularity, in fact, made possible the reforms of the late 2000s, some of the most dramatic since the 1960s expansion began. The Healthy Hunger-Free Kids Act of 2010 (HHFKA), led by the administration of Barack Obama and pushed as part of First Lady Michelle Obama's *Let's Move!* program, took a decidedly more progressive turn from the Reagan era decline. The HHFKA established the first calorie maximums for the program, added the first non-inflationary raise to per-meal reimbursements (6¢), made hundreds of thousands of children eligible for free meals by directly certifying those on other public assistance, and allowed the Secretary of Agriculture both to tighten nutritional standards and—for the first time since the 1970s—to set nutrition rules for "competitive" foods like à la carte purchases and vending (Samuels, 2010). Other key reforms included gradual targets for reduction of sodium, increases in whole grains, and more vegetables and fruits, including the requirement that schools serve students a half a cup of fruits and vegetables to have the meal reimbursed. Certainly it had problems—a lack of clarity about the extent of changes required to make nutritional standards work, a paltry rise in reimbursements, and not enough attention to infrastructural issues—but even as incremental as it seems, the HHFKA represented the biggest change since the NSLA's passage.

Amidst a global recession and still roiling from debates over health-care reform ("Obamacare"), HHFKA was a tremendous victory for Democrats, though the law was vehemently opposed and procedurally blocked at times by Republicans for its costs and its new federal rules (Associated Press, 2010). Sarah Palin, former 2008 vice-presidential candidate and at the time still a popular voice of Tea Party Republicans, even protested the law by bringing cookies to a Pennsylvania school visit; she sent a message to her Twitter followers in advance saying, "I'll intro kids 2 beauty of laissez-faire via serving them cookies amidst school cookie ban debate; Nanny state run amok!" (Palin, 2010). (More on such conservative beliefs in Chapters 3 and 4.) And the battling didn't end with the HHFKA's signing. Instead, what followed included numerous fights over proposed nutrition rules that would limit certain foods ("pizza as a vegetable," "french fries as a vegetable," "pink slime," and lamentations about hungry football players—most of which I discuss in Snacks at the end of chapters) and continued legislative maneuvers intended to roll back parts of the legislation.

When the conservative Trump administration took office after his surprise victory in the 2016 election, the rollback of nutritional standards installed during the Obama administration began immediately. The far-right House Freedom Caucus, a group of Trump's most ardent supporters in Congress, rushed together a list of "Rules, Regulations, and Executive Orders to Examine, Revoke, and Issue" in the first 100 days (Meadows, 2017). It was authored by Mark Meadows, then Republican representative from North Carolina, who in 2019 became Trump's chief of staff. The first of its 303 suggestions was to end reimbursements for full-priced meals served through the National School Lunch Program. Think of it: suggestion #1 was to reduce school food funding. Tenth was ending the mandate for schools to create wellness policies required by the HHFKA. Fourteenth was repealing the nutrition standards for food sold in schools under the HHFKA, those that had given the Secretary of Agriculture the power to set standards for food served in schools *outside* of school lunch, too.

Sure, the Department of Agriculture sits alphabetically first in the list of government agencies, but the order of individual suggestions within departments appears otherwise random. Meadows could have started slashing with the alphabetically first Agricultural Conservation Easement Program, which helps protect wetlands and grasslands from overdevelopment. But school lunch received first priority on his list to drastically reduce.

Trump's Agriculture Secretary, Sonny Purdue, also had the deregulation of school food high on his list of priorities. He was sworn into office on Tuesday, April 25, 2017. He had as his first three public events a Farmer's Roundtable with the President that same day, a "bipartisan" breakfast with four members of the House agriculture-related committees on Thursday, and then on Monday he was announcing his first policy initiative. You guessed it: school lunch reforms. He stood at a podium at Catoctin Elementary School in Leesburg, Virginia, to announce that the USDA's first move would be to "Make School Meals Great Again" (U.S. Department of Agriculture, 2017). (Insert your own joke about when school lunches were "great" before. This phrase played off Trump's campaign slogan in 2016, "Make America Great Again.") Purdue's plan—a granting of Meadow's 14th wish—was to cancel whole grain requirements, sodium reductions, and limits on higher-fat versions of chocolate and strawberry milk. These were agribusiness industry hopes come true, even after years of effort to reach near universal compliance with standards meant to reduce obesity and other health concerns. Once again conservatives' economic imperatives were coming to the fore in school meals policy.

With its history laid out before us, some distinct political patterns emerge that can inform our understanding of both the past and the likely future of US school food. If we want to talk of the future, we need theories that explain how school meals and the policies that shape them get made. I turn to that in the next section, and I demonstrate these theories' application in later chapters and "Snacks" between chapters.

Theorizing School Food Policy

School food policy in the United States has conformed well to Baumgartner and Jones's (2009) framework of *punctuated equilibrium*, where long periods of stability and status quo (the *equilibrium* part) get *punctuated* by moments of significant change. Because the status quo of an existing policy usually proves difficult to overcome (Baumgartner et al., 2009), the NSLP's history since 1946 has largely involved tinkering at the edges to expand the program or make it fairer, more efficient, or more nutritious, rather than undergoing radical reforms. This slow policy evolution has largely been due to incrementalism from progressive political forces, which have largely had to work against conservative resistance or outright hostility (see Chapter 3). (See Haskins [2005] for another explanation of progressive slowness: special interests and lobbying.) Looking at Table 2.1, one can see a large *quantity* of laws

Table 2.1 History of amendments to the National School Lunch Act, 1946–2012

Year	Public Law #[a]	Name
1946	79–396	National School Lunch Act
1952	82–518	[unnamed][b]
1962	87–688	[unnamed]
	87–823	[unnamed]
1966	89–642	Child Nutrition Act of 1966
1968	90–302	[unnamed]
1970	91–207	[unnamed]
	91–248	[unnamed]
1971	92–32	[unnamed]
	92–153	[unnamed]
1972	92–433	[unnamed]
1973	93–13	[unnamed]
	93–150	National School Lunch and Child Nutrition Act Amendments of 1973
1974	93–326	National School Lunch and Child Nutrition Act Amendments of 1974
1975	94–20	[unnamed]
	94–105	National School Lunch and Child Nutrition Act Amendments of 1975
1977	95–166	National School Lunch Act and Child Nutrition Amendments of 1977
1978	95–561	Education Amendments of 1978
	95–627	Child Nutrition Amendments of 1978
1980	96–499	Omnibus Reconciliation Act of 1980 (Title II)
1981	97–35	Omnibus Budget Reconciliation Act of 1981 (Title VIII)
1984	98–459	Older Americans Act Amendments of 1984
1986	99–500	School Lunch and Child Nutrition Amendments of 1986
	99–591	[corrected version of 99–500]
	99–661	Child Nutrition Amendments of 1986 [Division D]

Year	Public Law #[a]	Name
1987	100–71	Supplemental Appropriations Act, 1987
	100–175	Older Americans Act Amendments of 1987
1988	100–237	Commodity Distribution Reform Act and WIC Amendments of 1987
	100–356	[unnamed]
	100–435	Hunger Prevention Act of 1988
	100–460	Rural Development, Agriculture, and Related Agencies Appropriations Act, 1989
1989	101–147	Child Nutrition and WIC Reauthorization Act of 1989
1992	102–337	[unnamed]
	102–342	Child Nutrition Amendments of 1992
	102–375	Older Americans Act Amendments of 1992
	102–512	Children's Nutrition Assistance Act of 1992
1994	103–448	Healthy Meals for Healthy Americans Act of 1994
1996	104–149	Healthy Meals for Children Act
	104–193	Personal Responsibility and Work Opportunity Reconciliation Act of 1996
1998	105–220	Workforce Investment Act of 1998
	105–336	William F. Goodling Child Nutrition Reauthorization Act of 1998
1999	106–78	[unnamed agricultural appropriations] Changes name of the National School Lunch Act to the "Richard B. Russell National School Lunch Act"
	106–170	Ticket to Work and Work Incentives Improvement Act of 1999
2000	106–224	Agricultural Risk Protection Act of 2000
	106–472	Grain Standards and Warehouse Improvement Act of 2000
	106–554	Consolidated Appropriations Act, 2001
2001	107–76	Agriculture, Rural Development, Food and Drug Administration, and Related Agencies Appropriations Act, 2002

(continued)

Table 2.1 (continued)

Year	Public Law #[a]	Name
2002	107–171	Farm Security and Rural Investment Act of 2002
2003	108–7	Consolidated Appropriations Resolution, 2003
	108–30	[unnamed]
	108–134	[unnamed]
2004	108–211	[unnamed]
	108–265	Child Nutrition and WIC Reauthorization Act of 2004
	108–447	Consolidated Appropriations Act, 2005 (Division A, Titles IV & VII)
2006	109–97	Agriculture, Rural Development, Food and Drug Administration, and Related Agencies Appropriations Act, 2006
2007	110–134	Improving Head Start for School Readiness Act of 2007
	110–161	Consolidated Appropriations Act, 2008
2008	110–234	Food, Conservation, and Energy Act of 2008
	110–246	Food, Conservation, and Energy Act of 2008
2009	111–8	Omnibus Appropriations Act, 2009
	111–80	Agriculture, Rural Development, Food and Drug Administration, and Related Agencies Appropriations Act, 2010
2010	111–296	Healthy, Hunger-Free Kids Act of 2010
2011	112–55	Consolidated and Further Continuing Appropriations Act, 2012

Note Based on analysis of Title 42, Chapter 13, Sections 1751 to 1769j, of the United States Code. Laws current as of June 13, 2013. Retrieved 26 June 2013 from 143.231.180.80/browse.xhtml
[a]Public laws are designated by the Congress number, in order by two-year terms, and the numerical order in which it was passed
[b]Only laws given a title or short title within the act itself have been named

that have altered or that implicate the original NSLA. Most of these, however, made minor adjustments rather than major overhauls.

I argue, principally, that school food remains so controversial nearly 75 years after becoming federal policy, because the policy's fundamental political tensions have never been resolved. The United States still struggles with key debates: whether the government should provide nutritional aid to individuals; whether such aid robs individuals of drive and self-direction; whether federal aid infringes on basic, often religious beliefs about culture, gender, race, and class; whether the government can tell us what to eat; whether support for this program benefits children or corporations. Put simply, when arguing about school food, we are arguing over basic definitions of fairly common words and who gets to define them: What is *food, democracy, education, poverty, welfare, rights, freedom*? These current arguments, at heart, replicate arguments going on in the 1940s when the NSLA was created (see also Levine, 2008).

If I'm correct that fundamental tensions remain unresolved, it still begs a question: Why should so controversial a policy exist in such equilibrium? Why haven't these tensions been solved? Or at least, why wouldn't wild policy swings between the two poles of thought occur, varying by who has electoral power? These tensions, not unexpectedly, make US school food policy both hard to reform but rife with attempts to reform it. Following, then, I explain three dynamics—among other possibilities—that have helped determine the current school food system's stability.

Diffuse Policy Responsibilities

One major impediment to large-scale reform arises from the *diffuse* nature of school food policymaking and implementation. In the United States, the federal government oversees implementation by states that then oversee implementation by local school districts who usually oversee multiple schools. This diffusion produces a significant tension, namely that local control endangers major top-down reforms, for conservative forces can struggle for the status quo or undercut progress. In any event, though, local control has allowed for some localities to pressure the whole system to innovate in progressive ways. California's progressive laws restricting sodas in schools, for example, might not have happened without local control, and California's success has forced changes to the whole system given the state's huge population, like industry agreements not to sell beverages over a certain calorie count. If school food were completely the province of federal control, what recourse would progressives have when right-wing movements control governments (and vice versa)?

Multiple Competing and Cooperating Stakeholders

School feeding's wide variety of stakeholders present another major reform tension, for it has competing interests over its many "outcomes"—financial, health, ideological, military, religious, racial, cultural, nutritional, academic, and more. Even the policy preamble's split of purposes—military, child welfare, and agriculture—creates a three-way conflict of interests. That conflict both provides for, on one hand, equilibrium when none of the three domains suffers unresolved issues and, on the other hand, provides impetus for change when one purpose garners renewed public or media attention. When at war or feeling threatened, for example, the school lunch program's military purpose can push reform (e.g., Mission: Readiness, 2010). When poverty suddenly makes the evening news, child welfare concerns do the pushing instead.

We must not mistake school food politics as only local or national concerns. Indeed, the biggest impediment to major reform comes from the global interconnections of the *entire* food system. Any changes to school food now implicate global actors, both international and transnational in scope. For example, proposed rules from the USDA in 2011 that sought to serve fewer potatoes in school meals had wide implications, provoking resistance from numerous actors at every level of the ecology. Potato growers, of course, resisted losing any market, particularly in an increasingly competitive world food economy with constantly diminishing profit margins (Roberts, 2008). While farmers tend to be the face presented for the impacts of such "restrictions," messing with sure sellers like french fries caused grave concern for transnational corporations, too. Sodexo and other transnational school food contractors can buy french fries cheaply (often bolstered by rebates and bulk purchasing discounts), and fries store easily, require no cooking skill, and almost guarantee sales (Komisar, 2011). Restricting potato consumption thus would have hurt management companies' and school districts' bottom lines. Further, if the USDA Agricultural Marketing Service (AMS) were to reduce purchases of even surplus potatoes—never mind what schools spend out of pocket—some of the world's largest food manufacturers stood to lose millions. Based on my secondary analysis of 2013 AMS data alone, of its nearly $69 million in potato surplus purchases, the AMS bought $2,522,893.50 worth of potatoes in various forms from Allen's Inc.; $2,357,848.00 from ConAgra; $5,714,359.20 from Heinz Frozen Foods; $1,128,400.00 from J. R. Simplot; and a whopping $16,707,748.48 from McCain Foods USA (Agricultural Marketing Service, 2014). By 2019, based on my secondary analysis of the Fiscal Year 2019 Purchases summary, commodity potato purchases rose to nearly $75 million, including multimillion dollar purchases from 15 different suppliers; McCain Foods was again the largest at $19.7 million. That's for potatoes alone! Again, that doesn't begin to account for hundreds of millions school food programs likely pay from their normal budgets for fries and other potato products. The same resistance comes up from any other industry—dairy or beef, for example—when faced with a reduction in the key K-12 schools market.

Put simply, US school feeding has provided food manufacturers and growers a major advantage, shielding them from the true rigors of the international market—soaking up surpluses, keeping prices higher, generating revenue, providing subsidies, and ensuring a captive market of school children. Purchases in the 2012 K-12 school food market segment represented 4.4% of total US foodservice purchases—every fast-food outlet, restaurant, and cafeteria (School Nutrition Association, 2013). Food industries can't give up that amount of their sales lightly—not to mention inculcating future customers—so any suggestion that schoolchildren "eat less" of anything predictably causes massive resistance (Nestle, 2007).

Even amidst high competition for ever-scarcer food dollars, compelling evidence suggests that *cooperation* may cement the status quo of school food, too—or at least prevent progressive reform. Powell and Gard (2015), for example, argue persuasively that "ensembles" of interests have converged to put public health education under the purview of transnational corporations like Coca-Cola. Such cooperation provides a "win–win–win" situation for those involved. Corporations re-brand themselves as providers of healthy products for rational, freely choosing consumers who practice self-responsibility; neoliberal governments divest themselves of the responsibility for creating and paying for sustainable food environments (see also *heterarchies*; Ball, 2010); and overburdened schools and teachers can meet the mandates for health education despite any lack of independent training and resources. One can hardly consider these partnerships a "win" for students and parents, yet these shared interests forestall progressive reform, particularly given corporations' simplistic "eat moderately, exercise more" messages.

Internal Tensions in Political Ideologies

We must not forget that each ideology has its own internal tensions—contradictions in a stance's basic logic—such that even within a single political party significant disagreement can exist about how to proceed. Nutrition provides a prime example. Within the US Republican party, a strong libertarian streak argues against the government telling people what or how much to eat, so attempts to reformulate nutrition guidelines often rankle, particularly for those who sell that product, even if eating less of something represents the best nutritional advice (Nestle, 2007). Simultaneously, though, conservative ideology holds that government programs should operate with maximum efficiency, and poor nutrition would undermine that goal and increase healthcare costs. Hawkish Republicans also see the benefits of the program for military fitness, which requires a nutritionally balanced diet. These competing doctrines within conservative ideology make it difficult for Republicans to mount singular, coherent reforms to the school lunch program. The Democratic Party has similar internal contradictions it must confront, with its own

radical factions preferring one solution to school food problems (vegetarian offerings, say) over other less radical solutions (like adding a few
pennies per meal to the reimbursement rate).

Given the diffuse nature of policy responsibility, the multiple stakeholders, and the internal contradictions of the political ideologies that
fight over school food, reform has been understandably hard to come by.
Yet such fights do not occur between equal competitors. Instead, some
actors clearly have more social, economic, and cultural capital with which
to wage battles over school food. Some political ideologies clearly have
more media outlets blaring their messages. Some policymakers have more
policy levers at their disposal. Neglecting such power imbalances would
create a toothless, vapid understanding of school food politics.

In this section I have perhaps underplayed *structural* components that
shape chances of reform, choosing to focus instead on the agency of
particular actors. To redress that, I turn to a dynamic inherent with the
policy itself—one that incorporates the earlier discussion of history. This
dynamic involves the accretion of policy mandates, layering new ideas
on top of old rather than starting fresh, creating a status quo that has
remained difficult to overcome in the intervening 75 years.

US School Food Policy as Palimpsest

Centuries ago, writing materials like parchment, made from animal
skins, were relatively rare and valuable, so scribes often recycled them
by scraping off old texts and writing new ones over them. Curators
and historians call these *palimpsests*. Their value, though, comes from
still being able to read the original text underneath. The so-called
Archimedes Palimpsest, for example, has as its topmost text a thirteenth-
century prayer book—valuable enough in itself. Peeking through that
text, though, are seven texts by Archimedes, the famed Greek math-
ematician and inventor; two of those texts exist nowhere else. With a
palimpsest you can see valuable information at varying levels.

US school food policy acts much like such palimpsests. In making
changes to the NSLP and NSBP over the years, lawmakers have tended
to add rather than subtract, and much of its underlying structure has

remained the same, and visible, despite major changes to the US's social, economic, and health milieu. One might visualize the palimpsest of school food policy as in Fig. 2.2, where individual policies get rewritten over time, other policies get added, and so on, until it results in a deeply complex policy arena, with remnants of the original policy intent visible beneath subsequent fixes. Put concretely, you can still see most parts of the 1946 National School Lunch Act in current policy of the twenty-first century.

Lingard and Douglas (1999) were the first to use the metaphor of policy palimpsests, but they saw the palimpsest-like quality of policies in teachers' adjustments to the policy during classroom implementation. Think of it like this: When classroom teachers begin implementing a new curriculum or pedagogy based on a policy, the policy intention shows through, but the teachers will put their own stamp on it, their own approach that largely fit their previous stances on practice. Carter

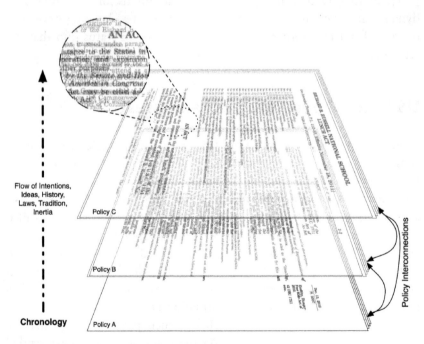

Fig. 2.2 Metaphoric diagram of a palimpsest policy

(2012) similarly uses the palimpsest metaphor as a "sensitising device" for understanding how policy departs from its legislated intentions during implementation—in her case focusing on childcare policy in England. This use bears a resemblance to educational sociologist Basil Bernstein's (1977) term *recontextualizing*, where local actors adapt knowledge or curriculum to meet local concerns.

Naturally, implementation-based reinterpretations occur in school cafeterias and state school food authority offices, much like a palimpsest of differing understandings overlaid across time. But school food policy itself, the actual legislation, shows that policy can be palimpsest-like *even before* it reaches the desks of implementers. I use the palimpsest metaphor for that purpose. My distinction shows policy as *officially* palimpsest, not only reinterpreted by every local context. Legislators rarely start without existing policy in an area; instead, they often work hard to stay within the existing frameworks of extant policies. Teachers and other implementers then add their layer of interpretations, too.

Looking closely at Fig. 2.2, the palimpsest metaphor becomes clearer. Policy A, at the bottom, is the original policy, the first legislative action on a social, cultural, economic, or legal concern. Policy B and, later, policy C represent replacements, revisions, and/or interconnected policies. Some policy areas, of course, might involve many more than three policies. In short, though, across the policy's chronology—from the diagram's bottom-up—certain elements of the original intentions, history, policy ideas, ideologies, laws, traditions, and the inertia of the status quo continue across time and influence the policy ecology, whether positively or negatively. The dotted line of the chronology suggests the punctuated equilibrium of policy processes (Baumgartner & Jones, 2009): changes occur periodically, but major elements show mostly continuity. We might also imagine each policy as having varying opacity, showing underneath them portions of previous and/or connected policies. In the diagram the callout detail (the dotted circle) imagines—like the palimpsest of the metaphor—the faint words of the original peeking through the topmost layer. Sometimes, of course, the original's words are literally still present from iteration to iteration (like the NSLA's preamble), but sometimes only the intent and structure remains.

Most policies are like this, as I said. Rather than starting over from scratch on a major policy, policies usually get constructed more like Frankenstein's monster, with new parts sutured onto existing ramshackle policies when the parts they replace stop working. There's a pragmatic reason for this: summoning the time, political will, and eventually the consensus for a major policy shift often proves difficult. Policymakers can more easily stick with the status quo (Baumgartner & Jones, 2009), or one can take an incremental approach of choosing between known policy alternatives (Lindblom, 1959).

For many policies, this palimpsest construction method works just fine. Policies require small changes here and there; implementation shows the limits of the original hopes for the legislation, which policymakers then patch; and radical changes to a policy's ecology happen infrequently enough to make needing total reconfiguration rare (Weaver-Hightower, 2008).

Sometimes though, I argue, a policy's palimpsest nature itself can cause problems. Some policies demonstrate more than just the inertia of the status quo. Instead, the origins showing through the patches and rewritings act antithetically to contemporary needs. Sometimes the dilemmas that prompted a policy have changed and sticking to the original framework makes the policy exacerbate those problems.

School food policy in the United States—with its founding as simultaneously an anti-hunger program, agricultural support, and defense program—shows well when a palimpsest policy becomes problematic. In the 1930s and 1940s, when the political settlements over school food policy were made, the major difficulty in child nutrition was *under*nourishment. Children were not getting the macro- and micronutrients they needed, and the citizenry worried that public health and national security would suffer. Thus the school lunch program established *minimum* caloric requirements for meals—no maximums, just minimums. Though it's hard to believe, *maximum* calories first appeared in the 2010 HHFK Act. Thirty years into a devastating obesogenic spike (Baskin et al., 2005), and the layers of NSLP policy—perversely—kept in place calorie minimums that did nothing to limit obesity's rise. The 1940s concerns about malnutrition—bolstered by the growing perception that school meals were solely for poor children who, some think, must get too few calories—continued to show through the palimpsest of school food policies, despite Congress tinkering with the NSLP dozens of times (see Table 2.1). Indeed, in some cases, because these calorie minimums were difficult to meet without running afoul of fat content restrictions, more sugar and bread was added to menus to meet requirements. Janet Poppendieck (2010, p. 112), for instance, tells of a school cook in Mississippi—the state with the highest childhood obesity rate—who was told to add fat-free but full-sugar chocolate pudding to her meals to meet the calorie minimum. Sugary desserts, largely because of food subsidies and mass production, remain cheaper than fruits, vegetables, and other healthier fare that the cook might have added instead.

Another holdover from the policy's origins is means testing for free and reduced-price meals. And like caloric minimums' impact on obesity, means testing has amplified inequalities rather than reducing them or, for that matter, bringing any hoped-for fiscal discipline to the NSLP. As the apparatus of US school lunch policy has grown from the original 5 pages to nearly 90, so too has grown an audit culture that accompanies managerialism movements globally (Clarke & Newman, 1997). Massive amounts of time and effort get poured into checking each child's eligibility for free lunches, 40¢ reduced-price lunches, or full-price lunches. Several automatic eligibility programs now ease income verification burdens—by, for example, "direct certification" of students on other forms of welfare or mass eligibility based on local socioeconomics. Yet most schools still send home eligibility forms for parents to fill out and return. And as Poppendieck persuasively shows, this 1940s-created system still presents four major obstacles to hungry children: the vagaries of the initial application; the error-prone certification process at the school or district level to make sure families' incomes are low enough; the subsequent verification audit involving a whole new round of paperwork for randomly selected parents to submit income proof; and the price, which even when reduced to 40¢ can prove too expensive for some families (Poppendieck, 2010, pp. 179–189). All that work to ensure that no child gets a "free ride" unless she "deserves" it. Despite drives to "eliminate the reduced-price" category (given its own acronym, ERP) led by the influential School Nutrition Association (2020), and despite persuasive arguments to make school meals universally free (Cohen et al., 2021; Poppendieck, 2010), the weight of policy history and conservative fiscal and social sentiments have maintained the three-price system for three quarters of a century.

Clearly, as I said, the status quo proves hard to change. The status quo has implications, though. To close out this chapter that theorizes school food in the United States, then, I explore various impacts—conceived of broadly—of the ways policymakers over the decades have structured school food.

A Broad View of Impact

For many, perhaps, this chapter's view of policy and history might seem rather wonkish. After all, only an amoral analyst could consider school food primarily important because of its legislative logistics and political science implications. I certainly don't think that way. In the remainder of this chapter, then, I consider the broader implications of school food for people (and non-people living creatures). These implications—all discussed at lengths and depths beyond my expertise by others elsewhere—should remain front and center when we consider feeding children. That's why they are crucial to lay out here. Still, such implications should not replace attention to politics. As I argue throughout *Unpacking School Lunch*, we must remember that policy and politics constrain or facilitate food programs—the whats, whys, hows, and whos that determine whether we reap the positive benefits.

Impacts on Students

Perhaps citizens and policymakers care most about the health, academic, and behavioral effects of the food. Are the meals "good" for children and their educations? It's a natural question, and it has several aspects to address.

Regarding healthiness, school food has improved dramatically since the passage of the HHFKA in 2010. Indeed, according to the most recent large-scale study in the *Journal of the American Medical Association* (Liu et al., 2021), school food now has the highest dietary quality—measured by the American Heart Association diet score and the Healthy Eating Index 2015—of any source of food, from grocery stores to restaurants. Even more than that, school meals had the lowest inequities across those same sources, meaning that even low socioeconomic status, race, and gender didn't prevent those gains.

Student weight holds particular interest to policymakers because of public concern about obesity and the hope that school meals might help reduce obesity and overweight. The research on the weight impacts of the NSLP has shown somewhat mixed results. Condon and colleagues' (2015) USDA study found, at each age group, "no differences between NSLP participants and nonparticipants in the prevalence of overweight or obesity" (p. xi). Taber and colleagues (2013) found that states with school lunch standards stricter than the NSLP guidelines had lower rates of childhood obesity in their sample than those whose standards simply matched federal guidelines. Yet Millimet and colleagues (2010) and Schanzenbach (2009) found, before the implementation of HHFKA, that the lunch program but not the breakfast program increases the likelihood of participating children being obese. More recent research noted above, however, seems to have trended toward better school food impacts on obesity. Overweight and obesity among children overall, though, has not abated (Fryar et al., 2020).

Food insecurity (hunger) and overall poverty have been alleviated for many children because of school lunch. For poverty measures, the US Census Bureau estimated that, in 2020, about 300,000 fewer children lived in poverty solely due to school lunches, but getting both school lunches and SNAP benefits (Supplemental Nutrition Assistance Program; formerly known as "food stamps") helped 3.2 million more students to live above the poverty line (Fox & Burns, 2021). One would expect positive flow-on effects of less food insecurity, and research has repeatedly found that true (Ralston et al., 2017).

Do children perform better academically with healthy school meals? While establishing causation can prove difficult with nutrition research, much evidence seems to suggest kids do better in school with healthier food. Anderson and colleagues (2018) found that California schools that switched to healthier school meal providers saw test score gains of three to five percent of a standard deviation—small but statistically significant. Belot and James (2011) utilized the natural experiment of Jamie Oliver's reforms in Greenwich, England, to show that educational outcomes in English and science improved significantly. Other studies find a mixed bag of evidence, with one review (Hecht et al., 2020) finding more studies of universal free meals that showed academic improvement than those with no change, and they mentioned no studies that showed a decline in performance. Regarding long-term effects, Hinrichs (2010) finds that lifetime health benefits were not evident from school food programs (though short-term benefits might have occurred), but that those adults that had participated as children had higher educational attainment over their lives. A similar Swedish study (Lundborg et al., 2021) found that there were health benefits long term in addition to the higher educational attainment and lifetime income.

While harder to measure, the impact of school meals on student non-academic aspects of performance—attendance, behavior, and the like—seems somewhat positive, as well. Bartfeld and colleagues (2020) found that low-income students, particularly, were more likely to attend after their schools began participating in Community Eligibility Provision (CEP) universally free school meals. Belot and James's (2011) study after Jamie Oliver's reforms found a 14% increase in attendance. School breakfast programs, especially, seem to improve attendance and reduce students being tardy (School Food Trust, 2008; Taras, 2005).

Regarding behavior and discipline, Gordon and Ruffini (2021) found that students generally were less often suspended when their school became eligible for free meals, particularly statistically significant for White boys in elementary schools. Gennetian and colleagues' (2016) work focused on SNAP benefits suggests that food assistance has a timing effect for behavior, too, as disciplinary rates spike at month's end when SNAP benefits run out. Even measures like on-task vs. off-task classroom behavior were improved in studies from England (School Food Trust, 2009a, 2009b).

Qualitative studies of educators' impressions support the vital impact of school food on students. Cassar (2018), for example, interviewed teachers at schools with both traditional and healthier school lunch programs or a mixture, finding that students' behavior, concentration, and hunger varied a great deal based on the type of lunch, the portion size, and whether children skipped breakfast.

Considering the impact of school lunch on students also requires that we consider the broader socialization from these meals. What does it mean for children to have school be a primary place they get and consume food? This invokes the key concept of *foodscapes*. According to MacKendrick (2014), one's foodscape includes "the places and spaces where you acquire food, prepare food, talk about food, or generally gather some sort of meaning from food," as well as the "institutional arrangements, cultural spaces, and discourses that mediate our relationship with our food" (p. 16; see also Vonthron et al., 2020). Children certainly learn from these foodscapes, but what, precisely, do they learn? Increasingly it appears they learn a great deal.

Indeed, we see the breadth of what children could potentially learn by looking at scholars' attempts to define, explicitly, the aim of most programs: *food literacy*. In Truman and colleagues' (2017) scoping review of 38 definitions of the term *food literacy*, they found that six themes emerged: skills and behaviors, food/health choices, culture, knowledge, emotions, and food systems. As they explain,

> *Skills and behaviours* describe physical actions or abilities involving food; *food/health choices* describe actions associated with informed choices around food use; and *culture* describes societal aspects of food. *Knowledge* refers to the ability to understand and seek information about food (i.e., nutrition education); *emotions* cover the influence of attitudes and motivation; and *food systems* describes understanding the complexity of food systems (i.e., environmental impact, food wastage, food risk/safety, and so forth). (p. 367, emphasis original)

In follow-on work, Truman and a larger group (Truman et al., 2017) added a seventh theme, "tool use," meaning the ability to utilize the growing, harvesting, preparing, cooking, serving, and eating utensils necessary to carry out their foodways.

Certainly not all schools do this level of explicit teaching on food. Yet I would argue that whether part of the *explicit* curriculum (what schools say they teach), the *implicit* or "hidden" curriculum that students learn from schools' structures and interactions, or the *null* curriculum (what schools avoid teaching or under-teach [Eisner, 1992]), students always learn something from the experience. If a school has 15 minutes for lunch (and some do), it teaches students that food should be hurried through, not savored. If a school uses disposable plastic sporks every meal, it teaches students that distinctive uses for utensils (forks, knives, spoons, chop sticks, hands) don't matter, and it teaches poor lessons about waste and environmental disregard.

Students learn food literacy lessons from nearly every aspect of the school foodscape, from where, with whom, what, when, how, and how long they eat. They learn what behavior they can and cannot do during a meal. Some schools have instituted "silent lunches" for all students (e.g., Caruso & Rosenthal, 2020), a collective approach not just an individual punishment, aimed at keeping discipline , getting kids to eat, and—during the COVID-19 pandemic—limiting the spread of the virus during mealtimes. Other schools have lunches that feature crowding, excessive noisiness, and frequent incivilities that make eating school lunch less than positive for children (Caruso & Rosenthal, 2020).

Many students learn about their value and the value of others from what schools do and don't do in the cafeteria and the academic curriculum. What must vegans and vegetarians learn from the constant salad and cereal schools offer them as their only vegetarian entrees? Only 56.5% of schools in the United States serve vegetarian options, but a lowly 13.9% have vegan meal options (School Nutrition Association, 2018). What do immigrant children learn about their value when the menu rarely or never includes their cultural foods, like Indian foods or kosher and halal foods? Only 1.9% of US school districts serve kosher or halal items (School Nutrition Association, 2018). How do obese children experience the school environment, particularly if their schools treat it as a disease to actively cure (Crosnoe, 2010)? How do children with eating disorders experience school lunch, either before diagnosis when eating creates significant stress or during treatment when parents or school personnel often strictly monitor their eating (e.g., Loeb et al., 2011)? What do children who receive special education services or who have visible disabilities learn about their place in the social order (Bashinski & Smilie, 2018)? What do children learn about the experience of being hungry at schools (Cassar, 2018)? What do children learn about social class, work, and justice from how cafeteria staff are paid and treated (Gaddis, 2019)? What do children learn about the animals that eventually end up on their plate, and what do they glean about how to treat those animals and their meat (DeLeon, 2011; Dolby, 2015; Rice, 2013; Stewart & Cole, 2009)?

Impacts Beyond Schools

While students naturally demand our attention when considering school food's impacts, I began this section promoting a "broader view of impacts." School meals touch many aspects of the world beyond the school's walls, consistent with my notion above of schools existing within a complex ecology.

For one, the benefits of school food's impacts on the health of individuals at large scale—30 million lunches a day—contributes to numerous social gains. Though I personally tend to avoid human capital arguments, school lunches do indeed alleviate poverty and associated negative health implications, allowing students to remain in school, learn better and longer, and ultimately increase the population's productive capabilities.

US school food has long had a connection to the geopolitical interests of the United States, as well. School feeding had military purposes domestically, as I discussed above, but school food has played a major part in the peacetime missions of US foreign policy, too. Rutledge (2016) details the many ways that US school food programs were used as a policy and ideational template for the World Food Programme and its focus on school meals. In creating this and other food aid, like the McGovern-Dole Food for Education Program, the US government has hoped to relieve poverty and famine, create new markets for US agriculture, and "win the hearts and minds" of people globally to the US's values.

School food also makes a tremendous economic impact. US federal school food programs themselves circulate roughly $18 billion through the economy each year from 2016 to 2019 (U.S. Department of Agriculture, 2021), paying the wages of everyone from cafeteria workers to food distributor salespeople to farm workers. Those workers go out to buy things themselves, and school nutrition programs also pay for electricity, equipment, uniforms, transportation, professional development, trash services, software, maintenance, printing, and on and on. The spending on school food programs thus gets distributed widely across the economy. We must thus view school meals as benefitting more than just the children who eat them.

Indeed, the economic ripples of school lunch spread to the larger community, whether one has kids eating it or not. A recent working paper by Handbury and Moshary (2021), for example, suggests that grocery store prices go down for everyone in the community when a school participates in Community Eligibility Provision universally free meals. Grocers might not care much for that, but it makes necessities more affordable for entire communities. Even beyond the local grocery store, school nutrition programs have significant influence on US agriculture writ large. School's market share and nutrition standards influence what farmers grow, and the commodity system keeps crop prices higher than the market otherwise would (Poole et al., 2020).

School lunch and breakfast of course have impacts on the natural environment, as well. School cafeterias expend tremendous natural resources: the various energies to freeze, refrigerate, process, and heat food; the water used by school kitchens in cooking, dishwashing, and cleaning; the energy used in cooling, warming, and lighting kitchens and cafeteria spaces. Numerous chemicals get used in refrigeration, air conditioning, and cleaning. Getting the food from farm to processor to distributor to the cafeteria also requires tremendous "food miles," a general measure of the polluting and fuel consuming costs of transporting food. Then add in the frequent use of disposable implements, like plastic foam trays, plastic serving containers, plastic wrap, cardboard boxes, plastic cutlery, and so on. Multiplied over nearly 100,000 schools making school meals, these consumptions and impacts grow substantially.

Consider the environmental impacts of the food on the tray, too. What foods child nutrition programs serve have implications for greenhouse gas emissions, land use, water use, pesticide use, biodiversity loss, and pollution of water, land, and air. Poole and colleagues (2020) show that current US school meals have a tremendous carbon footprint, easily exceeding the EAT-Lancet standards for an ecologically sustainable diet (Willett et al., 2019). A similar study (Wickramasinghe et al., 2016) shows the same for English school food. The over-reliance on dairy and beef in school lunch guidelines prove particularly environmentally taxing, because raising cattle for milk and meat generates tremendous greenhouse gas emissions, land use requirements, deforestation, and pollution in local watersheds (e.g., Lappé, 1971; Pollan, 2006). The EAT-Lancet standards thus suggest a move toward a more plant-based diet, which would require substantial rethinking of current school meals (Poole et al., 2020).

Conclusion

Given what I've discussed in this chapter, I hope it's now possible for readers to see school food as both complicated and broadly impactful. It has a lengthy history, replete with multiple stakeholders, full of competing interests with competing ideas, and constructed in complex and layered ways through politics, policy, and practical necessity.

Now, though, I shift focus in Chapters 3 and 4 to examine how this reality has been built and maintained through political ideology, part of Rutledge's (2016) notion of the "ideational" dynamics of creating school lunch programs. In the United States, this particularly involves an ongoing battle between progressive and conservative political ideologies. In the next two chapters, then, I illuminate the ways that conservative politics, especially, has shaped whether, how, and what students eat.

Snack Two: Pizza Is a Vegetable

In November 2011, Congress officially decided that pizza—or, technically, the two tablespoons of tomato sauce on it—counted as a serving of vegetables. To be fair, that Congress didn't invent the rule; they only prevented the USDA from changing it. The USDA, acting on the Institute of Medicine's (2010) advice, had wanted kids to eat a half cup of any vegetable to count as a serving. Two tablespoons of tomato sauce just don't pack the same nutritional value as a half cup of, say, broccoli.

The political dimensions were hard to miss. In the November 2010 elections, Republicans had taken over the US House of Representatives and narrowed their minority in the Senate to just two (51 to 49), and they used their newfound power to directly challenge the Healthy Hunger-Free Kids Act that President Obama signed the year before. It was among Obama's signature accomplishments, not to mention a victory for the First Lady, Michelle Obama, who had made healthy eating and exercise her priority goal.

While "owning the liberals," in the parlance of Internet trolls, might have been reason enough for Republicans to attempt gutting USDA school lunch rules, they—and their Democratic colleagues—were also vigorously lobbied by manufacturers and industry groups (Associated Press, 2011). The rule changes, besides defining pizza sauce, also contained reductions to sodium, a requirement for more whole grains, and limits on "starchy vegetables," especially white potatoes, so that kids would get a variety of vegetables—beans, broccoli, carrots, sweet potatoes, lettuces, and so on, rather than just daily french fries—in amounts that offered wide nutritional benefits. The salt industry didn't want any rule suggesting sodium isn't great for you. Those who make fortunes from selling pizza and a multitude of pizza-like products stood to lose substantial money. They stood to potentially lose the existing tomato sauce rule and their products wouldn't count as vegetables anymore, and they faced having to spend money to reformulate products with less salt and whole-grain crusts, which would threaten sales because such pizzas aren't as tasty. Potato industry groups also revolted, and they got their senators, both Democrats and Republicans, to reject the USDA's changes. Yes, they said, we always want fries with that.

Obviously, designating pizza as a vegetable and blocking healthier school food reforms demonstrates vividly the political and economic dynamics of school food. I'm sure few were surprised to learn that many in

Congress care more about (voters') jobs and industry's (campaign donatable) profits than they do about how much sodium kids consume. After all, industry-sponsored studies give them plausible deniability, and many believe that government should stay out of school feeding altogether, as I'll explain in the next two chapters. This side of school food politics perhaps leaps off the page.

Less obvious but perhaps more important, this political fight over what counts as a vegetable represents a battle to define basic concepts of our lives *and* to do so in a particularly conservative way that benefits certain people over others. Political groups want to cement particular beliefs in our imaginations and ways of living. In this instance, the very definition of *vegetables* was at stake. Who profits from the definition, consumers or producers?

Important for much the same reason, the techniques of governance that ultimately defined pizza as a vegetable deserve scrutiny. To the public, government rulemaking seems arcane, only something that policy wonks care about. Industry and government often like it that way, I suspect, keeping the public from getting meddlesome about things that damage their bottom lines. Yet this kind of definitional work has important implications. As Verlyn Klinkenborg, an agriculture and environment writer for the New York Times put it,

> For me, the most interesting thing about this is how you turn language of the kind you find in the ag appropriations bill into "pizza" and "vegetables." On the face of it, it's almost impossible to tell what's being said. But then, that's part of the point. Rather than revealing what the real subject is—and who stands to lose or gain from it—we're left with this truly indigestible wordstuff. Even ag experts ... have a hard time moving from the text to the fact that this is really an industry move to feed school kids pizza. The thinking seems to be that anything that has once been a vegetable remains a vegetable, no matter what form it ultimately takes. And it has the unique property of turning anything it touches into a vegetable too. (quoted in Rosenthal, 2011)

This kind of thinking springs from our cultural obsession with "nutritionism" (Scrinis, 2013), where "food" no longer means just whole foods (an apple, a steak, a potato) but rather what swirls around in them at a microscopic level (their potassium or iron, their Vitamin B, their protein). Such language and policymaking confuses citizens, though, and allows those with profit motive to continue arguing that anything goes—all the pizza and potatoes kids can eat—provided they have a little more of some vitamin or mineral than something else. Those who aspire to reform school food must wade into such definitional battles, too, if they want to make kids healthier.

3

Conservative Resistance to Progressive Incrementalism: The Political Terrain of School Food in America

In the last chapter, I showed that the lingering political tensions created at the National School Lunch Program's origins still haunt contemporary school food politics. In this chapter, I define these tensions further and give them a more precise ideological basis. Discussions of "conservative" and "liberal" (hereafter "progressive" for the latter, to avoid confusion with other terms I'm using) can destroy the nuances and complexities of any debate (Jost et al., 2009). Yet sorting arguments over school food into these camps helps illuminate a central dynamic (Lusk, 2012). Put simply, school food in the United States and many other countries has been characterized by conservative resistance to food provision and regulation alongside progressive incrementalism toward healthier, more just food provision. Thus far, neither ideological position has completely gotten its way, but not for a lack of trying.

In this chapter and the next, I focus specifically on conservative resistance. I do this not to ignore progressive contributions or efforts; indeed, Chapter 6 details a progressive vision of school nutrition, and it explores several innovative progressive programs. If you need an inoculation of progressivism before diving in, perhaps skip to Chapter 6. I focus on political conservatives here because rightist resistance *explains*

M. B. Weaver-Hightower, *Unpacking School Lunch*, https://doi.org/10.1007/978-3-030-97288-2_3

progressives' incrementalism. My discussion thus focuses on the less understood and publicized positions of the political right, seeking to explain what conservatives believe about school meals and why. Though a progressive myself, I believe an important component of progressive strategizing involves understanding and acknowledging conservative ideologies' "good sense"—in Antonio Gramsci's (1971) meaning of an ideology's appeal to people's lived experiences—while also critiquing the "bad" sense. In that way we can move toward productive collaborations among everyone—whether on the left, the right, or somewhere in between—to improve children's health and education.

Conservative Modernization

In the academic study of education, particularly the study of pre-K-12 reform efforts, scholars have lavished much attention on the dominance of conservative reform ideas. Nearly all major public education transformations since the 1980s have particularly conservative origins: standardized high-stakes testing, voucher and tax credit programs for private school attendance, public school choice systems, accountability measures, parent triggers, school turnaround and takeover policies, curriculum standards, scripted pedagogies, and much more. The Democratic party has largely come to adopt these same policies rather than asserting progressive, oppositional ideas (Weaver-Hightower, 2012).

In general, conservative educational reforms have been developed, advocated for, and implemented by a coalition of disparate conservative groups coalesced and energized in what Michael Apple (2000) called the "conservative restoration." *Restoration* here refers to a returning to dominance of conservative political, cultural, and economic beliefs that held sway prior to post-World War II liberal, Keynesian welfare policies. As Apple noted, the resurgence of conservative "common sense" did not happen suddenly. Rather, it resulted from numerous coalitions' creative struggles to win public consent on broad policy fronts at many legislative levels, from school boards to federal office. One field on which conservatives have battled over the years—with varying amounts of publicity—is school food.

Chapter 2 outlined the historical progression of school feeding programs, showing the moments where conservative politicians have tried to socially engineer, quash, reduce, streamline, or severely restrict the program. For some conservatives across the decades and even now, the federal school feeding programs variously represent (a) welfare, which, they believe, saps the industriousness and self-reliance of individuals; (b) a source of unnecessary regulations on states and schools; (c) an overly expensive handout; (d) a source of considerable waste and fraud; (e) an unconstitutional venture not anticipated by the country's founders; and (f) meddling in the God-given roles of parents—particularly women—in raising their children. Many of these core concerns remain for conservatives today, as I explore below.

To better understand the current positions and goals of conservatives regarding school nutrition, I find it helpful to use Apple's (2006) typology of conservative groups described in *Educating the "Right" Way: Markets, Standards, God, and Inequality*. He identifies four partly overlapping groups—neoliberals, neoconservatives, the professional and managerial new middle class, and authoritarian populists—who together define the US's education reform agenda. I define these groups and positions below. Importantly, I argue that these same standpoints, roles, and belief systems apply to the debates over school *food* reform as much as educational reform generally. As mentioned above, conservative restoration has been advanced by conservatives' willingness to engage every issue, no matter how seemingly peripheral. So while, to many, school feeding might seem like a minor concern compared to vast inequalities and achievement gaps, conservatives have seen it as one more place to fight the destructive forces they see within progressivism. Indeed, as perhaps the United States' most successful and widely supported "welfare" program, school meals have become a prime target; school feeding programs represent the antithesis of some core conservative tenets. Examining the stances on school food by each group illustrates why.

Neoliberals

Perhaps the most important conservative impulse toward school food is neoliberalism. David Harvey (2005) concisely summarizes neoliberalism's basic tenets:

> Neoliberalism is in the first instance a theory of political economic practices that proposes that human well-being can best be advanced by liberating individual entrepreneurial freedoms and skills within an institutional framework characterized by strong private property rights, free markets, and free trade. The role of the state is to create and preserve an institutional framework appropriate to such practices. ... But beyond these tasks the state should not venture. (para. 3)

Neoliberalism privileges the "market *über alles*" (McChesney, 1998, para. 9). Several components of Harvey's description bear emphasizing, for it encapsulates complex beliefs about human freedom and motivation, the role of governments, and conditions for the success of society.

First, neoliberalism proposes that humans—particularly as atomistic individuals—function best in markets, provided they have "entrepreneurial freedoms and skills." Human motivation, they believe, comes primarily from competition and self-interest, a cornerstone of capitalist markets. That individual, however, must have "freedom" to participate in the market (though we hardly have a choice, ultimately). Similarly, the market must be free from government regulation, manipulation by powerful interests, or trade restrictions. The market also must feature choices, for, without choices, "consumers"—what individuals become rather than citizens (McChesney, 1998, para. 10)—find themselves at the mercy of monopolies. Individual consumers must also have free access to information to make rational choices.

The major concern for neoliberal theory, then, involves limiting the state's role. The ideal "neoliberal state," as Harvey notes above, simply makes conditions right for market operation and otherwise stays out of the way. Neoliberal theory distrusts the state *explicitly*. As McChesney (1998, para. 2) asserts, neoliberals believe they must "undermine the dead hand of the incompetent, bureaucratic and parasitic government, that can never do good even if well intended, which it rarely is." The state should be vested only with protecting private property rights—by force if necessary—and ensuring the freedom of markets. Yet post-World War II governments rarely fit this mold because of their various social safety net programs and because most regulate or administer parts of the economy considered indispensable, like water, electricity, health care, and education. Because such arrangements supposedly interfere with markets, the major objective of neoliberal policymaking has been to dismantle welfare programs and to deregulate government-run sectors and/or sell them to private interests. One sees such objectives through global efforts to deregulate utilities, open free trade in key sectors like agriculture (Patel, 2007; Roberts, 2008), and to scale back social aid (Chomsky, 1999; Clarke & Newman, 1997). In education, one sees these objectives in allowing for-profit companies to run public schools and to provide parental "school choice" through charter schools and vouchers or through tax credits for private schooling (Apple, 1996, 2000, 2006).

Attending to the implications of neoliberalism has become crucial because, as McChesney (1998, para. 1) notes, "Neoliberalism is the defining political economic paradigm of our time." Apple (2006, p. 31) notes further, "neoliberals are the most powerful element within the alliance supporting conservative modernization." This dominance applies to education powerfully because, more than simply an economic theory, neoliberalism acts as a political and cultural force as well. In other words, neoliberalism has asked the public to *think* as economic actors, to consider economic markets as a model for all human endeavors, including basic human support systems like education and health. Such efforts have been remarkably successful. As Harvey (2005) explains,

> Neoliberalism has, in short, become hegemonic as a mode of discourse. It has pervasive effects on ways of thought to the point where it has become incorporated into the common-sense way many of us interpret, live in, and understand the world. (Introduction, para. 4)

Perhaps worse, advocates of neoliberalism present this "common sense" as if no rational or fair alternative exists (Apple, 2006, p. 35).

As applied to school food, neoliberal political theory focuses on the atomistic economic individual as consumer of the food, free and open markets for selling and distributing meals, and limited roles for government regulation. Neoliberals frequently critique school food provision—particularly free and reduced-price meals—as welfare, which supposedly weakens recipients' entrepreneurial skills and unfairly taxes others. They critique school food as interference in free markets, for the US programs provides protectionist agriculture subsidies. And neoliberals critique government involvement in nutritional, advertising, and other regulation, both because these constitute interference in choices for parents and students and because these regulations create burdens on businesses' free-market participation. Neoliberals want the government out of school food provision and regulation, preferring instead to let private companies operate programs, deciding based on "market signals" (i.e., profitability) who eats and what gets eaten.

An Example of Neoliberal Discourses

To illustrate neoliberal discourses around food policy, consider the *Wall Street Journal* editorial (2009), "The Fat of the Land: A Soda Pop Tax and Government Health Care Won't Cure Obesity." The piece argues that neoliberal economic principles can fix obesity better than government taxation and restrictions, the latter being the antithesis of the ideal neoliberal state's behavior. Instead, they suggest ending agriculture subsidies, which, from a neoliberal perspective, interfere with the market's natural self-corrections. The *Wall Street Journal* editors suggest that the "Government could also free up the private market to change the economic incentives to have better health." Becoming *homo economicus,* the paragon and avatar of the neoliberal individual, thus becomes the solution to every social illness. The government often only blocks this economic self-realization.

Another neoliberal tenet comes through the editors blaming obesity on individuals. As they say, "Unlike traditional illness, obesity is largely the result of individual choices about diet and exercise." While of course many decisions leading to obesity are indeed made by individuals, this ignores the ubiquitous obesogenic environment beyond individuals' control (Hojjat, 2021, Chapter 2; Popkin, 2009). The editorialists' attribution becomes simple, though: "Americans are eating too much. ... We are eating larger portions and more snacks." Not that restaurants "offer" or just "give" people larger portions; that manufacturers engineer food to contain more calories for taste; or that restaurants and grocery stores design their environments, menus, and advertising to nudge us to eat more (e.g., Pollan, 2006; Popkin, 2009; Schlosser, 2001; Wansink, 2007). According to neoliberal ideology, we simply make our own unfettered choices.

The editors object to "taxpayers"—all readers thus being reduced to primarily economic entities—"footing most of the medical bills" for obesity because of government-subsidized health care. Indeed, economics becomes the primary cost in neoliberal positions, rather than say the human toll or family distress caused by debilitating illness. No, instead, the key concerns include Medicare spending, the threat of what they call the "McLawsuit" "transferring wealth to the trial bar" (US conservatives detest "trial lawyers"), and the "fatter and sicker workforce" that will prove "a drag on economic growth." As they say, by becoming an obese nation, "In effect, we're eating money."

Interestingly, the editors recognize a tension between neoliberal theory and the necessity to curb obesity for economic prosperity: "Namely, the food market reflects what people want. A business that disregards consumer preferences is unlikely to survive for long in today's ultra-competitive food industry." In other words, one cannot rely on the so-called invisible hand of the market if that hand is reaching for super-sized fries. In classical neoliberal theory, economic rationalism prevails given free access to quality information; people will do the right thing if they have enough information to make the right decision. The editorialists, though, note that we have an "obesity paradox." We know more about nutrition than ever before—we have reliable information thanks to "label laws, education campaigns and so forth. ... anyone mainlining mayonnaise knows the risks"—but that still has not prevented the obesity spike.

This tension does not cause them to give up on neoliberal solutions, though. Policymakers must still reject government market intervention

because "the policy quiver is not well-stocked, and the arrows are dull."
Banning and taxing certain foods—including, notably, "prohibiting soda
and candy machines in schools"—usually prove "unpopular." If we
pattern obesity intervention on smoking prevention, they say sarcasti-
cally, "we'd ban eating in restaurants." Bans also present a slippery slope,
they contend; after "sugar-sweetened drinks, no doubt [reformers will
start] moving on to fat, salt or calories." Government intervention, like
preventive care through Medicare and Medicaid, also lacks private solutions' appeal because "it would take years for the health benefits to
materialize, and even longer to reduce overall health-care costs. More
preventive care is very expensive and almost never produces cost contain-
ment." Here again, the primary goal is economic—its expense—rather
than human. And they prefer short-term results, not long-term effort on
thorny problems.

For the editors, then, neoliberal policy provides the only real solution.
"Start by reforming agricultural 'policy,' meaning subsidies that help
make unhealthy food artificially cheap." As I noted above, agriculture
subsidies—what they deride through scare quotes as poor policy—represent an unwarranted government intrusion in the free market, making
prices "artificial." Furthermore, they contend that these discourage
competition. As the editors highlight, "Most farmers receiving ag subsidies are actually prohibited by law from growing 'specialty crops'—
i.e., fruits and vegetables—as protectionism for California and Florida
produce growers." The thinking holds that if subsidies disappeared,
competition would grow, prices would reflect actual costs, and consumers
would make better decisions because calories would cost more.

The only role for government they suggest comes from pure neoliberal
theory: "Government could also free up the private market to change the
economic incentives to have better health." In their view, the "private
market" includes individuals and businesses. Again, the individual will
supposedly make the right economic decisions when they have something to gain or lose: "If people have skin in the game, preventable
costs fall." That "skin in the game" comes down to individuals having
to pay their own health care costs; if it came out of their pocket, they
wouldn't become obese, the editors reason. Businesses, too, can engineer obesity prevention, they suggest. "[C]ompanies have saved a lot of

money with wellness programs, and increasing cost-sharing also has a huge effect." In neoliberal theory, businesses (like individuals) will voluntarily do things in their own best financial interest, and company wellness programs lower healthcare expenses and make for a less ill, and thus more productive, less absent workforce. By "cost-sharing," they mean having individuals pay more for their insurance and health care. In other words, companies can give individuals more "skin in the game" by lowering their contributions to employee benefits. In suggesting this, they ignore the ruinous effects of catastrophic events on individuals when both worker benefits and social safety nets get stripped away.

This editorial crystalizes well the neoliberal stance toward food policy, including school food. Remove the government totally, except to enforce the efforts of private individuals and companies. The informed economic actor, if given an unfettered market to operate within, will make the right choices and economic growth will ensue along with good population health outcomes. The next two conservative factions—authoritarian populists and neoconservatives—also want the government out of the school food business, but they have different rationales, which I discuss next.

Neoconservatives

A second major impulse in conservative critiques of school food comes from neoconservatism. Neoconservatives, importantly, reject neoliberalism's ideal of atomistic individuality and a weak state. It holds instead that a strong nation requires a strong (though perhaps smaller) state to provide common purpose for a cohesive citizenry. Jack Kerwick aptly summarizes core neoconservative beliefs:

First, morality consists primarily of "self-evident" *principles* specifying "natural" or "human *rights*" that belong to *all* human beings just by virtue of their humanity. Second, because these principles are "self-evident," they are rationally or intellectually accessible to *all people* in *all places* and at *all times*. Thus, according to the neoconservative,

neither reason nor morality is encumbered by the parochial considerations thrown up by tradition, custom, or habit. Reason and morality are
unitary phenomena that, as such, ultimately owe *nothing* to the contin-
gencies of place and time. Third, since "liberal democracy" is the only
kind of regime that embodies principles of "natural rights," and since the
United States is *the* "liberal democracy" extraordinaire, ... "liberal democ-
racies" in general, and the United States in particular, have an obligation
to advance "the human rights" of people *everywhere*. Finally, the only
alternative to the "moral realism" of "natural rights" is "historicism" or
"relativism." (Kerwick, 2013, pp. 8–9, emphasis original)

As Kerwick showed, neoconservatism repudiates "moral relativism," cele-
brating instead bold declarations of what is good and what is evil, as if
these too are universally self-evident. Of course, the principles invoked
most often derive from a particularly Anglo-Saxon Judeo-Christianity.
From this basic core grow numerous key practical implications for
policymaking.

Most people encounter the term "neoconservative" related to foreign
policy. The bellicose and militarily hawkish policies of neoconservative
pundits, military officials, and policymakers certainly grow from the idea
that the United States' supposedly universal principles of liberal democracy ought to get exported everywhere, by force if necessary. Importantly,
though, just as neoliberalism has exceeded its economic origins, neoconservatism goes beyond foreign policy to act as a cultural form, too,
notably in education.

Neoconservative educational reform efforts, Apple (2006) argued,
have centered largely on "issues of knowledge, values, and the body."

> It is largely, though not totally, based in a romantic appraisal of the past,
> a past in which "real knowledge" and morality reigned supreme, in which
> people "knew their place," and where stable communities guided by a
> natural order protected us from the ravages of society. (p. 39)

Thus reforms have sought national curricula based on classical Western
knowledge, rigorous testing to ensure adherence to "worthwhile
learning," and particularly conservative character education program-
ming. Neoconservatives, in other words, call for the reestablishment of

core texts including the US Constitution and literary and historical "classics," which they see as inerrant, just like the core values such texts impart, like patriotism, loyalty, self-sacrifice, and entrepreneurialism. For neoconservatives, a "return" to such standardized, "traditional" education would instill values that unite the nation toward a common purpose and act as a bulwark against the national decline, moral decay, and relativism that they see all around.

Regarding school food, neoconservative arguments reflect many such beliefs. One major argument critiques school food as welfare because it weakens families and their self-sufficiency; for neoconservatives, the family represents the core unit of social stability and moral training. One can also see elements of cultural nativism—"a fear of the 'Other'," as Apple notes (p. 39)—particularly in attempts to keep non-Western, "cultural" foods off school menus; the protests over halal meats in England and other parts of Europe provide a clear example (e.g., Bisserbe, 2021; Osowski & Snyder, 2020). Neoconservatives correctly see school meals as inculcating culture, so they often focus on ensuring that a *particular vision* of culture gets established through school food.

The military and political beliefs of neoconservatives also have relevance to school feeding. Concerns that the American military has been imperiled by school food, for instance, have clear neoconservative underpinnings. Mission: Readiness, a group of retired US military generals and admirals, released a report called "Too Fat to Fight" (2010; see also 2018) that shows this well.

> The United States military stands ready to protect the American people, but if our nation does not help ensure that future generations grow up to be healthy and fit, that will become increasingly difficult. The health of our children and our national security are at risk. America must act decisively. (2010, p. 7)

In Chapter 1, I detailed the NSLP's military history, and Mission: Readiness explicitly invokes this to implore Congress to reform school meals and limit junk food's availability. For Mission: Readiness, national interests demand school food reform, more so even than the health of individual citizens. Our global geopolitical dominance requires it, and to do anything less means putting the entire nation "at risk" militarily.

Yet neoconservative concerns for school meals' national security benefits produce friction with strict neoconservative interpretations of the US Constitution. For many neoconservatives, the government should not feed children at all because the Constitution has not granted it that function. In their view, the literal Constitution and the timeless, universal wisdom of the "founding fathers" represent unchanging expressions of "natural rights," starkly opposed to a theory of governance that shifts—to neoconservatives' eyes—with societal whims (Kerwick, 2013). For neoconservatives of this ilk, then, only families should provide food, or, in dire need, local charity.

An Example of Neoconservative Discourse

As an illustration of common neoconservative discourses, consider Vin Suprynowicz's (2010) editorial, "Choosing 'Profusion and Servitude' Over 'Economy and Liberty'," in the *Las Vegas Review-Journal*, that city's largest newspaper. Suprynowicz complains of the passage of the Weekends Without Hunger bill by Nevada congressperson Dina Titus, whom he non-parenthetically refers to as a "permanent UNLV politics professor … (gubbimint jobs are like that)," apparently a dig at university tenure systems. (Full disclosure: I have tenure.)

For Suprynowicz, some of his complaints about the bill fall under neoliberal and professional/managerial concerns, discussed in other sections. He doesn't approve, for instance, of the lack of income proof requirements; "no child will be required to prove he or she is 'poor' to get the free stuff." Ultimately he rejects needing such a program altogether. We should wage a battle over "childhood obesity, not emaciation." Such an argument, of course, misunderstands the hunger-obesity paradox, a well-documented phenomenon in which the most food-insecure populations also suffer the most obesity (Dietz, 1995; Scheier, 2005; Tanumihardjo et al., 2007). Nevertheless, Suprynowicz claims that the government has squandered resources on the wrong problem.

Further, as neoliberals frequently claim of any public enterprise, "Waste, fraud, and contract kickbacks will ensue, as the night follows day."

While other conservative tendencies peek through, most of Suprynowicz's argument evinces a classic neoconservative approach. He presents a list of reasons to reject the bill. For one, it endangers the United States' sovereignty. As he says, "Washington currently borrows 40 cents of every cent [sic] it spends, much of that from the Red Chinese, whose goals are seldom ours. Will the federals be able to kick this addiction, cold turkey, when the borrowers start demanding higher interest rates, or other geopolitical concessions?" Cold War references to communism, like "Red Chinese," clearly delineates a neoconservative argument, a rationale for thrift in government. "Geopolitical concessions," or challenges to the United States' unquestionable might and right globally, could be the ultimate consequence of feeding kids who supposedly don't need it anyway.

Moreover, Suprynowicz calls child nutrition programs "unconstitutional." "Nowhere," he says, "in Article I, Sect. 8 is the Congress authorized to spend a single penny of anyone's tax money feeding anyone's kids, anywhere." It's an old argument, whether Congress can legally spend on social safety programs. The debate typically centers on the Constitution's phrase "promote the general welfare," which progressives often interpret as giving Congress considerable authority. Neoconservatives, particularly those with strict, inerrantist interpretations of what the US's "founding fathers" would have wanted, take exception to such broad interpretations. Quoting Thomas Jefferson, a favorite among neoconservatives (though not on church-state separation), Suprynowicz notes that Jefferson "dismissed" broad interpretation of the general welfare clause "as a rhetorical trick." If Congress can raise money for any purpose, Suprynowicz writes, "Jefferson warned we would have not a limited government, but a 'complete government,' by which he meant a tyranny." Here we see exemplified a constant conservative refrain in arguments over school food: the government wants to take over our lives. While most do not cite constitutional articles and sections or quote the founding fathers' correspondence, the underlying sentiment remains. We should, from neoconservative viewpoint, avoid nutrition regulations and subsidizing meals because it represents stripping local control and substituting government intrusion in individual lives.

Also among the most visible neoconservative arguments within school food debates, Suprynowicz decries the expected toll on families from government intervention. He notes that the weekend feeding program

> is yet another step in reducing the value, the importance, the need for and thus the durability of that institution to which children have always in the past looked for their sustenance—the family—replacing it with the presumption, ingrained from the cradle, that the institution to which all voters should look for their sustenance is ... The State. (para. 16; as written)

For Suprynowicz and other neoconservatives, the only proper place for feeding, educating, and providing health care for children is the family. (And, yes, he does specifically say education and medical care). In their view, assisting families who cannot afford these breeds dependence and sloth. It also breeds fealty to the government, which Suprynowicz translates into "keeping Democrats in office." This will supposedly prove detrimental to family stability, a cornerstone institution, and social grouping. One wonders, though, where he and other neoconservatives find evidence of the family-strengthening influences of poverty, hunger, lack of education, and illness.

In sum, one can see neoconservative influence on school food debates in idealized notions of families (while ignoring many families' dysfunctions and hardships); unceasing loyalty to the intentions of the framers of the Constitution, who were writing more than 200 years ago; and worries that debt will undermine American exceptionalism and geopolitical dominance. While clearly melding occurs between Judeo-Christian beliefs within neoconservatism, we can see even more of that influence among authoritarian populists, discussed next.

Authoritarian Populists

A third conservative impulse relevant to conservative modernization comes from authoritarian populism. To explicate this term, *populism* comes in two basic flavors: democratic populism and what the eminent British cultural studies scholar Stuart Hall (1979, 1985) called "authoritarian populism." The distinction, of course, comes between democracy and authoritarianism; both try to harness the allegiance of "ordinary" people. The term *authoritarian populism,* though controversial (Bonnett et al., 1984), offers an important contrast for identifying some underlying political philosophies. Authoritarian populism seeks to "return" society to a sense of order through external authority, whether through the cultural elites, the state, the military, religion, or some other social control. Think of it as something like "I personally don't believe in evolution, so no one can discuss it in schools." Importantly, though, authoritarian populists still seek this control while appealing to popular sentiments and discontents. Generally it establishes an "other"—immigrants, say, or people of color or progressives—who needs to be brought under control again. As Hall (1979) noted, the successful populism of the New Right in 1980s England—and, I would argue, in international conservatism since then—

> is no rhetorical device or trick, for this populism is operating on genuine contradictions, and it has a rational and material core. Its success and effectivity does not lie in its capacity to dupe unsuspecting folk but in the way it addresses real problems, real and lived experiences, real contradictions—and yet is able to represent them within a logic of discourse which pulls them systematically into line with policies and class strategies of the Right. (p. 20)

Authoritarian populism, that is, takes the real discontents of everyday life—in Hall's case, for example, dissatisfactions with trade union practices—and sutures them to conservative political solutions, all while *rhetorically* disavowing government intervention.

Michael Apple (2006) focuses his analysis of conservative modernization in the United States on authoritarian populists, showing convincingly that the Religious Right provides the dominant role in US authoritarian populism. Building on the sentiments of "those who feel disen-
franchised by the absence of religion in schools" (p. 20)—a resentment
over what they see as irrational overreactions to "harmless" expressions of
faith, like prayers at public events—the conservative coalition has been
able to capture support for its policies, even those unrelated to religion.
The major impetus behind the authoritarian populist impulse in the
United States, though, remains focused on a return to the social stability
that (conservatives' particular Christian) religious beliefs would purportedly provide to everyone if those beliefs were just "returned" to schools
(p. 19).

Though perhaps the least influential and least visible in school
food debates, authoritarian populist impulses are clearly present. These
include religious impulses, as in Apple's analysis. The focus on school
food in the United States, however, has largely avoided overt appeals to
religion; religious politicking has been more evident in other countries
with, for instance, larger and more visible Muslim populations. Not to
say that *covert* appeals to religion don't occur, particularly in coded arguments about the family impacts of "the government" making lunches
for children instead of mothers (the gendered specificity completely
intended). Instead of explicit religious discourses, though, US authoritarian populists have generally fought school food battles by appealing to
the broad population's dissatisfactions with perceived class-based elitism
and government overreach.

Charges of elitism are rife within debates over school food policy, and
such rhetorical moves clearly indicate an attempt to invoke populism.
"They" don't think "your" food is good enough, these charges seem to
say, and such accusations strike at very real class anxieties, for food has
always been a realm of class distinctions and classed resentments (Bourdieu, 1984). John Fund (2014), writing in the conservative *National
Review*, for instance, says reforms have been made to school food because
"Too many people eat too many white potatoes, Mrs. Obama believes."
Stated that way, as Mrs. Obama "believing" that "people" eat too
many white potatoes—not coincidentally the US's most popular, most

consumed vegetable (Agriculture et al., 2010), in the form of chips and fries ranking 11th and 17th, respectively, in the list of sources of calories in the overall US Diet (no other vegetable made the top 25)—puts Mrs. Obama in the role of snob or scold against the larger population. The calculated misrepresentations, of course, include (a) that reducing potato consumption marks only one of many proposed changes following from the Healthy Hunger-Free Kids Act's (HHFKA) and (b) that the source of the recommendation was not Mrs. Obama's "beliefs," but rather the findings of the Institute of Medicine (2010), the independent medical arm of the National Academy of Sciences. To reinforce the characterization of the First Lady as a nag, Fund refers to an interview in which Obama was "stern" and "uncompromising" and that "other people's kids" will be treated just like her own, by making them "eat all their vegetables." The word choice has little ambiguity here: Michelle Obama wants to interfere in your parenting.

Such rhetoric clearly intends to persuade readers toward Fund's policy recommendation, ending federal regulations (and perhaps funding) and having local institutions make decisions. The key point is that *the allegiance to the policy perspective derives from playing on the popular resentment*. Online reader comments for the article suggest this strongly. As "annieoakley53" said, "Are her kids being fed this crap at their expensive private school? No. Not even close. Why doesn't she take her nanny act to her own children's school?" The explicit mention of "*expensive private* school" signals classed resentment and implies Obama's hypocrisy. Crucially, Fund's policy argument grows from neoliberal theory, but his rhetorical strategy draws on authoritarian populism. That adopting his policy recommendation could mean devastating cuts to a hunger program seems beside the point, just so long as adherents boil over Michelle Obama's bossiness.

Authoritarian populists frequently play on popular dissatisfactions with government services and a sense that the government intrudes, or "overreaches," into the lives of individuals. If you want to stir up objections to a policy, just compare it to many people's experiences with the local department of motor vehicles, where long lines and grumpy civil servants have become the avatars of supposedly inherent problems of the public sector doing anything. One might see similar resentment of government in an opinion piece by Chuck Norris (2011)—yes, the actor and martial artist. In objecting to the HHFKA, he argues,

> I just don't think it should take the federal government's overreach into our lives and lunches to make that happen. I think local citizens, communities and counties should rally together, show a little neighborly love and discover solutions for their own issues and downtrodden. That's the way it used to be done in America before the federal government overreached its limits to try and solve most of our community problems. Is the federal government really our "only savior," as the president [Obama] purported in 2009?

For authoritarian populists, then, resentment over intrusion into "personal choices" about what we eat compels policy adherence. They connect policy adherence explicitly to neoconservative pining for the golden age of "the way it used to be done in America." Even though Norris agrees with nearly every component of the legislative changes— "More fruits and vegetables, whole grains, less fat, sugar and salt is always the way to go"—he rejects the HHFKA because of the "overreaching food tampering" and the "bloating-kids'-cuisine-bureaucracy trend" it seems to entail.

An Example of Authoritarian Populist Discourse

Given religious and community organizations' long traditions of feeding the poor, religious arguments appear least often when arguing against school food reforms. They do exist, though, and some populist beliefs have been reshaped to fit conservative resistance to school food reform. Consider a speech by Representative Paul Ryan, Republican from Wisconsin and 2012 vice-presidential candidate for Mitt Romney's losing presidential campaign. Ryan's speech was given to the Conservative Political Action Conference, an annual meeting of conservative activists, on March 6, 2014. About 11 minutes into the 14-minute speech, he said,

The Left is making a big mistake here. What they're offering people is a full stomach and an empty soul. The American people want more than that. This reminds me of a story I heard from Eloise Anderson. She serves in the cabinet of my buddy, [Wisconsin] Governor Scott Walker. She once met a young boy from a very poor family, and every day at school, he would get a free lunch from a government program. He told Eloise he didn't want a free lunch. He wanted his own lunch, one in a brown-paper bag just like the other kids. He wanted one, he said, because he knew a kid with a brown-paper bag had someone who cared for him. This is what the left does not understand. (American Conservative Union, 2014)

A minor firestorm erupted in the national press after this speech. Commentators from the political center and left condemned Ryan's implication that families who have their children eat school lunch—the families of 31.6 million kids at the time—don't care about them.

It only got worse for Ryan when his anecdote was fact-checked later that same night in *The Washington Post* by Glenn Kessler (2014). As Kessler shows, Anderson's story that Ryan retells didn't even happen to Anderson. She read it in a book, Laura Schroff's 2011 *The Invisible Thread*, which tells the story of Schroff befriending an 11-year-old panhandler named Maurice Mazyck. He asks Schroff to put the lunches she (not the government) was going to give him in a paper bag because the other kids, who have someone that cares for them, have theirs in a paper bag. As if these mis-tellings weren't enough, Schroff and Mazyck actually partner with the national organization No Kid Hungry to, among other things, *increase* access to free school lunches and food stamps (now called SNAP benefits).

Perhaps more important than the dishonesty and sloppiness involved in Ryan's anecdote, though, his reshaping of the story gives us insight into authoritarian populist beliefs, ones underpinning many conservatives' policy positions. Certainly, as Apple (2006) showed, religious fundamentalists have deeply influenced the US brand of authoritarian populism, particularly those from a Judeo-Christian background. Ryan's catchphrase about "a full stomach and an empty soul" clearly conveys the religious message. The danger to one's "soul" from government feeding programs proffers a moral conclusion—from Ryan's own religious background—that self-reliance is morally superior to accepting charity. This represents, in other words, not a rational policy conclusion but a morality judgment.

The populist appeal of Ryan's story—which the conservative *National Review* called "moving" (Brennan, 2014)—seems obvious. The unassuming "brown paper bag" holds a special place in American culture, particularly among the working class, for whom it remains a symbol of class solidarity and identity (Lautenschlager, 2006, pp. 47, 151). In this mythos, those who work hard and need to save their pennies don't eat in the factory cafeteria; they bring leftovers or a sandwich in a cheap paper bag. Ryan clearly plays up this Americana appeal. Yet he's also referring to the rags-to-riches, pull yourself up by the bootstraps, Horatio Alger story that sits so centrally in the American meritocracy ideal. The little boy in Ryan's story seems morally courageous because "he didn't want a free lunch. He wanted his *own* lunch," one bought through the "dignity of work" that Ryan made a central theme of his speech. Ryan tells a morality tale rather than proffering a policy rationale, and the moral of the story "is what the Left does not understand." The "American people want more" than the "empty soul" offered through "a government program"—namely free school lunch.

Authoritarian populist arguments, then, hold that school lunch represents a moral issue, usually judged against Judeo-Christian thought and belief. While sometimes God and biblical values receive explicit mention, often the references come in more oblique forms—words that have entered common vernacular, like *souls*—particularly because of the historical conflict presented by suggesting that feeding the poor is anti-religious.

The Professional and Managerial New Middle Class

The professional and managerial fractions of the new middle class are the final, highly necessary group within the conservative project. They rival neoliberals for dominance in political school food debates. The "professionals" provide expertise in the form of technical knowledge about causes and solutions to social problems, while "managerialists" provide bureaucratic administrative and logistical functions (Clarke & Newman, 1997, pp. 4–8). These individuals do not *necessarily* provide ideas and ideology to the conservative cause, nor do they *necessarily* profess diehard belief in the conservative cause. Indeed, as Apple (2006, p. 24) shows, this group has been "relatively autonomous" from the other conservative factions; members of this group may not even consider themselves conservative. Yet their work creating and maintaining systems of efficiency, accountability, and standardization remains indispensable for actualizing reforms initiated by other conservative factions. Neoliberals need professional/managerial individuals and organizations, to monitor and ensure market freedom and to produce the technical knowledge required for rational economic decision-making. Neoconservatives, too, need them:

> The neoconservatives are the advocates of a new managerial state—a state controlled and regulated by a mandarin class of conservative virtucrats who think the American people are incapable of governing themselves without the help of the neocons' special, *a priori* wisdom. (Thompson, 2011, penultimate para.)

In sum, the professional and managerial new middle class provides the knowledges, skills, and acumen—usually emulating business practices developed for private markets—to make conservative reforms implementable.

Professionals/managerialists, far from wishing to uniformly reduce the state's role, actually gain mobility and prestige from enhanced governments. Managerialism offers them new identities, new roles, and new power and status. As Apple (2006, p. 25) describes this new identity,

> They are not passive, but active agents—mobilizers of change, dynamic entrepreneurs, shapers of their own destinies. No longer are the organizations they inhabit ploddingly bureaucratic and subjected to old-fashioned statism. Instead, they and the people who run them are dynamic, efficient, productive, "lean and mean."

As Apple further argues, conservative policies "enable such actors to engage in a moral crusade and enhance the status of their own expertise."

Not coincidentally, such policies also provide "mechanisms of restrat-ification" that favor this class's children and the kinds of credentials they will likely earn (pp. 48–49). Thus, as it was for neoliberalism and neoconservatism, managerialism has distinct political and cultural impli-cations, exceeding its origins in the logics of practice (Clarke & Newman, 1997). That is, such movements encourage the public to *think* and *act* in ways that accept efficiency, transparency, accountability, and standard-ization as common sense—as the *only* way—even in domains of life previously exempt from such calculations. In various food policies, for instance, professional/managerial groups urge the public to rely on "pre-dominantly technocratic framings of policy debate ... around food and nutrition" as universally applicable (Timotijevic et al., 2011).

In education such professional/managerial workers have made possible conservative reforms like vouchers, standards, and accountability systems. They provided the technical expertise needed to construct tests and measure how students, schools, and even teachers perform on them. They create new "evidence-based" policies, implement them, and eval-uate their success. They implement financial systems for tax breaks and voucher payments. Their academic expertise helps construct curricula that conform to standards. They develop systems of evaluation and verify the metrics for measuring educators. They cultivate incentive systems, like merit-based pay, to engineer behavior toward specific policy ends.

Specifically in school food policy, the professional/managerial faction has had a dominant role; only neoliberals rival their influence. Partly this results from the successful entrenchment of nutrition professionals in policymaking right from the early days of school nutrition programs (Levine, 2008, especially Chapters 1 and 3). Across the programs' histo-ries, nutritional requirements have closely followed the professional expertise of nutritionists. Contemporary school food has thus followed the entire food system's push toward what Scrinis (2013) calls "nutri-tionism," an ideology holding that "Foods are essentially the sum of their nutrient parts" (Pollan, 2008, p. 28), that eating functions solely for bodily health, that nutrients are either good or bad, and that the source of nutrients—whole foods or processed foods—hardly matters. As any school nutrition director can tell you, current regulations reflect this way of thinking, for directors often find themselves having to include particular menu items to meet recommendations for this or that vitamin; to hold down fat, salt, or sugar; or to sneak in requisite amounts of whole grain. Importantly, nutrition directors frequently accomplish such nutritional feats through fortified, processed foods rather than substituting more expensive and harder to prepare whole foods. The managerial/professional class has made this possible by providing expertise on what kids should eat, how to plan menus, and how manufacturers can engineer products' nutrition.

More than just nutrition, though, New Right attacks on the welfare state in the 1980s brought intense managerialist scrutiny on costs, efficiencies, waste, and fraud in the NSLP (Levine, 2008; Poppendieck, 2010). Cost focus, firstly, became a crucial bureaucratic imperative amid drastic Reagan-era cuts, forcing cafeteria managers to accede to "consumer preferences" and selling à la carte items. Cost focus also pushed cafeterias toward processed, no-cook convenience foods that did not require pricey skilled laborers.

The NSLP and NSBP have also come under scrutiny for how much food students throw into garbage cans, whether because of its quantity or quality. Mid-1970s shifts toward "offer versus serve" attempted to reduce such waste, as has the increasing attention to "consumer" palates (Poppendieck, 2010, pp. 64–71). Technical and managerial solutions have been hard to come by, though, and still conservatives rail against limiting consumer choice or tightening nutritional standards, positions which almost guarantee more waste.

Fraud has similarly been a concern, the worry being that more children than truly entitled to will take free or subsidized meals. As part of a larger project of rooting out welfare abuse under Reagan—think of his influential "welfare queen" image (Gustafson, 2011, Chapter 2)—new requirements for income verification were added to the free and reduced-price lunch eligibility process. As I note later, such efforts found only minor cases of fraud. Nevertheless, the hunt for fraud has empowered managerialists in new ways.

In the end, the managerial and professional middle-class stay generally agnostic (literally and figuratively) about the state's level of involvement in school food. They leave that basic decision to the other ideological groups. Their role, instead, involves providing the expertise to make the system run, and they do this both in the private and public sectors. Yet we ought not misrecognize this faction as apolitical. Indeed, their participation has largely worked to resist progressive food reform by facilitating plans of the food industry, neoliberals, and neoconservatives.

An Example of Professional/Managerial Discourse

Professional and managerial new middle-class discourses differ, often, from other conservative fractions by not condemning or seeking an end to free lunches or nutritional requirements. Instead, such discourses often argue for more accountability, less waste, more efficiency, and more accuracy in the systems. That these often mean many kids will not eat often seems beside the point. Because of the highly respected skill sets involved in producing these discourses—statistics, efficiency, measurement, and evaluation—neoliberals and neoconservatives frequently incorporate or co-opt professional and managerial discourses to broaden their messages' appeal.

Take for example David N. Bass's (2010) "Congress Should Shore Up School Lunch Reliability," published in *Education Week,* the United States' largest education trade newspaper, with a circulation of around 35,000. It's important to consider that Bass worked as an "investigative journalist" for the conservative-libertarian John Locke Foundation, which advocates for educational privatization and school choice, and which seeks a "limited, constitutional government" (à la neoconservatives) by working to "transform government through competition, innovation, personal freedom, and personal responsibility" (many of these the ideals of neoliberalism; see http://www.johnlocke.org/about/). This editorial typifies the professional and managerial approach, though, by arguing that lawmakers must consider the statistical dependability of free and reduced-price school meals counting. This is crucial because school districts, other federal programs, and even academic researchers rely on this data as a stand-in for socioeconomic status (SES) and poverty.

Of course, others have noted problems in using eligibility for free and reduced-price meals before Bass. Scholars Harwell and LeBeau (2010, pp. 124–126) argue that free and reduced lunch eligibility makes for a poor indicator of SES, largely because eligibility poorly measures access to financial resources, often because of certification errors (the checks on family incomes); participation rates decline as kids go up in grade even if family income does not improve; and inferences about eligibility's impact are inherently confounded because it comes with an intervention (how much worse, in other words, would students achieve without the nutrition gained through the program?).

The problems using free and reduced-price meal eligibility get compounded by certification errors, on which Bass focuses his attention. He claims that the eligibility data are "skewed," largely because "parents are required only to self-report income on the application and needn't provide proof, such as a pay stub or W-2 form [that reports annual income]. Because of this, the potential for error, whether intentional or by mistake, is real." His proposed solution relies on verifying self-reported parental income, asking for documentation so that school districts can "weed out cheating."

Income verification has deep historical roots in the pantheon of conservative policy desires. President Reagan insisted on installing such requirements in the 1980s, during his bid to dramatically reduce the NSLP. It didn't work, though; verification netted little new fraud in the program. Instead his administration discovered relatively common income fluctuations for poorer Americans that changed their eligibility month to month (Levine, 2008, pp. 174–175; Poppendieck, 2010, pp. 198–206). What the Reagan administration's new requirements actually accomplished, though, was driving *eligible* students from the system (Poppendieck, 2010, p. 204). Income verification was thus abandoned, and now districts could not verify more than three percent of free and reduced lunch applications—the three percent targeted at the families around the income cutoffs, where most errors would likely occur. The USDA does not allow districts to verify more than this—indeed, it may constitute grounds for getting funding withdrawn, as Bass recounts nearly happened in North Carolina's Charlotte-Mecklenburg district—because verification carries high stakes. If a child's parents do not submit income verification when required, the child *automatically* loses meal eligibility. It doesn't matter whether the parents simply forgot, accidentally lost the form, or were trying to avoid being caught for fraud. The child pays the price by not getting to eat.

Bass seems undeterred by this history, though. He suggested that lawmakers "revamp" the law that prohibits requiring full verification. He presents verification softly, as a way to "review their work for accuracy" and "make some strides to ease errors." He presents it as commonsensical, that "Bringing greater accountability to the school lunch program shouldn't be controversial," but that it only becomes controversial because of "the politics of poverty" and "a political alliance between agricultural-area Republicans and metropolitan-area Democrats." And he makes a valid point, that great sums of money ("taxpayer dollars") get devoted to the NSLP and NSBP and that "policies and research are based on it," so accuracy should not be an afterthought. He does not say, however, that the costs of this policy move include more hungry children and tremendous administrative time and expense—potentially more than saved through catching any fraud. Perhaps though, given the political stances of his think tank, fewer children accessing school meals would serve their aim of a more "limited, constitutional government."

Throughout the editorial, Bass shows professional and managerial hallmarks that support conservative positions on school food. Frequent use of "business speak" and "data speak" appeal to the fiscal conservative—words like "data," "evaluate," "allocate," "verification summaries," "reliability," "evidence," "accuracy," and more. Such terms present a common sense built on "proof" and "accountability" that appeals to reasonable desires for efficient and honest government. Professional and managerial approaches, though, just like neoliberalism, reduce citizens to "taxpayers" and they ignore deep questions about morality and human costs by focusing on purely economic calculations and fidelity to theoretical ideals.

Conservatives Together and Apart

Together, the four conservative stances described above form the backbone of resistance to progressive school food reform. Neoliberals want school food privatized and subjected to free-market forces. Neoconservatives want school meal provision to support social stability and military preparedness. Members of the professional and managerial new middle class want school meals rationalized, countable, and accounted. Authoritarian populists want elitists and governments out of kids' lunches.

Importantly, despite whatever appearance my characterizations give, political ideologies rarely separate cleanly in practice. Rather than thinking of these four as clear-cut "groups," with defined boundaries and identifiable organizations representing coherent, singular ideological positions, I find it more helpful to think of this conservative typology as a set of *tendencies*. Given the ideological intermingling within the pan-Western conservative modernization since the 1970s, contemporary conservative arguments often draw from a spectrum of political beliefs. Much of this resulted from the hard work of conservatives to organize coalitions and to reduce tensions between positions. As Apple (2006) convincingly shows, for instance, the amorality of modern capitalism had an uphill climb among religious conservatives, and much creative ideological work has been done to make capitalism into "God's economy" (p. 21). Similar creative work gets undertaken, for instance, to help biblical inerrantists reconcile the presence of dinosaur skeletons in a world they believe is around 6000 years old—a necessary step for cooperation with professional and managerial factions that rely on traditional scientific skillsets for their standing in the conservative movement (for another example, see Weaver-Hightower, 2008). Still, this work of smoothing out tensions has not been completed. Deep divisions remain within US conservatism, and anyone analyzing food policy, including *school* food policy, must keep account of such rifts.

Take, for example, Rod Dreher's (2006) interesting examination of "crunchy conservatives," or "crunchy cons." As he defines his own conservatism and that of the people he featured,

> We are conservatives by conviction and temperament, and usually vote Republican (though to call us "liberal Republicans" is to fundamentally misunderstand us), but we're "crunchy"—as in the slang for "earthy"— because we stand alongside a number of lefties who don't buy in to the consumerist and individualist mainstream of American life. (p. 12)

Conservatives of Dreher's ilk reject some central tenets of conservative modernization espoused by mainstream Republicans, including neoliberalism's focus on consumerism and unregulated free markets, the crassness and over-sexualization of popular culture, and—importantly for my purposes here—the reflexive bashing of organic food, slow food, and alternative agriculture as elitist. To this latter point, Dreher's discussion of food policy and agrarianism doesn't sound much different from progressive critiques. Indeed, he admiringly quotes Wendell Berry, long a darling of progressive food policy groups, as well as Joel Salatin, an organic farmer featured in the popular documentary *Food, Inc.* (Kenner, 2008) and in Michael Pollan's (2006) *The Omnivore's Dilemma,* two touchstone texts for progressive food movements. Clearly, for Dreher's conservative faction, many important tensions in conservative ideology remain.

This diversity within conservatism serves as a good reminder that party affiliation does not always prove the best predictor of school food stances. Most Republicans take a moderate stance on the necessity for government involvement in school feeding. On the fringes, though, some reject the federal role altogether. In 2010, just a couple of months after President Obama signed the Healthy Hunger-Free Kids Act, the House voted on a simple resolution (H. Res. 362, 2010) expressing that the House "supports the goals and ideals of the National School Lunch Program"— not the precise policies, just the goals and ideals—and that "America's pupils deserve access to high-quality, safe, nutritious meals available in the school setting." Thirteen Republicans voted *against* it; no Democrats did. We must remember, though, that 155 Republicans voted *for* the resolution. So, whatever the disagreements over the details, the vast majority of conservatives support (or don't *publicly* reject) the program generally. Still, for some at the extremes of conservatism, the program is anathema.

Even alert to such divisions and nuances, one can still point to some core conservative thinking about school food that has defined rightist attempts at policymaking (and *un*making). In the next chapter, I thus explore examples that vividly illustrate the conservative approach to school food policies, the kinds of arguments they make publicly, and the rhetorical strategies involved.

Snack Three: The Pancake that Never Spoils

In late June 2009, while the world roiled from an economic crisis, I attended the School Nutrition Association's (SNA) annual national conference in Las Vegas. The SNA represents the interests of more than 58,000 members across the country (School Nutrition Association, 2019), including the gamut of the school food industrial complex, from frontline servers to district directors, university nutritionists specializing in schools to mega-corporation employees. SNA, because of its size and links with the food manufacturing and distribution industry, has an enormous role in federal policymaking, including its own lobbyist and an annual legislative conference that sends members to "charge the Hill." It receives frequent invitations to anything school food-related going on in Washington, DC, to appear in photos alongside presidents, senators, and representatives. Nancy Rice, SNA's then-President attended the signing of the Healthy Hunger-Free Kids Act (HHFKA) in 2010, for example. Michelle Obama spoke at a different SNA conference—live, too, not a recorded hello. The SNA has real clout.

I regarded the conference fondly as "the lunch lady conference," because thousands of school nutrition professionals were gathered—mostly women who looked just like the lunch ladies that fed me as a child, in their khaki capri pants, polo shirts, and sensible shoes, alongside the occasional suited salesperson or administrator. Assuming they weren't playing hooky in the casinos, attendees could go to sessions about a range of topics. At 9:45 a.m. on Wednesday, for example, they could attend presentations on equipment safety, emerging academic research in school nutrition, avoiding kitchen gossip, promoting the school food program, cost savings by using canned and frozen food, celiac disease and allergies, how supermarkets and fast-food restaurants market to kids (the one I attended), professionalism, the USDA Summer Food Program, or the HealthierUS School Challenge. I learned a huge amount at the conference, for at the time my understanding was inchoate at best. This included the difficulties of "charge policies" which would later blow up into the lunch shaming controversy (discussed in Snack Five) and the "indirect costs" that cafeterias frequently get charged for, like renting their space, paying electricity, having the garbage taken out, and cleaning by the school's janitorial staff. Sometimes, allegedly, districts just skim right off the top of nutrition budgets for other things they need for the schools. Managers and nutrition directors deal with a dizzying amount of complexity in their jobs, and attending the conference made that clear.

SNA conferees could also attend keynotes featuring high-dollar motivational speakers. There, for a mere $20,000, corporate sponsors could place their advertising on each chair, get recognized during the presentation, and even show a video. The opening session was sponsored by SweetSurprise.com, a public relations website for high fructose corn syrup producers. Each chair had a booklet about the safety, utility, and cost efficiencies of the much-maligned sweetener, which they clearly hoped would produce evangelists (or at least defenders) in cafeterias across the country. It's not just industry groups that dole out for the chance to influence what's served, either. The Physicians' Committee for Responsible Medicine, a vegan advocacy group (described in Weaver-Hightower, 2011), hosted a lovely four-course vegan dinner for over a hundred, featuring a dinnertime address on the dangers and politics of cheese, meat, and milk. This wasn't an official SNA event (it would clearly offend some of SNA's patron companies), so I don't know the price tag, but serving all those people and renting a huge ballroom couldn't have been cheap. These high-dollar attempts to sway the crowds at the SNA conference show the stakes of school cafeterias in the fights over food policy, and those stakes are clearly high.

Oh, and there was a closing night concert by Frankie Valli and the Four Seasons. It was delightful to see lunch ladies cutting loose to "Dawn," "Working My Way Back to You," and the theme to *Grease*, screaming like teenagers when the Four Seasons whipped off their jackets.

If there were any doubt that money makes the school food engine turn, that dissipated as soon as one walked into the wonderland that was the exhibit hall. It featured 760 booths, according to the program, in a massive 169,587-square foot hall. The first thing to greet everyone was a towering milk industry booth, where waitresses (basically) were handing out pint bottles of various flavors of milk to a continuously long line of thirsty conferees. Tyson was giving away branded stuffed chickens (like, the toy kind) dressed like chefs. Indeed, nearly any massive US food corporation you've heard of—ConAgra, Simplot, Kraft, Kellogg's, PepsiCo, Schwan Foods, Dole, ADM, and more—was there vying for lucrative space on school menus. At the back, at sad little tables in the prosaically titled "USDA Lane" (near to "Dairy Way" and "Produce Row," which were clearly the better side of the tracks in the SNA's fictional town) were the USDA divisions with connections to the school lunch programs. The USDA booths mostly had only pamphlets to give out and lonely looking bureaucrats-cum-booth attendants. They certainly couldn't compete for pizazz with the person in the Smucker's Uncrustables costume (Fig. 3.1).

Fig. 3.1 A person in an Uncrustables costume at the School Nutrition Association Conference, June 2009 (Photo by author)

Almost anywhere one strolled other than USDA Lane, someone had tasting samples of "super maxed out pizza roll sliders" or some such concoction. Live cooking demonstrations showed attendees how to cook in bulk with whatever sauce or ingredient. Others had booths where you could get a souvenir photo taken, or you could pick up a souvenir plate or tote bag. Indeed, so much was being given away to the lunch ladies and school nutrition directors that the conference had to have a strict "no rolling carts" policy. I was feeling cheeky, I admit, so I set myself a goal of collecting everything that I possibly could from the exhibitors in just two hours. While a rolling cart would have helped, I still managed to collect an impressive haul of freebies, samples, and promotional products with my arms, which you can see in Fig. 3.1. (Tip for the wise attendee: Find a booth giving away tote bags first, which you can use to hold a great deal more.) Mine would have been a bigger pile, but I ate the unpackaged samples while in the hall. Imagine what I could have gotten in four hours! As fun as it was, though, more importantly this haul highlights companies' desperation to get districts to buy their value-added products. School food isn't charity work for these companies, and schools in no way represent an undesirable market (Fig. 3.2).

The food sold by these mega-companies doesn't resemble what one might imagine to be "healthy" food. It's not *un*healthy, per se, but it was a lot of carnival fare food. Sure, this was the year before the HHFKA was signed, but based on the advertising and regulations I've seen, the industry continues much of the carnival fare approach. Take breakfast foods, for example. As Siegel (2019, pp. 94–95) has explained, breakfast regulations for grades K-12 have no cap on added sugar except in certain products, like canned fruit (see CFR Title 7(B)(II)(A)(220)). And, since the guidelines also don't require a protein at breakfast like eggs or cheese, cafeterias instead fill breakfast with carbohydrates, like cinnamon buns, danishes, pancakes, and muffins. Cafeterias like such sugar-glazed products because kids like them, and these confections come shelf-stable and wrapped in plastic, able to last for months. So if the bear claws don't sell one day, cafeterias can use them the next. In fact, my title for this section refers to one such product I collected at the conference. It showed no signs of rot or mold for years—literally—not until I accidentally punctured a small hole in the wrapper during a move. Then a tiny dot of green mold appeared under that exact spot, but never spread anywhere else for months after, until I finally threw it away. Sure, it's not a scientific study, so I'm not impugning the product overall, but having seen that, I don't think I'd want my children consuming one.

Fig. 3.2 Items collected from the School Nutrition Association Conference Exhibit Hall in two hours (Photo by author)

The SNA itself, even though a nonprofit, reaps substantial money from their work in representing *both* the lunch ladies *and* the companies trying to sell them equipment, supplies, and especially food. Sure, they got membership dues from individuals ($130 in 2021) and conference registration fees ($249 for regular members, $399 for industry members, and more for non-members). Their "Patron" industry members, numbering about 90 in 2018, could pay $12,500 yearly and get a host of benefits and discounts, most valuable being what the membership webpage describes as "greater exposure and access to foodservice professionals nationwide"—meaning the SNA membership directory. The SNA mails members a full-color printed magazine, *School Nutrition*, 11 times a year, filled with helpful advice and hot topics in the field, and of course a bevy of advertisements. The ads ranged from a quarter-page ad run once for $3556 (discounts add up for multiple runnings) to a one-time full-page spread for $14,812 (School Nutrition Association, 2021). As you can see in Table 3.1, the biggest, most frequent ads that year I attended the conference were for software—subscriptions, technical support packages, and user fees provide steady income for software makers—and for highly processed carnival-type foods, the biggest profit makers. The SNA also offer their industry members numerous sponsorship opportunities at their meetings and conventions, like the ads on chairs I mentioned above. For $3,000, too, companies could add something to the tote bag that every attendee got. The SNA also runs professional development training for a fee. From these varied sources, the SNA had yearly assets of $13,386,699 in 2018–2019. This amount and kind of money explains some of the difficulty in shifting the status quo of school food. Entrenched interests—in many sectors—have made their livings and, for some, tremendous profit from the federal school meals programs *as they are*. One can understand their reluctance to jeopardize that. That's not a moral judgement from me, either; I feel the same way about funding research universities! Economic and political self-interest is just an inescapable human truth to be grappled with for those who want to reform school food.

Table 3.1 Products and services advertised in *School Nutrition* magazine, May 2009 through April 2010

Product(s)[a]	# of times advertised [b]
Computer software and online services	27
Burgers (beef, turkey, and other meats)	26
Cookies, cakes, pudding, rice cereal treats	23
Pizza and pizza hybrids (e.g., baked pizza nuggets)	20
Pasta (dry and prepared)	20
Sandwiches	20
Industrial ovens, stoves, steamers, presses, and holding cabinets	18
Milk	18

(continued)

Table 3.1   (continued)

Product(s)[a]	# of times advertised [b]
Complete breakfasts in a bag or box	17
Pancakes, waffles, french toast and breakfast sausage	16
Dairy industry-sponsored programs	14
Steam tables, serving lines, displays, transport bags, salad bars	14
Sauces and gravies	12
Asian foods	11
Cereal and cereal bars	11
Company reputation or full line of products	11
Cheese, yogurt and miscellaneous dairy (not milk)	9
Chicken nuggets, patties, and tempura	9
Salsa, ketchup and other condiments	8
Bread, rolls, pastries, buns, biscuits, and bagels	7
Fruit (canned, in cups, or pre-sliced in plastic bags)	5
Fruit or tea beverages (not 100% juice)	5
Knives, sharpeners, and slicers	5
Turkey products (other than burgers)	5
Blueberries	4
Corndogs	4
Crackers, chips, and pretzels	4
Juice (100%)	4
Mexican or Tex-Mex	4
Cleaning and sanitation	3
Egg products (not whole eggs)	3
Nut butter spreads	3
Packaging	3
French fries (white or sweet potatoes)	2
Ice cream	2
Oils	2
Popcorn	2
Soy products	2
Vegetarian specialty items	2
Walnuts	2
Chilies and stews	1

(continued)

Table 3.1 (continued)	
Product(s)[a]	# of times advertised [b]
Complete snack in a bag or box	1
Conferences	1
Food preservatives	1
MyPyramid.gov	1
Pan liners	1
Refrigeration machinery	1

Note. School Nutrition editorial guidelines deny any advertising for products that "run counter to the U.S. Department of Agriculture's Foods of Minimal Nutritional Value Policy." The table is sorted first by number of times advertised and then alphabetically.
[a]Does not include SNA's self-advertising. Also does not include brand-name products or companies referred to or pictured in the articles. Only the featured product(s) are counted, not things simply mentioned or in the background (e.g., a milk carton as a prop in an ad for spaghetti sauce).
[b]Some ads are counted more than once because they advertise multiple products; thus, these counts cannot be used to count the total number of advertisements in the magazine.

To be fair, in addition to its neoliberal and purely economic positions, the SNA also has progressive impulses to celebrate and help build upon. The organization has for decades advocated eliminating the reduced-price category of subsidized lunches (the ERP campaign) and raising the income threshold for free meals. They advocate ensuring that kids have sufficient time to eat, rather than 15- or 20-min lunch periods. Conference attendees were trying to work through the difficulties and injustices of "lunch shaming" students whose parents hadn't paid their lunch accounts years before it became a national issue. Easily 300 people attended the conference session on this topic, by far the largest breakout session audience I saw. And the biggest applause line I heard at the conference was when C. Lincoln Pierce, from the Bethel School District in Washington State, suggested that a universally free school food program would solve many of these problems. Many, many school nutrition professionals want free meals for kids, too. Yes, such policies enjoy popularity in part because they make school lunch programs more economically stable and ensure more participation, but we must remember that these professionals want the best for kids, too. They deeply believe in giving kids the healthiest meals they can within the system's constraints. Most personally hand food to individual kids every day, often knowing the kids by name and knowing what struggles they have in their classrooms and at home. Progressives must learn to work within otherwise conservative, economically oriented systems by seizing on those progressive impulses to form "strategic alliances" (Apple, 2002). That's how progress will get done.

4

Conservative Talk: The Techniques for Dismantling Faith in School Food

Conservative approaches to school food reform evince more than just the underlying ideologies described in the previous chapter. They also involve rhetorical techniques. These techniques, I assert, have largely been used, as this chapter's title suggests, to undercut faith in lunch and breakfast programs, their expansion, and their regulations. Don't just take my word for it, though. Even the Secretary of Agriculture in both the Obama and Biden administrations, Tom Vilsack, sees delegitimizing programs like school meals as conservatives' goal. As he said, "The reality is a lot of our nutrition programs are under attack. They are under attack in a very consistent, thoughtful campaign to delegitimize the programs. … Make no mistake, this is a battle" (Doering, 2013).

I try my best in this chapter not to mischaracterize conservative positions, particularly with the cartoonish version of conservatives hating children or heartlessly stealing food from them. Conservatives have sincerely held beliefs, just as progressives do. Still, I do believe conservative positions generally get a lot wrong, and I endeavor to say so—with evidence—throughout.

M. B. Weaver-Hightower, *Unpacking School Lunch*, https://doi.org/10.1007/978-3-030-97288-2_4

This chapter also aims to have practical purpose, not just theoretical understanding of conservative positions, interesting though they may be anthropologically. Rather, when understood *as* techniques, conservative resistance to school food reform can show ways progressive reformers might better craft their own strategies and better communicate with the public. Such communication underpins whether we will have democratic or authoritarian school food policies.

In the following analysis, I analyze primarily rhetoric and discourse in public media to understand how conservatives view the roles, meanings, and impacts of school feeding. While I could have employed many other means—research interviews, floor debates in legislative bodies, and so on—news stories, opinion-editorial essays, televised speeches, and advocacy group reports provide perhaps the clearest, most widely accessible forms for communicating political ideologies. This has certainly been true of school food, where conservative discourses and rhetorical tactics appear across many stories and media types.

I based this analysis on a corpus of online articles collected using Google Alerts, daily emails sent from a search engine looking for user-defined terms. Using various search terms used in English-speaking countries to refer to school feeding—including "school lunch," "school meals," "school dinners," "school canteens," and "school food"—I received lists of hundreds of stories daily from 2010 to late 2021. Certainly these included stories, both progressive and conservative, related to school food. As I said, though, my focus was specifically conservative arguments. Just remember as you are reading that, for every conservative story or complaint about school food reform, there was generally another progressive story or hope for reform. I come to those in Chapter 6.

I identified conservative stories in the corpus either by their authors' explicit claim of conservatism, the author being a self-confessed conservative, their presence in an avowedly conservative source, or my recognition of conservative lines of argument based on my more than two decades of doing political analysis. My inquiry was based on critical discourse analysis methods (Fairclough, 1995; Gee, 2014), which pay close attention to language, assessing how language carries ideology and reproduces social inequalities.

The following sections lay out two general aspects of the conservative discourses around school food. The first includes the *specific arguments* that conservatives have used to resist school food and/or its reform. Then I explicate the *rhetorical tactics* that have been used by conservative thinkers in the school food debates, going beyond just the content of arguments to examine style. Naturally, arguments and their tactics closely intertwine, and overlaps almost inevitably occur.

Arguments

The specific arguments made for and against policies and reforms fall under the larger conservative tendencies described above—neoliberal, neoconservative, authoritarian populist, and professional/managerial. A set of arguments overlap these groups, too, which I include as "cross-group" arguments. So here are the kinds of beliefs conservative individuals and groups have about changes proposed or made in school meals.

Neoliberal Arguments About School Food Reform

Reforms would have unreasonable or ruinous costs to business and industry. Numerous companies and agricultural product organizations depend on the National School Lunch Program (NSLP) and National School Breakfast Program (NSBP) for tremendous portions of their profits. Milk producers, for instance, likely sold around 4.244 billion half-pints of milk in 2014 through the NSLP alone (National Dairy Council, 2015). Reactions to attempted reforms to any milk requirements thus bring immediate pushback, including public advertising blitzes (Associated Press, 2009). The United States Potato Board was also alarmed by the Institute of Medicine suggesting serving kids fewer potatoes in the NSLP. While school sales make up only about 1% of national sales of potatoes, the real threat was to the potato's reputation:

[T]hat relatively small impact of schools doesn't defuse the issue. "Even though the percentage is small, no one likes to lose any market share," [USDA representative Gary] Lucier said. "That's business."

And while the potato industry is far from going bankrupt, even if the nation's schools pull out every last baked tater tot, the school kids of today may be influenced to eat fewer potatoes as adults, said Lucier, who last year authored a report that examined how children carry vegetable eating habits into adulthood. ... The potato industry is concerned that a decision by the USDA to embrace the IOM's recommendations would send a message to parents who shop for groceries that other vegetables carry a higher value than the potato. (Kawamoto, 2010)

Industries often warn of ruining or unfairly tarnishing their reputations. This takes an economic perspective on school lunches, usually pushing the product's major nutrient profile (calcium for milk, no cholesterol and low calories for potatoes) rather than, say, its role in a holistic diet for students. Such arguments urge policymakers to privilege economic interests over that of students, based on a partial view of the stakes.

Subsidized meals are wasteful handouts to middle-class and wealthy people. Naomi Riley (2017), in responding to the New York City Public Schools' creation of universally free school lunches, particularly that the program, in part, avoids the stigma of free meals, acerbically conjectures

Maybe middle-class families should receive food stamps so that poor families don't feel stigmatized. Perhaps we should send the 1% to eat at soup kitchens, so people in desperate straits won't feel bad about their situations. Or maybe we should offer public housing to the rich, so no one who is forced to use it will get self-conscious. The left says it wants a safety net, but if everyone falls into it then the safety net is properly called socialism.

Her arguments ignore the cost savings involved in utilizing community-based certification, forgoing costly management of free and reduced-price meal paperwork, and the relatively small cost of a school lunch compared to that bureaucracy. We should also remember that the moral cost of letting a student go hungry because they sit at the cusp of eligibility but can't afford the meals or can't get their parents to return the paperwork.

Market-based solutions work best. If the world runs best by turning everything into a market, then neoliberal adherents believe the invisible hand of the market can guide them out of every problem. They praise corporate proactiveness, like the beverage industry voluntarily—though under increasing threats of regulation—agreeing in 2006 to remove full-sugar sodas from schools (William J. Clinton Foundation, 2010). Former food executive Hank Cardello (2010), though, believes that we can rely on the market to do the right thing without government interference. He suggests,

> From a corporate perspective, having the flexibility to determine which products to change or promote offers a huge advantage over a government imposed one-size-fits-all tax mandate. And progress would be easily tracked, since every company knows how much of each individual product it sells and the calorie content (one of the side benefits of those bar codes on the label). (para. 16)

Cardello suggests that the government instead need only let food companies keep their current tax deductions on their advertising ($15 billion of it annually) if they reduce calories in their products 2% each year for 10 years. The challenge, of course, comes when an industry sees no incentive for market reforms. What levers would public health have then?

Market-based solutions, moreover, have a patina of morality for some conservatives. Teresa Mull (2017), a fellow at the free-market advocating Heartland Institute, illustrates:

> Enacting free-market solutions would go a long way in stimulating the economy and empowering parents to provide for their families.

> The number of low-income kids relying on government schools for food would decrease, and so would everyone else's tax burden. Parents would also be reminded of the pride and joy that comes from providing for one's family, and they need to know that bonding with a child at the

grocery store and the dinner table is a thousand times better for his or her development than any government-subsided meal could ever be. (paras. 15–16)

Yes, the language here focuses on child development, but it's wrapped in the moralistic language of "provide for their families" twice, not being a "burden," as well as "pride and joy." These rely on the readers' alignments with emotional valences rather than more objective policy decisions.

Unions, trial lawyers, and bureaucrats benefit disproportionately from reforms. Michelle Malkin (2010), former Fox News contributor and now a host on farther-right Newsmax TV, believed that Michelle Obama's efforts to improve school lunch were not meant for children's interests.

Who really benefits from the ostensible push for improved nutrition in the schools? Think purple—as in the purple-shirted army of the Service Employees International Union. Big Labor bigwigs don't care about slimming your kids' waistlines. They care about beefing up their membership rolls and fattening their coffers. (para. 1)

Like numerous conservatives before her, Malkin leans on the trope of left-wing labor advocates as pulling the strings of the Democratic party. Trial lawyers are frequently seen as beneficiaries of any Democratic policy, too. The Wall Street Journal editorial board (2011) seemed incredulous at claims that voluntary advertising restrictions on unhealthy food wouldn't eventually provoke lawsuits by the US Federal Trade Commission. "It doesn't have to. That job will be cheerfully assumed by consumer activists and their allies in the plaintiffs bar" (para. 4).

Other welfare makes free school meals "redundant." Howard Portnoy (2010) complained that the United States has too many welfare programs, and the poor shouldn't need school meals on top of those others. He praises a letter written to the conservative *Washington Times*:

The writer, James Gill, notes that the law provides breakfast, lunch, and dinner to children at the schools they attend. "That being the case," Gill writes, "should we expect the dollars spent on food stamps that go toward the feeding of families to drop correspondingly?" In other words, will taxpayers be double-billed for the cost of feeding other people's children?

The fear that "other people" might get one over on the system has long roots within welfare opposition (Gustafson, 2011; Schram et al., 2003). But to suggest that free school meals should reduce the modest amount the average eligible child gets in SNAP benefits—less than $1.40 per meal for 2019 and 2020 (Center on Budget and Policy Priorities, 2021, p. 4)—seems particularly miserly, especially because the vast majority of students nationally do not actually get three meals at school each day.

Private sector actors do it best. While the *Wall Street Journal* frequently rails against school food programs, it apparently depends on who does the reforming. When it involves philanthropy, they celebrate reforms because this fits the neoliberal worldview of capitalism and markets functioning to make the world a better place. For instance, their "Donor of the Day"—an occasional feature from 2010 to 2016— on March 18, 2011 (West, 2011) was The Palette Fund, who funded a grant to Wellness in the Schools, which "will place a part-time chef alongside the kitchen staff in a high-poverty public school for one year. The chef will help the staff initiate a cook-from-scratch menu" and teach four cooking classes. They can praise this reform because it comes from a market actor without the involvement of the state.

Focus on "moderation," because individuals are to blame for poor choices. In neoliberal thought, the ideal market provides a person with choices, and if one makes bad choices (either as a producer or consumer) only the chooser can take the blame. It represents the market's "invisible hand" working to ensure that good ideas and a good society flourish. Neoliberal arguments thus blame obesity, food insecurity, and poor nutrition solely on the choices of individuals. Take as an example Whole Foods founder and CEO, John Mackey, who said in an interview with the *New York Times* (Gelles, 2020) that the market would provide if only people "want different food."

> Whole Foods has opened up stores in inner cities. We've opened up stores in poor areas. And we see the choices. It's less about access and more about people making poor choices, mostly due to ignorance. It's like a being an alcoholic. People are just not conscious of the fact that they have food addictions and need to do anything about it. (para. 26)

Industry tends to put the onus on consumers, too, arguing that "moderation" should be the goal rather than restricting snacks or sodas. Seeking "energy balance" seems the term of art for suggesting that it's more about individuals needing to exercise if they indulge in too many calories. Take Ben Boychuk's explanation:

> Of course, every expert on nutrition and good health will tell you diet is part of the anti-obesity equation. Another factor is exercise. Kids are more sedentary. Usually, television and video games get the blame. Some blame also falls on parents unwilling to say "No" to their kids at the fast-food drive-thru. (Boychuk & Lopez, 2010)

Thus, parents' and students' individual choices about food and exercise deserve the blame, not systems. It's thus not a matter for the market (and definitely not lawmakers); the choosers simply must choose better rather than putting restrictions on everyone.

We should "empower" consumers with more information (i.e., advertising). The choices prized by neoliberals require, in their thinking, the fair and free flow of information needed for consumers to make decisions. If markets become skewed by misinformation, market competition becomes unfair. The theory seems straightforward enough. In some cases, though, this argument becomes a defense of advertising. As Beth Johnson (2011) succinctly puts it in her criticism of the Interagency Working Group's suggesting voluntary limits on advertising unhealthy food to children, "I believe the government should be empowering consumers with more information, not less." Ads for children are, in this way of thinking, information to be weighed, no different from any other. Yet children's inability to fully process such "information" does not seem to give them pause. According to the Institute of Medicine (2006),

> Before a certain age, children lack the defenses, or skills, to discriminate commercial from noncommercial content, or to attribute persuasive intent to advertising. Children generally develop these skills at about age 8 years, but children as old as 11 years may not activate their defenses unless explicitly cued to do so. (p. 5)

It strains credibility to believe that the Trix Rabbit or Ronald McDonald have information to share about wise food choices anyway. And when the advertising budgets of international food behemoths so utterly eclipse those of more credible, unbiased information from the USDA or nutrition scientists, one can hardly see this as "empowering" consumers. As Talbot (2013) wrote in the *New Yorker*,

> Information and moral suasion ...are important, but in the salty-sweet sea of temptation we all swim in, they're not really enough. Big Junk Food, with its ubiquity and its advertising juggernaut, will always swamp earnest nutritional pamphlets and public-service announcements. (para. 11)

Reforms present overly burdensome regulations on local schools. Many neoliberals believe that government, when it regulates school food, oversteps the bounds of simply ensuring market fairness and instead creates distortions in the market. A commentary on the conservative think tank Heritage Foundation's website (Bakst & Sheffield, 2017), for example, suggests that

> Policymakers should end this federal overreach into school cafeterias by rolling back these heavy-handed standards [of the HHFKA] and allowing school districts to develop their own standards. This would allow local officials to tailor school meals to the needs of their communities and better respond to the demands of parents and students. (para. 6)

Should taxpayer-citizens want more than 13,000 school districts in the United States each doing whatever they want with nutritional standards? What if 1000 of those districts want to do away with standards altogether, allowing for deep frying everything, candy at every meal, and full-sugar sodas? And what of the cost of duplicating the efforts of working out healthy meals district by district rather than having national-level nutritional advice? After all, food's propensities for healthfulness, obesity, or disease risks don't vary when they cross school district lines.

Students should have choices. A *Las Vegas Review-Journal* editorial (2011), in lambasting the supposed failure of Los Angeles' food reforms because some kids were instead eating Hot Cheetos, suggested kids need choices about whether to have nutritious meals at school.

> Should kids be taught about health and nutrition? Sure. Should they be given healthier alternatives to corn dogs, doughnuts and nachos? Sure. But "alternatives" imply choice. ... If you want to run a successful Nanny State, you've got to eliminate this "competition" business, this idea of "choice." In the end, they're going to end up needing a lot more guards and some barbed wire.

One wonders if the editorial board also wants kids to choose not to take algebra or history. Maybe schools should make vaping optional, just like Hot Cheetos. Why should food be treated differently from other things we mandate or restrict in schools?

Neoconservative Arguments About School Food Reform

Follow history, especially the "founding fathers." You might remember Vin Suprynowicz's (2010) editorial, "Choosing 'Profusion and Servitude' Over 'Economy and Liberty'," from the previous chapter. He argued that providing weekend meals to students was a form of tyranny-by-debt from the government, and a main argument was that Thomas Jefferson warned us of such a possibility.

I also categorize this as a rhetorical tactic, discussed next. After all, pundits commonly designate whatever policy they dislike as contravening what the US's "founding fathers" forewarned. Yet this theme particularly appeals to neoconservatives. It suggests an inerrantist reverence for the thinking of "our" heroes. (Understandably, many US citizens consider some of these "fathers" as tainted by Native American genocide and land theft and African American slavery, not as heroes). Neoconservatives forward arguments that only by going back to the original intent of the framers of Constitution can we preserve society, individual freedom, and democracy. It always seems better in the past.

Take as another example a short essay by Brian Vanyo (2014), where he moves from school nutrition regulations back to Franklin Delano Roosevelt's New Deal and then back to quotes from James Madison and Thomas Paine. For Vanyo, the "path toward tyranny" from school nutrition regulations is clear: Give the government an inch and it will take your liberty. (See also the slippery slope technique discussed below.)

Reform jettisons traditional, deeply adored comfort foods and Americana practices from the past. A key tipoff for neoconservative arguments, according to Apple (2006), comes from longing for the past, a mythical "golden age" when things were simpler and everyone "knew their place." Sometimes this shines through in arguments about school food with a longing for iconic "American" foods and how school cafeterias and parents used to provide lunch. For example, David Smith (2011) received an email from a healthcare provider about lunch packing tips that sent him down memory lane. "When I was a youngster my mother packed my lunch …. Those lunches generally included a sandwich and a snack. We bought our milk at the school for 4 cents a bottle." With a start that makes any whippersnapper recoil, he continues, "In my day, we ate our lunch because we were, well, hungry, and we weren't so picky." *He* survived potential food poisoning, he says, so why should modern parents make sure to pack ice in a lunchbox?

A major backlash from neoconservatives regarding school food was to the 2014 SmartSnacks regulations on foods sold outside of the NSLP (like vending, snacks, fundraisers), the first time a US secretary of agriculture had set standards for so-called competitive foods. Conservatives immediately seized on cupcakes and other nostalgic foods. As former Texas Rep. Ted Poe (2014) argued, "Bake sales in schools are as American as apple pie and the flag. … But now the almighty federal government has cooked up new rules controlling public school bake sales." Such arguments rely on icons and symbolism, the fear of losing tradition and culture, to sway people against policy positions.

Stop accommodating small minorities. Lisa Barone (2011), complaining with her headline that "*Schools Exaggerate Food Allergy Concerns,*" notes that only 150 people a year die from allergies, whereas gun and vehicle accidents claim thousands. So even if a peanut could make a child sick in her daughter's school, it's not a big deal. "In the US, the minority historically has yielded to the majority." She asks, "When have our school officials become the food police? Maybe they should put more energy into teaching our kids so they can compete better in the future with the rest of the world." Alongside the nationalistic discourse, such arguments suggest that "our" culture (the majority) shouldn't have to compromise with minority needs. One could easily extend this to refusing to provide non-dairy alternatives to the lactose intolerant, culturally inclusive foods for significant populations of non-White or international students, and more.

Being poor in the US isn't as bad as being poor elsewhere— American exceptionalism. For neoconservatives, one cannot admit to anything wrong about the United States—apart from progressives and the peace movement, I suspect. The US even does poverty and hunger the best! (Or, at least, the least bad.) Take Rector's (2007) claim from a report for the Heritage Foundation:

> Roughly a third of poor households do face material hardships such as overcrowding, intermittent food shortages, or difficulty obtaining medical care. However, even these households would be judged to have high living standards in comparison to most other people in the world. (p. 16)

Julie Gunlock (2011) doubles down on this exceptionalism, complaining that a new *Sesame Street* muppet, Lily, who suffers from intermittent food insecurity, misleads the young impressionable minds watching. "Lily's lucky to be 'poor' in this country. *Sesame Street* would be wiser to educate America's children about the real poor and hungry—the 98 percent of the world population who live outside the United States" (para. 2). No one should complain about hunger, such arguments seem to say, unless your conditions resemble charity infomercials about the most desperate African famines.

Authoritarian Populist Arguments About School Food Reform

Reformers are elitist. You will remember from the last chapter that populism centers on rejection and resentment of elites. This happens regularly in arguments against school food reform (e.g., Lusk, 2013). Representative Ted Poe's (2014) diatribe against snack food regulations, noted above, also raises the specter of elitism, both in choice of schools and food choices when he says, "The Washington regulators, many of whom have their kids go to private schools that are not covered by the new rules, say kale chips and quinoa are to replace snow cones and Valentine candy. Isn't that lovely?" Elites like quinoa and kale. Regular ol' folks like Valentine candy and snow cones. Whatever his policy position—that we need no policy whatever—Poe's argument revolves more around the reader's distaste for snobs and hypocrites.

Similar arguments have a long history in England, as well, where critiquing the posh for their classist attitudes seems almost like a sport. Brendan O'Neill (2011) makes his feelings about England's attempts to curb obesity plainly about "class hatred" with his editorial, "This Jihad Against Junk Food Is Driven by Naked Snobbery for the Lifestyles of the Lower Orders." Rather than seeing regulation and reform as attempts to undo the legislated unhealthiness of food deserts and unregulated school meals—a potential benefit to working-class peoples—such policies provide

> another way to express their fear and loathing of the strange, unknowable blob that inhabits council estates and inner cities. And they increasingly do it through the issue of food, fantasising that Those People spend all day munching on recklessly unhealthy fare. (para. 2)

Here again the hoped-for rejection of a policy follows an emotional appeal to reject the policymakers' supposed snobbery, not any health or social merits of the policy.

"They" want to take foods away—banning. Naturally, a tendency to refer to a shadowy Other of elites and bureaucrats, typically just a vague *they*, can creep into arguments of any political persuasion, conservative or progressive. It has a key populist appeal, thus making it rife within authoritarian populist arguments. This holds particularly true with food reforms because "They," supposedly, will take away the grub you love. Take for example the Elyria pink cookie, described by Owens (2014) as "a velvety, cake-like, scrumptious delicacy glazed with a huge dollop of sugary pink icing" made from "lots of butter, a couple different kinds of sugar, some Crisco and sour cream." But now schools can't sell this local treat, enjoyed only in Elyria, Ohio, "thanks to federal intervention that first lady Michelle has made her signature issue." The cookie runs afoul of the 2014 SmartSnacks regulations. Nothing says that students can't eat them at home, of course, but it becomes a federal infringement of basic freedoms, neoconservatives seem to say, to not have them at school.

Refusing government assistance is the moral choice. Part of the *authoritarian* impulse of authoritarian populism comes from installing one group's morality—Judeo-Christian, especially—and using it as a point of judgment against those who disagree with them or who come from marginalized groups (the working poor, racialized minorities, immigrants, and those of other faiths). Think of Paul Ryan's speech about children eating school lunch having an "empty soul" from the previous chapter (American Conservative Union, 2014). Consider, too, Marilyn Tarkalson's (2012) opinion piece, "It is My Responsibility to Feed My Children Not the Government's." She recounts,

I grew up in a family of eight and I remember bringing home a free school lunch form for my parents to fill out to see if they were eligible. My parents told me it was their responsibility to feed us and they felt it was more important to teach their children to be self-reliant than to accept government handouts. (para. 6)

While Tarkalson was at pains to emphasize that summer feeding programs, the focus of her essay, were fine for truly needy people, only those who refuse assistance achieve the morally high position of "self-reliant."

Having traditional, conservative family values will fix everything. Robert Rector's analysis of poverty, noted above, presents a straightforward fix for child poverty:

The main causes of child poverty in the United States are low levels of parental work, high numbers of single-parent families, and low skill levels of incoming immigrants. By increasing work and marriage, reducing illegal immigration, and by improving the skill level of future legal immigrants, our nation can, over time, virtually eliminate remaining child poverty. (p. 16)

The racial subtext here isn't even subtext. Moreover, though, Rector—and many who argue similarly—present a basic policy prescription that has guided welfare policy since the mid-1990s. Make people work for benefits, incentivize marriage, and provide job training. Rector throws in immigration limits, too—not so much a family value as a conservative vexation. Such prescriptions for welfare, though, have done little more than make it hard to access financial assistance for those especially in need (Tach & Edin, 2017).

Professional-Managerial Arguments About School Food Reform

Nutrients mean particular foods are good. Western ideas about food have largely been overtaken, as I said previously, by "nutritionism" (Scrinis, 2013):

> Nutritionism—or nutritional reductionism—is characterized by a reductive focus on the nutrient composition of foods as the means for understanding their healthfulness, as well as by a reductive interpretation of the role of these nutrients in bodily health. A key feature of this reductive interpretation of nutrients is that in some instances... it conceals or overrides concerns with the production and processing quality of a food and its ingredients. (p. 2)

This kind of argument, focusing on one or a handful of nutrients regardless of holistic health or processing concerns, rears its head almost any time food gets reduced or restricted in school food regulation.

Milk provides an ideal example. When full- or reduced-fat chocolate milk was being restricted in favor of only *fat-free* flavored milk in the HHFKA, conservative pundits were apparently alarmed that children might never get calcium or vitamin D again. Singer (2011) said that her son needed the chocolate milk when he was in elementary school because it was the spoonful of sugar—or four—that made the medicine go down. He got his vitamin D and calcium, plus some protein, and I got peace of mind.

The dairy industry had a similar message (Shoup, 2017), including from the then-president and CEO of the National Milk Producer's Federation, Jim Mulhern:

> "Milk is the number-one source of nine essential vitamins and minerals in childrens' [sic] diets, and when its consumption drops, the overall nutritional intake of America's kids is jeopardized," Mulhern said.
>
> …
>
> When kids don't drink milk, it's extremely difficult for them to get sufficient amounts of three of the four major nutrients most lacking in childrens' [sic] diets: calcium, potassium, and vitamin D. (paras. 4 and 12)

In fact, one can find calcium, potassium, and vitamin D abundantly in foods. According to the National Institutes of Health (2021a, b, c), people have many, and sometimes even better, ways to get these nutrients besides just milk. Vitamin D one can get from direct exposure to sunlight, as well as fish and eggs; even soy, almond, and oat milk have nearly as much or more vitamin D than cow's milk. One can get three times the potassium from half a cup of dried apricots as from a cup of milk. Indeed, lowering the fat percentage of chocolate milk, as the regulations recommended, *increases* the calcium, as nonfat milk usually has more calcium than whole milk. While I wouldn't personally like it, one can consume more calcium from a tin of sardines than a cup of milk.

The point, however, remains: arguments based on nutritionism can lead us astray. Professional/managerial thinkers appreciate the countability, regulatability, and accountability of nutrient-based planning. Readers and policymakers, though, can get lost in a maze of shifting nutritional advice and scientific terms, and they forget the holistic role of food and even the pleasure, environmental impact, and social justice implications of a food.

Data usage and accuracy are key. The *professional* part of professional/managerial generally entails making the program countable, controllable, and accurate through technical knowledges and skills. If you can't count on the data (pardon!), you can't ensure the program has done what it should for who it should. Paul Gregory (2011), writing for *Forbes*—a venue usually most enamored with the wealthiest 400 Americans—does his own dive into USDA statistics and finds that the "hunger lobby" supposedly exaggerates the claim that one in five children—nearly 16 million Americans—are "hungry" or "food insecure." The red flags he notes to discount food insecurity include that "almost half [of poor households] own their own homes, three quarters own a car, and almost all have a color television." How removed must someone be from the plights of poverty that they imagine having a place to live, a car to get to work—particularly necessary in suburban and rural areas— or a *color* television (did they even sell black and white TVs in 2011?) should exempt a person from being hungry? Nevertheless, he claims that anti-hunger activists err when they say "one in five" children in the US suffer food insecurity. He cites USDA data (likely, Nord et al., 2010) to suggest anti-hunger advocates should instead say about one in ten or 10%. He stresses that inaccurately using statistics like this could skew policymaking, urging legislators to act in ways they wouldn't if they knew the true extent.

Yet Gregory misreads the data tables, or he mischaracterizes his opponents; 21.3% of food insecure households in 2009 did indeed have children living in them. The 21.3% figure was not all food insecure households, including those without children, as he claimed (see Nord et al., Table 1B, p. 7). In fact, because many households have more than one child, obviously, the percentage *of all children* who live in an insecure food household in 2009 was 23.2%. Even considering fewer children experience food insecurity themselves *within* otherwise food insecure households—because they are "shielded" by the adults or by social programs like school food or the Special Supplemental Nutrition Program for Women, Infants, and Children (WIC)—the percentage should actually be 13.4%. That includes 12.1% in "low" and 1.3% in

"very low" food secure households. But that's largely arguing over seman-
tics, and it's simply inaccurate to chide hunger advocates for peddling
"folklore" statistics.

Other critiques of data are more technical. The use of free and
reduced lunch data for other educational decision-making has some well-
established problems (e.g., Harwell & LeBeau, 2010), so conservatives of
this ilk commonly criticize the data and its usage. Take the opinion piece
by Ann Helms (2011), who questions whether high-poverty schools
get more teachers and other aid than they ought to, based on free or
reduced-price meal eligibility.

> Some say the lunch-aid data are too shaky to form the foundation for
> such spending. Eligibility is based on self-reported family income, and the
> small sample of applications that are checked typically turn up problems.
>
> For instance, [Charlotte-Mecklenburg, North Carolina, schools'] most
> recent check of 236 applications found 30, or 13 percent, that weren't
> eligible. And 36 families, or 15 percent, didn't respond to the request for
> documentation.
>
> If 13 percent to 28 percent of all students getting the aid were not
> really eligible, that would translate to roughly 9,600 to 20,700 students
> inaccurately tallied as "poor." (paras. 5–7)

Helms goes on to suggest, mainly with quotes from school board
members and conservative pundits, that much of this inaccuracy comes
from fraud, that "Many families in North Carolina lie about their
income" (Bass, 2008). The true reliability of this data is vastly more
complicated than simply branding it "fraud" or accusing parents of
lying. As Poppendieck (2010, Chap. 7) details, reviews of free and
reduced-price meal applications may prevent more *eligible* children from
participation than they catch fraud. Many families lose or forget to
return paperwork (let he or she who has never missed a form crum-
pled in a backpack cast the first stone!). And income verification checks
by law focus on those closest to the cutoff incomes, so statistically more
honest mistakes and recent income changes will occur among those families than would be found among families farther from the cutoff incomes.

It hardly seems fair or accurate to characterize everyone in such situations as liars. It betrays a rather uncharitable view of the poor as morally corrupt.

We must focus on efficiency and cost-effectiveness. For professional/managerial conservatives, "it's all about getting the most for our money" (Hovde, 2010). Frequently arguments against increasing school food funding point out the sheer size of overall welfare spending and the numbers of programs receiving this money.

> The average family with children in the lowest-income third of the population, [Robert] Rector [from the conservative Heritage Foundation] noted, already receives more than $30,000 in assistance annually from these programs. The total amount of spending on this population exceeds $475 billion annually—which is only about half of all welfare spending. … "Before you propose spending even more money, you ought to at least have a reasonable accounting of where this money is currently going in 70 different programs, all of them going effectively to the same population." (Franc, 2010)

Franc seeks to "demand real evaluations of whether anti-poverty programs actually help the poor, and then defund those that do more harm than good while expanding those that actually lift the poor out of poverty." The charge boils down to duplication of services and lack of accountability for what works. Certainly citizens should ask their government to spend their tax dollars wisely and effectively, and proof of that would be ideal. Yet accounting like this overly simplifies where welfare money, after mid-1990s welfare reform, goes. The libertarian Cato Institute, in a study of welfare benefits versus salary from work (Tanner & Hughes, 2013), concludes that there were then actually 127 programs focused on "anti-poverty" (they may be counted differently), many of which don't even distribute individual benefits but rather run community programs. He also rightly corrects the impression of major overlap: "Clearly no one receives benefits from all of these programs. Indeed, many federal welfare programs are so small or so narrowly targeted that few receive benefits. Yet many recipients do receive benefits from multiple programs" (p. 14), though these don't duplicate the same types of aid (utilities assistance, food assistance, medical care, housing subsidies, etc.). In other words, the worry about duplication is overblown. If anything, many low-income people find it difficult to access even one program for any particular need (Tach & Edin, 2017).

Develop systems of accountability and economic incentives. Neoliberals believe deeply in market-driven psychology that economic rationality and incentives can shape behavior in positive directions. But it's the professional/managerial new middle class who design and implement those systems at scale. One approach involves accountability, designing systems that ensure people can't cheat, and holding programs responsible for their progress. One can see the accountability approach in means-testing for free and reduced-price lunches, for example. Bass (2008), you might remember, wanted a more robust system of checking family applications for subsidized meals, and Rector (quoted in Franc, 2010) wants a "reasonable accounting" of where anti-poverty programs spend their money.

Another approach to designing systems revolves around incentives; it's the carrot to accountability's stick. Take the example of Denver, Colorado's, attempts to apply a "pay-for-performance" scheme for cafeteria workers. (Teachers have been used as guinea pigs for incentive programs for many years, with generally disappointing results [Kozlowski & Lauen, 2019].) As Garcia (2011) reports,

> Lesh [executive director for enterprise management at Denver Public Schools] says the plan for food service workers will focus on getting more kids to eat better at school. One measure could be the number of students who purchase lunch.

> "If our participation rate say at this school is 50 percent and someone brings it up to 60 percent and 70 percent, that's a measure of efficiency," Lesh said.

> …

Lesh says other measures could be health inspection scores, profits, grades on customer service.

"Smiling at a child, making the food right, garnish it, having it look good, having it taste good," said Lesh. "They do that, [students are] going to come back." (paras. 9–14)

Certainly few would question the value of treating children well and making the food and experience appealing and pleasurable. And certainly Garcia rightly emphasizes the "positive" approach of rewarding people for doing their job well rather than punishing them. Rather, note the underlying philosophy: Nutrition professionals on the front lines would largely find their motivation in data targets and economic incentives and that the professional/managerial class has the logistical means to make it happen. Such a system, furthermore, still surveils workers through analytics and metrics, and it depends upon new expectations of emotional labor ("Smiling at a child") that can have negative impacts on workers and their performance (Hochschild, 1985). Smiling can feel great, don't get me wrong, but smiles are emotionally best and most effective if one *wants* to do it rather than simply doing it as performance to bump up their metrics.

Cross-Group Arguments

The following arguments combine central tenets of certain of the four conservative positions covered earlier. In parentheses I note specific traditions each attracts.

Focus on "freedoms" (neoliberal, neoconservative, authoritarian populist). The editorial board of *The Wall Street Journal* (2011) saw free speech violations in the Interagency Working Group on Food Marketed to Children's (2011) suggestions that corporations *voluntarily* reduce marketing of "foods with significant amounts of nutrients that could have a negative impact on health or weight—specifically, sodium, saturated fat, trans fat, and added sugars" (IWG, p. 3). In this view, corporations have freedom of speech and advertising should remain unfettered, even from government suggestions.

Freedom also apparently means deep fat frying for some conservative politicians. Sid Miller, the controversial Texas Agriculture Commissioner, made an oily splash in 2015 by proposing returning deep fat fryers to Texas school cafeterias. "We're about giving school districts freedom, liberty and individual responsibility… We're all about local control and not big brother, big government control" (McGee, 2015). In response to criticism, he continued,

> The school districts that disagree with my decision, I just have to say, don't get a deep fryer! Don't let the room mothers bring cupcakes to school. That's your decision, [and] I'll support you on that. That's what this is all about. It's not about cupcakes. It's about freedom and liberty.

Of course, one person's freedom—to not wear a mask during a pandemic, say, or deep fry whatever you want—represents another person's removal of freedom—to not get sick or to have healthy food at school. Nevertheless, such arguments have tremendous appeal, for no one likes to feel controlled, and the federal government as boogieman has a long rhetorical history.

Reforms create socialism (neoliberal, neoconservative). If one wants to get conservative readers' blood boiling, few concepts do it as reflexively as the specter of socialism. As noted above, Riley (2017) cries socialism when New York City made school lunch universally free. Krayton Kerns (2012), writing for *The Laurel Outlook* in Montana, reacts to an unfortunate incident when a 4-year-old in North Carolina was forced to buy chicken nuggets (Burrows, 2012), and goes so far as to say "Marxist philosophy did not break the American family overnight. It took decades to systematically disassemble the backbone of our great republic." It seems bombastic to suggest from one regrettable incident that Marxism has taken over. Most Marxists I know would be surprised by the news of their conquest.

Science and experts are wrong or self-interested (authoritarian populist, professional/managerial). Conservatives of many stripes have increasingly come to distrust scientific research, experts, and "consensus" (e.g., Mooney, 2012). Naturally, we want every citizen to critically appraise science, not simply take it for granted. Yet across issues, one can see a reflexive rejection of science, of institutions, and of consensuses that governments rely on to make policy (Mooney, 2012), including in the arena of school food.

Earlier I cited Gregory (2011)—the color television guy—about his skepticism of how many children truly count as food insecure. His questioning of the statistics fits this category, too. The core argument holds that "experts" willfully try to mislead the public and lawmakers.

Consider, too, William Hoar's (2010) essay for the *New American,* "Feeding Insatiable Government Appetite Won't End Obesity." He casts doubt on the World Health Organization, the Centers for Disease Control and Prevention (CDC), "anti-fat activists," and the body-mass index (or BMI, which does have real limitations). These sources have obesity wrong, he seems to say. He feels especially in the know because of his independent research, mostly using a right-wing think tank's book written by Patrick Basham and John Luik, whose previous books have argued that smoking isn't that bad and gambling is good. For obesity, Basham and Luik use two CDC studies (probably Flegal et al., 2010, and Ogden et al., 2010) based on BMI—the CDC and BMI apparently now OK to use when they supposedly prove one's conservative point. Yet they mischaracterize (or misunderstand) the CDC authors' findings that obesity had reached a "plateau" for the past decade by suggesting that means obesity panics have become overblown. The CDC papers were hardly that sanguine; their conclusion was that the plateau was not good: "The prevalence of obesity in the United States continues to be high" (Flegal et al., 2010). So Hoar's initial confidence that he had seen behind the fraud of the experts—because "Governments ... want to hop on the soda-pop bandwagon ...to collect more levies to improve their bottom line"—seems overblown. Nevertheless, it illustrates well the kinds of arguments that some conservatives utilize to shake confidence in school food programs.

Waste, red tape, and "unfunded mandates" are rife (neoliberal, professional/managerial). I described earlier the professional/managerial penchant for focusing on bad data, particularly when it comes to the certification of eligibility for free and reduced-price lunches. The technical aspect of catching fraud, along with the poor decisions that might arise from bad data, concerned them most. Neoliberals also respond to such arguments because they generally believe the state is feckless and inherently more wasteful than the private sector. A related argument thus underscores this general belief, emphasizing waste and fraud as a feature rather than a bug, as the saying goes, of government programs.

Arguments in this vein usually focus on what students will waste: all that "healthier" food. Take for example Ben Wolfgang's (2011) editorial, "'Healthier' School Lunch at What Cost?" He quotes at length a director of food services in Pennsylvania, who believes meals under the rules would become "unpalatable" to students:

> For example, Ms. Castaneda said, the proposed sodium restrictions for student lunches resemble diets previously reserved for those battling serious illnesses such as kidney disease. The rules also would require students to eat more fruits and vegetables, forcing schools to serve extra apples and broccoli even if experience shows that children can't—or won't—eat them. (para. 4)

What good does it do, this argument poses, if students hate the food and throw it away? Plate waste certainly presents problems for the NSLP and NSBP (Buzby & Guthrie, 2002; U.S. Department of Agriculture, 2019). That isn't new, though. Waste has been a problem for a long time (see Poppendieck, 2010, pp. 64–71). US adults, I feel obliged to note, waste food at rates incredibly similar to those of children. Students in the school lunch program wasted 21% of available calories (U.S. Department of Agriculture, 2019) while consumer-level losses, meaning food adults wasted, was that same 21% (Buzby et al., 2014, p. 19). For conservative pundits to suggest that the NSLP creates a unique waste problem is simply disingenuous.

Nutrition directors did report initial waste increases after the HHFKA, but after taking some time to adjust and developing innovative approaches, they also reported that plate waste returned to "levels comparable to pre-HHFKA levels" (USDA, 2016). While a valid concern, plate waste has solutions, so it should not be a disqualifying metric for the whole program or needed reforms.

Welfare trains people for sloth, idleness, and dependency (neoconservative, authoritarian populist). As the COVID-19 pandemic raged on and schools reopened in the Fall of 2021, one—and only one—school district in Wisconsin decided to forgo the federal waivers allowing universally free school meals. Members of the Waukesha School Board were worried that their students would suffer a "slow addiction" to this federal freebie (Linnane, 2021). As board member Karin Rajnicek explained of her vote,

> I had three kids. I had them and so I'm going to feed them. I feel like that's the responsibility of the adult. ... I feel like this is a big problem, and it's really easy to get sucked into and become spoiled and think, "It's not my problem anymore — it's everyone else's problem to feed my children." (Sheffey, 2021)

The idea that most people who get public assistance stop working and become dependent has become a cliché, both among conservatives and among center-left politicians and social scientists of the 1990s who crafted welfare reform (Gustafson, 2011, Chap. 2). Changes since those reforms have largely focused on tying poverty assistance to work, a reflection of US culture's (and neoliberalism's) foundational belief in the *moral* value of paid work. Anyone availing themselves of resources seen as welfare—and school meals have unfortunately been tagged with that label because *some* get it for free or reduced prices—still get their moral responsibility and work ethic challenged. No one advancing this argument seems to realize they are ultimately advocating harming children to punish the morality of "spoiled" or lazy parents. Nor do they realize that curtailing meals does not punish the poorest students, who get their meals for free already, but rather working parents who struggle to stay just above the poverty line (Colicchio, 2020).

Perhaps the worst misinformation perpetrated in conservative school lunch arguments—knowingly or not—comes from suggesting that the program was always "meant" as welfare, only or mainly for poor children. That is simply not historically accurate. The focus on poverty reduction since the 1960s has led the public to think so, but as I detailed in Chapter 2, the original intent was a program for all students. Remember, the preamble to the NSLA said preparing for national defense, helping farmers, and "safeguard[ing] the health and well-being of the Nation's children"—not just poor children, but "children." Purposefully or not, though, connecting the program to welfare serves as an easy means of attacking it for the same reasons the public has been conditioned to dislike welfare and judge its recipients. If they simply focus on the free school meals to the exclusion of paid meals, conservatives can continue to suggest its moral and administrative failings with slogans rather than evidence.

Parents' rights and states' rights are most important (neoconservative, authoritarian populist). Whether the federal government should have any business in providing school food has been hotly debated since the beginnings of the program (Ruis, 2017, Chap. 7), and it continues to this day. Shoshanna Weissmann (2019), writing for the *Wall Street Journal*, suggests that if states disliked the Trump Administration gutting the HHFKA's nutrition regulations, rather than sue they should make their own higher standards. Chuck Norris (2011), you might remember from Chapter 3, felt the same. Let individual districts or schools decide whether meals should be healthy, they seem to say.

A similar appeal comes from those who argue parents know best what their kids will eat. Jen Singer (2011), for instance, advanced a kind of "you don't understand the pressures of parenthood" argument in reaction to the proposed removal of chocolate milk (though ultimately only milk containing fat couldn't be flavored). Certainly individual parents might feel adverse impacts from nutritional requirements, but at the population level policymakers must make choices about how to best address most children's nutritional needs.

Using "celebrities" and children's characters is wrong (authoritarian populist, professional/managerial, neoconservative). Julie Gunlock's (2011) critique of using *Sesame Street* to tell "lies" about hunger embodies this argument. She says,

> despite the grim "facts" and figures thrown around by children's television programs, celebrity spokespersons, and the mainstream media, the vast majority of children living in America are healthy and well fed.

The facts about hunger in America really aren't that alarming—certainly not alarming enough to warrant a whole new Sesame Street character! (paras. 3 and 4)

And it's not just children's celebrities that come up for criticism. Celebrity chefs like Jamie Oliver and political celebrities, especially Michelle Obama, frequently receive criticism for daring to advocate for healthier food in school lunchrooms.

"One-size-fits-all" solutions from the federal government don't work (neoliberal, neoconservative, professional/managerial). While definitely aligned with states' and parents' rights noted earlier, this argument adds in the subtext that local custom or context necessitates local solutions, and bureaucrats in Washington, DC, can't understand. The solution usually posed involves letting localities do what they want or depending on corporations to voluntarily cast aside profit considerations. Republican Kansas congressman Tim Huelskamp made a similar observation regarding portion sizes in the HHFKA during a visit to Abilene High School, whose students had been protesting (see also Snack Four):

"The obesity crisis in this country affects perhaps less than 20 percent of the kids," he added. "But with this new program it means 100 percent of the kids go on the same diet. We have 100,000 schools across the country. We put them all on a diet. I believe in local control and I think most Kansans do as well." (Horan, 2012, para. 16)

Naturally the language here exaggerates; the calorie maximums for school meals in no way represent a "diet" in the sense of restricting calories. The minimums and maximums were based on giving average students slightly more than a third of their daily calorie needs for lunch (750–850 calories for 9th–12th grades, less for younger grades). Sure, some football players and other athletes might not have been satisfied by those meals, but school nutrition programs can hardly base their menus on linebacker needs (see Snack Four).

The government wants to control us. The editorial board of the *Wall Street Journal* (2021) has a simple explanation for why President Biden and Democrats in congress wanted to increase social spending for families in poverty, including on school lunch universalization: "This is now about mainlining benefits to middle-class families so they become addicted to government—and to the Democratic Party that has become the promoting agent of government." While the editorial suggests that vote getting for Democrats provides a strong motivation, a more sinister undertone of addiction metaphors and control lurk here. Tennant (2010), though, provides the most bombastic warning about government control:

> There is, indeed, no such thing as a free lunch. A people that expects to be given bread and circuses from their government without being controlled by that same government expects what never has been and never will be. After all, slaves in the antebellum South got free meals, too.

Comparing school nutrition regulation to slavery is preposterous and reprehensible, but the subtext about those who support the policy goes beyond the bounds of goodwill in civil discourse. Couldn't Democrats' motivation simply be wanting to cut down on child poverty and making the economy more broadly fair for the fully employed but still struggling? And couldn't supporters of such policies be genuinely, morally in favor of such a vision of society rather than just addicted or controlled dupes?

The government has no constitutional right or responsibility for school lunch programs (neoconservative, neoliberal). Tennant (2010), who we just heard compare nutrition guidelines to pre-Civil War slavery, starts his essay with a common complaint among neoconservatives. "Remember that clause in the Constitution that gives the federal government the authority to regulate school bake sales? Even if you don't, Congress does." Whatever one thinks of school food nutrition, the thinking goes, it's not in the enumerated powers given to Congress in the US Constitution, thus invalidating any such laws. Vanyo's (2014) editorial, "Regulating School Lunch Oversteps Government's Authority," illustrates the argument: "To begin with, the Constitution, which establishes the federal government's limited authority, says nothing about a federal power to regulate school lunch menus—this power is actually reserved to the States under the Tenth Amendment." One could, of course, make this argument about thousands of issues, so Vanyo uses it quite selectively here. Many who argue that such regulation does exist in the Constitution cite the "General Welfare Clause"—Article I, section 8, Clause 1, "to provide for the common defense and general welfare." It is among the most contentious of the Constitution's phrases. Whatever one's preferred understanding of it, to say that regulation has *no* basis in the Constitution discounts even the framers' disagreements about the phrase's meaning (Schwartz, 2022).

Rhetorical Tactics

Every political position uses rhetorical techniques, above and beyond the specific arguments made. Progressives do it. So do conservatives. Often, in fact, they use the same tactics. Both poles of the political spectrum and everything in between, for example, tend to pick singular enemies to use as metonymy for a particular issue they don't like. Progressives like to blame everything on Donald Trump or the billionaire conservative activist Koch family, for instance, because doing so enflames the passions of progressive readers. So do not take the following list to imply that only conservatives practice rhetorical trickery; rather conservatives often use these *particular* tactics when addressing school food issues.

Killing the Messenger

The first general group of tactics focuses on the people involved in the debate, sometimes instead of the warrants of the argument. Many of these techniques mirror arguments made in the sections above.

Most prevalently, the op-eds in my corpus were prone to **creating singular enemies.** Former First Lady Michelle Obama and *Food Revolution* star and celebrity chef Jamie Oliver were the obvious targets during the era of this study. Policies and programs thus became "Michelle Obama's MyPlate food guide" (Portnoy, 2011) or regulations "trumpeted by" or "championed by Michelle Obama." True, she did advocate for the HHFKA and other school food regulation, but she certainly wasn't the only one. Clearly some of the authors seem to think pinning it on her will reflexively raise the ire of conservative readers.

Conservative pundits frequently **focus their criticism on particular organizations**, too. Often, in the vein of trying to pin disagreements on singular enemies, they deride left-leaning nutrition organizations. Margo Wootan from the Center for Science in the Public Interest provided quotes frequently, and sometimes she was the target for ire. Michelle Malkin (2010) went after the Service Employees International Union, saying that "SEIU fat cats" were behind the anti-obesity push. The same focus accrues to friendlier organizations to conservative arguments. Industry lobbying groups frequently get tapped to comment, like the Grocery Manufacturers of America, the American Frozen Food Institute, the National Dairy Council, and the Independent Dairy Farmers of America. The conservative pundits generally give rebuttal opportunities to those groups even if they don't always extend the same courtesy to progressive groups.

Name-calling and loaded descriptions were part and parcel of many arguments, too. Horan (2012) talks about how the HHFKA's regulations were putting students on a "diet," though no regulations called for diet levels of calories. That just sounds more inflammatory, so it stays. Bronwyn Eyre (2011), just before becoming Minister for Education in Saskatchewan's provincial government in Canada, complained of "nutrition Nazis"—yes, she went there—when her child's school sent home a note with tips for packing healthy lunches. Much more common was decrying "food police" (Lusk, 2013) or "food cops," as in Wilson's (2011) "Enjoy Halloween Candy Despite the Food Cops." Hoar (2010) called President Obama simply "the thin smoker in the White House."

A favored way to attack progressive policy positions, aligned somewhat to elitism, involves **charging hypocrisy**—that the person suggesting the policy doesn't or wouldn't eat the same way themselves, nor feed their own children that way. One can see this frequently with conservative commenters, gloating when they get a picture of Michelle Obama eating junk food (or photoshopping their own). They also suggest she's a hypocrite because her daughters' school while in Washington, DC, had fancier food (Owens, 2014). In a cheeky bit of legislative tomfoolery, Representative Rodney Davis, Republican from Illinois, introduced a symbolic bill, the "School Nutrition Fairness Act" (H.R. 3686, 2014), that would require White House state dinners to comply with the rules for school cafeterias (Gore, 2014). If school kids must do it, this suggests, President Obama would have been a hypocrite not to do the same.

Charging that **reformers don't understand children's eating habits** occurred often. Justin Wilson, quoted by Pham (2010), provides the typical thinking: "if what they want isn't in the vending machines, kids will bring food from home or buy it outside of school. In other words, the government can't force kids to eat their vegetables." Others, like Singer, discussed above regarding chocolate milk, suggest the same goes for their *particular* kids.

Reformers try to "frighten" people according to some conservative commentators. Lyons (2010), for example, complains of the various "panics" and "scaremongering" that have attended school food reform in England. The revolt over using "pink slime" in school meals (see Snack One) was simply "hysteria" and "pointless panic," according to Carl Shaffer (Shaffer, 2012).

Numerous conservative commentators also suggest that **supporters of regulation miss the "real" issue**—the real issue being whatever issue the pundits think more important. Glenn Cook (2010) blamed lack of exercise, particularly outdoors. An expert quoted in a News 4 Jacksonville story ("Ban on sweet drinks in schools on hold," 2010) thinks "You've got refined carbs like white breads and cereals that are a problem, as well. ...The veggie amount that should be served—there are a lot of things that can be thought of" instead of Florida's proposed ban on chocolate milk and "sugary drinks." Whatever the food regulation being argued against, this technique says we should blame something else.

Blowing Events Out of Proportion

The second group of techniques involves focusing on a small, usually outlier event or outcome. The writer seizes on splashy incidents, despite their rarity, as if emblematic that progressive reform has gone awry.

Highlighting singular failures counts as the most prevalent use of this technique. For example, the Hoke County, North Carolina, child with a packed lunch who was forced to eat chicken nuggets instead was a widely reprinted story, even overseas (e.g., "US teacher suspended over chicken nugget spat," 2012). A similar incident happened to "dozens of children" at Uintah Elementary School, in Utah, when the children's lunch accounts ran out of money. Their lunches were "snatched away" (Shoichet, 2014), a practice now widely known as "lunch debt" and "lunch shaming." Eyre (2011) tells us that "a six-year-old Quebec boy was barred from a drawing contest because his mother sent a Ziploc bag in his lunch box" in contravention of the school's plastic reduction efforts. Amidst serving 31 million lunches a day at hundreds of thousands of schools across the United States, of course some cafeteria employees will occasionally do something wrong, perhaps even cruel. We shouldn't excuse or overlook these incidents. Yet an incident making the news doesn't make it common nor a reason to jettison progressive school food reforms.

Some conservatives declare reforms a failure prematurely. Sometimes commentators find it difficult to give policy and practice reforms a proper chance to be implemented and for those affected to become acclimated. They pounce on reforms as "failed" within months. The editorial board of the *Las Vegas Review-Journal* (2011) didn't wait six months to declare the Los Angeles Unified School District's healthier menu a fiasco. Their proof? Some kids disliked the food and the district said it would make adjustments. Howard Portnoy (2011) gave the MyPlate food guide, which replaced the food pyramid on June 2, 2011, that same six months before declaring it a "spectacular failure." His evidence? Americans weren't *already* eating by the guidelines according to a market research firm.

Some focus on a small number of complainers. Conservatives could hardly contain their glee when a Twitter hashtag (#ThanksMichelleObama) began circulating with pictures of skimpy, unappetizing school lunches students were served (e.g., Confessore, 2014). Tweets and focusing on football players who complained about portion sizes (e.g., Yee, 2012; see also Snack Four) takes a relatively small group and makes it seem big. And naturally Michelle Obama didn't make, nor would she have approved of, those photographed meals.

Focusing on the Impacts for Conservative Groups

The third group of techniques concerns itself with assessing policy impacts only for traditionally conservative groups and concerns. While certainly all groups deserve consideration for intended and unintended consequences, the problem often comes from these being the only groups or considerations remarked upon. Or, at least, editorialists give them priority over wider public concerns.

Conservative pundits in the corpus focus much criticism on **the impact on "taxpayers,"** a not-subtle suggestion, by negation, that those whose children eat school meals are *not* taxpayers. It demonstrates an underlying resentment of those who might take free or discounted meals and dare to comment about their composition or quality. And while the US tax system seems somewhat progressive in that wealthier people pay higher percentages in taxes at the federal level (at least if they don't have shell corporations and bank accounts in the Cayman Islands), even people living near the poverty line contribute taxes, including payroll taxes, state taxes, and sales taxes. As the non-partisan Institute on Taxation and Economic Policy's analysis shows,

> The national effective state and local tax rate is 11.4 percent for the lowest-income 20 percent; 9.9 percent for the middle 20 percent; and 7.4 percent for the top 1 percent …. This means the poorest Americans are paying one and a half times as much of their income in taxes than the top 1 percent. (p. 4)

As Vanessa Williamson (2017) puts it, "If one's fiscal contributions are measured in the hardship they impose, the poor are paying dearly" (para. 4). The conservative arguments, willfully or not, overlook this reality.

Conservative arguments frequently emphasize reform's **cost to businesses and lunch programs**. Such arguments often prioritize economics over human and public health considerations. One can almost guarantee that saying "eat less" of anything will receive instant pushback from industries and their lobbyists (Nestle, 2007). The dairy and potato industries both mobilized when chocolate milk and white potato limitations were considered in 2010–2011. Congressional Republicans also railed against the policy changes on the assumption that such reform might cost schools nearly $7 billion. The USDA, though, said the savings from Republicans scrapping those reforms would have "little to no effect" (ElBoghdady, 2011). Such arguments also overlook the gains and savings for businesses and lunch programs, such as improved employee productivity and health.

Focusing on regulations and standards—rather than, say, health benefits—seemed almost mandatory. Certainly many instances of the almost obligatory "we've got an obesity problem, sure, but..." appear, yet pundits mainly fume over regulations, their sinister or authoritarian intent, and their being unnecessary. Authors also spent much space reporting anti-regulation advocates' views.

Sometimes the regulations aren't even about school meals, but the impact on school meals gets used to garner sympathy. Mike Stuart (2010), former president of the Florida Fruit and Vegetable Association, noted in an opinion piece that the US Environmental Protection Agency shouldn't enact clean water mandates on Florida because, if growers must spend time and money to protect water, "Where will the nation's public schools get the fresh fruits and vegetables they need to support the increased nutritional standards for school lunches?" (para. 6).

Conservative arguments often **give industry representatives ample opportunity to respond to stories.** Journalists routinely get responses from the multiple sides of an issue as a standard practice, but in conservative arguments industry representatives receive more opportunity than proponents or occupy more visible spots in the story. In an article (Gray, 2010) on lowered sodium recommendations in the 2010 Dietary Guidelines for Americans, for example, only one supporter of the guidelines gets quoted. Yet both the Salt Institute and Kraft Foods provide quotes for the industry perspective, and they get the last word.

Frequently, articles **allow industry groups to quote their own research** (as if it were unbiased) or to **critique the research methods**

of scientists (when they aren't qualified to do so). That same Dietary Guidelines panel article (Gray, 2010), for example, gives the following from the salt industry:

> Lori Roman, president of the Salt Institute, an industry group, said 1,500 mg is a "make-believe" number that is not based on scientific research. She said the human body needs more salt. "People all over the globe eat between 2,700 mg and 4,900 mg of salt daily because they have a physiological need to do so," she said. (para. 10)

Sodium recommendations, while not having absolute scientific certainty—a state common to nutrition research because of its complexity (Weaver & Miller, 2017)—hardly counts as "make-believe" or not based on research. The Dietary Guidelines (Agriculture et al., 2010) based their sodium recommendations on advice from the Institute of Medicine (2005), which included 26 pages of references to scientific studies. The Salt Institute quote is self-serving misinformation, but the reporter leaves it unquestioned, along with the unsourced reference to a "physiological need" for nearly 5000 mg a day. For many conservative arguments, the deference of not fact checking goes to other conservative voices that agree.

Language and Logic Techniques

The fourth set of techniques apparent in conservative arguments involves the purposeful use of language and logic approaches to persuade, shame, inflame, or misdirect. This list is not comprehensive, of course, but the following tactics are particularly prevalent.

Using what I call "*Declaration of Independence*-speak" stands out in the corpus, not as prevalent necessarily, but as uniquely part of conservative arguments. You might remember Vin Suprynowicz's (2010) essay from the previous chapter, in which a bill to create federal supper programs for schools leads to "profusion and servitude." Such arguments not only reference founding documents of the US, but they sometimes begin to sound like them with inflated diction and slogans intended to capture the patriotic high ground for the author.

"**Of course I support children, but…**"—and similar statements—appeared often, used to deflect criticism of the not so pleasant ideas presented. North Dakota Senator John Hoeven, when asked about changes he wanted to the HHFKA, said, "We're all about making sure the kids are healthy—that they eat in a healthy way—but we have to work on it in a way where you have that local control and flexibility" (Severns & Parti, 2014). As the old saying goes, when there's a *but,* ignore what came before because everything after that represents what the person really thinks. Naturally, arguing that children's health is less important than adults' profits and ease won't prove politically popular. This frequent tactic shows at least rhetorical support to avoid most backlash.

Some conservatives suggest **reformers and reform make us "soft" or "timid"**—a nuanced challenging of American masculinity. The "man-on-the-street" portion of the story "Ban on Sweet Drinks in Schools on Hold" (2010) clearly connects nutritional reform with being too risk averse:

> "I think there's too much government in our lives now, too much in schools," said Michael Stover.

> Stover thinks that if anything should be mandated, it should be exercise.

> "How about letting them eat what they want and then making them go outside to play?" he said. "Put the GameBoys down, go out and play a little football, wrestle. God knows, take off the helmets and ride a bike." (paras. 8–10)

To my mind, it's a strange argument, suggesting that kids shouldn't wear bike helmets, often on the grounds that younger generations didn't have them and those kids "turned out fine" (though many didn't). Connecting eating any food one wants with the "manly" acts of playing football, wrestling, and braving traumatic brain injury on a bike makes plain that part of the objection to food regulation comes from a perception that risky behavior builds character.

Kerns (2012) similarly suggests that American parents have become "timid," proved by their inability to make lunch for their children. "Back then [in the 1960s], parents demanded the freedom to raise their children as they saw fit, but the '60s began the conditioning of parents to be meek and yield to the whims of an all-knowing big government." Meekness, timidity: these challenge the masculine character of readers and the nation.

Psychoanalyzing the opponent effectively allows conservative pundits to pathologize arguments they disagree with rather than engaging philosophical differences. Those who support regulations for tackling unhealthy eating Giuda (2012) diagnoses as "insecure," and "desperate for power and dominance over the masses" (para. 16). Many other pundits think progressives have "trust" problems. Hovde (2010), as so many others do, wants the government to *trust* school districts to make their own menus and nutritional goals.

Slippery slope arguments suggest that if we permit one thing to happen, an inevitable and increasingly bad series of events will follow. Glenn Beck, conservative radio and television host, relies on such arguments to an extreme extent. Speaking of Michelle Obama and her attempts to reform food policy, he said,

> You're going to have to tax, you're going to have to make it more and more difficult. But when those options don't work, how do you get people to stop eating French fries, because French fries still beat carrots. What's left? Well, now you have to start thinking about punishments — maybe a fine, maybe even jail. But it always starts with a nudge. (quoted in Media Matters, 2010)

Not stopping there, he suggests that eventually the government will shoot citizens for eating cookies and french fries. He says it will lead to "global government." Later in the same article, John Stossel suggests that the next step includes "deciding who we'll marry, where we'll work." All this from suggesting federally provided meals feature carrot sticks rather than french fries!

Word choices and metric choices often slant toward conservative positions in many of the arguments presented. Regulations "tighten"

(Zhang, 2007) rather than, perhaps, "protect." "Flexibility" sounds so much nicer than "letting cafeterias have no standards or requirements." Another frequent argument poses that welfare and President Johnson's "War on Poverty" has been a "failure" because poverty still exists. The Heritage Foundation's Robert Rector, for example, notes that the same percentage of the population was poor as he was writing as there were in 1967 (Rector, 2014). But what if the metric was "misery averted" through the money spent? Certainly one hopes for the total elimination of poverty, but total reform would be needed for that, and conservatives have traditionally supported only subsistence-level aid.

Frequent use of neoliberal buzz words stands out in the corpus. *Choice* stands chief among these. Giuda (2012), for example, uses *choice* 18 times in his essay for *Forbes*. To his way of thinking, everything the government does takes away an individual's choice. Don't want to pay your fair share of taxes for public schools? That restricts your choice to send your kids to private school. Limitations on soda sizes and nutrition guidelines for school lunch restrict everyone's choice to join in the obesity and diabetes epidemics. Of course, such discussions about the relative weight of personal freedoms and community responsibilities have been going on for centuries; they represent the fundamental left–right divide in politics. What's new, however, is the suturing of economic terminology, particularly neoliberal terms, onto these debates, blurring the lines between political and economic interests.

Invoking Race

The final theme within my exploration of conservative rhetorical techniques involves the invocation of race, even bald racism, as an explanation for poverty or a reason to reform the school food programs. Racial politics remain central in both conservative and progressive movements, though in differing ways. While Donald Trump made racist dog whistles a standard practice—so much so that they were often less like dog whistles and more like fog horns—usually the racial politics of school feeding seem more subtle, more polite.

Paul Ryan, the former Republican House Speaker and vice-presidential candidate, for example, the week after releasing a Budget Committee majority report on poverty that reviewed school meal programs and other federal aid (House Budget Committee Majority Staff, 2014), got into trouble for his diagnosis of poverty on the radio show of President Reagan's Secretary of Education, Bill Bennett. Ryan said:

> We have got this tailspin of culture, in our inner cities in particular, of men not working and just generations of men not even thinking about working or learning to value the culture of work, so there is a real culture problem here that has to be dealt with. (Whitaker, 2014, para. 3)

Political analysts easily recognize the barely coded racial language of "culture" and "inner cities" (e.g., Anspach, 2021). Yet language and discourse are not most important in this discussion, for such attitudes have clear material consequences. Just months later, the Republican agriculture budget sought to give schools waivers for the HHFKA's nutrition requirements, allowed white potatoes for WIC after intense lobbying from the potato industry, and, most controversially, restricted a program for summer feeding to rural areas only (Rogers, 2014). The latter rural exclusivity, critics asserted (e.g., Smith, 2014), was intended to move money away from largely Black urban areas to majority White rural areas.

Or take as an example the 2011 institution of a free breakfast in the classroom program in all Chicago Public Schools. When the school board considered and passed the measure, a group of parents presented them with a petition with 1100 parent signatures opposing breakfast during class time (Hood & Eng, 2011). Their explicit objection was to the loss of 10–15 minutes of instructional time. Another quote from the article gives a different impression, though. Sandra Hamilton, one of two parents quoted in the article who had children at Blaine Elementary School, said "We fully support breakfast in the classroom for schools that need it, and we think it's marvelous there, but we think it's not right for our school" (para. 10). What's so different about Blaine Elementary from "schools that need it"? Well, Blaine is an arts magnet school in Lakeview, a wealthy neighborhood that houses Wrigley Field, home of the Chicago Cubs baseball team. And its community is 77.6% White within a larger city that's with only 33.3% White residents (Chicago Metropolitan Agency for Planning, 2021). The school has 53.1% White students in a district that overall, at that time, had only 8.5% White students in its elementary schools (Chicago Public Schools, 2011). No, when the parents say that breakfast is less important for their kids, but "marvelous" for kids over "there," they mean that free breakfast in the classroom is for children of color.

Other race references are more explicit. For example, pundits make several references to China, generally as a specter of fear. Suprynowicz (2010) laments that the US government borrows money to pay for social welfare programs "from the Red Chinese, whose goals are seldom ours," and Hoar (2010) says he "hesitates to note that a lack of exercise also plays heavily into the equation, lest the federal government have us all doing mass exercises similar to Communist Chinese calisthenics" (para. 7). Yes, these authors foreground communism here, but the *us vs. them* language, paired with a historic and current US antipathy for Asian cultures and peoples, not so subtly racializes the debate.

I certainly don't want to suggest that principled stands on the size and roles of government somehow equal racism. They don't, and arguments like that from progressives are intellectually dishonest or lazy. Yet it would be disingenuous to assert that school feeding policy debates have no racial overtones, given its history in race politics (see Chapter 2) and its strong conflation with welfare, which has its own deeply racialized history (Schram et al., 2003). In a country so deeply scarred by the sins of slavery, forced removals, legalized racism, historical use of the police and military as racial enforcers, segregation, and deeply unequal economic and social indicators, how could school lunch *not* be tainted with racial politics? "Other people's children" hardly feels like a phrase of love and human community—it means poor kids, immigrant kids, Black kids, and kids on the reservation—but it shows up often in school food debates, both explicitly and implicitly, as a reason to ignore, castigate, or strip down school food programs.

Conclusion

Let me reiterate that conservative resistance to school food is about more than just rhetoric. Material effects and implications come from these debates, actual policy maneuvers that conservatives have attempted over the program's history, that have endangered, rolled back, or stalled progress. These are things like draconian reporting requirements, redefining what counts as healthy or includable, cutting budgets, and privatizing. Progressives must guard against such effects, not just counter the rhetoric. I will say more about how to do that in Chapter 6. In this chapter, though, I have taken the important step of showing the *whys* of conservative resistance and *how* they justify resistance to the population they serve.

Arguing over food reform, as I mentioned earlier, ultimately means arguing over the ability to define the basic terms of our lives. Neoliberalism, for one, attempts to install as common sense thinking of ourselves as primarily consumers and social life as primarily competition. That holds true in food debates, as well, for conservative movements want to define some basic things: What is a "vegetable" (is it a green bean or pizza sauce)? What is "water" (solely H_2O, or "nutrient-enhanced water beverages")? What is "healthy"? What is a society's responsibility toward its least fortunate members? Whose culture will be represented on the plate? Whose religion? What rights do minorities (including food minorities, like vegans) have? What technologies and industrial processes will we accept in the food system, and what won't we accept?

School lunch, like other seemingly peripheral issues, plays a part in conservatives' larger project of school reform. It isn't enough to push vouchers and back-to-basics education in the curriculum. The conservative project is holistic, and we should pay attention to every facet of the policy milieu (Anyon, 2005), including food. Conservatives do.

More than that, though, progressives need to push back against reforms that ultimately function in un- or even anti-democratic ways. Rather than democratic systems, neoliberalism subjects everyone to the tyranny of the market (more money = more voice; business interests eclipse public health). Authoritarian populists and neoconservatives subject us to the tyranny of the cultural majority. Technicists and managerialists subject us to the tyranny of statistical systems and cold, amoral policy techniques. This will not do.

At the beginning of the previous chapter, I said right-wing resistance *explains* progressives' incrementalism. In part, one might attribute that to some timidity within the US left, particularly centrist Democrats, who cling to bipartisan traditions of the past. It's a pragmatic stance, sure. Take small wins (like the 6 cent per meal increase in the HHFKA). Fiddle with nutrient rules (like sodium caps) to push health goals. Fight attempted roll backs (like ketchup as a vegetable). We lack, though, a progressive vision within national-level politics to fundamentally rethink and improve school food. I will return to this in Chapter 6, giving one possible progressive vision.

In the next full chapter, though, I turn to a place where they have already tried progressive reforms to their national school meals program: England. It tells a story of amazing reforms, unintended consequences, and the constant threat of conservatives trying to undo reforms. The England case study explores the possibilities of working within a neoliberal/neoconservative political context toward progressive reform. In part, it answers the question, how do you get a staunchly conservative, neo-Thatcherite government to give free meals to all children? And how can everything go wrong when that government undercuts progress? The upcoming chapter on England provides the detailed brushstrokes on top of this chapter's sketching. Before that, though, a linebacker-sized snack.

Snack Four: Hungry, Hungry Linebackers

In 2013 and early 2014, the face of undermining Healthy Hunger-Free Kids Act (HHFKA) nutritional regulations was my own senator (at the time), John Hoeven of North Dakota, a Republican who had recently been the state's governor. He toured a handful of lunchrooms in the state, announcing that his "Sensible School Lunch Act" (Senate Bill, S.427, 2013–2014), cosponsored by a few other agriculture and ranching states' senators, was going to fix the lunch problems that constituents, he said, had frequently contacted him about. According to his press release (2014),

> "A one-size-fits-all standard *for school lunches left students feeling hungry and our schools struggling to meet* unnecessarily strict *new meal requirements,*" said Hoeven. "*North Dakota* students spoke up and made it clear that the program wasn't working. Together we were able to get the USDA to agree to provide permanent *flexibility in the school lunch program to make it work for our students, for our school nutritionists and for our school districts.*"

> *Hoeven sponsored the Sensible School Lunch Act, which provides school districts with* greater flexibility *to meet the nutritional needs of all students,* after hearing from North Dakota students *who were left feeling hungry due to new,* strict *school nutrition standards enacted at the beginning of the 2012-2013 school year. The rule attempted to curb obesity by* strictly limiting calories, *protein and grains for all students* without any flexibility *to meet the* needs of athletes *or others whose dietary needs do not fit the guidelines.*

I have italicized words here that illustrate the basic lines of argument for Hoeven, ones which appear in each press release and news report about the bill, and not coincidentally conform to conservative rationales explored in Chapters 3 and 4. "Flexibility" for cafeterias seems always to appear, as does that phrase "one-size-fits-all" which serves as the natural foil to flexibility. "Strict" functions the same way. "[S]trictly limiting calories" he meant to sound like a diet, but an 850-calorie ceiling for lunch hardly represents a strict limit. Here, though, Hoeven and his staff added the wholesome notion of a groundswell of students—particularly athletes—and concerned parents as a rationale for the bill. As he said in his visit to Century Elementary School, just about 3 miles from my home at the time,

> *I heard from kids across the state saying Senator Hoeven will you help us with school lunch we're not getting enough to eat we're not getting the foods we want can you help us the kids were so creative they sent in letters they sent in videos [sic]. (C. Johnson, 2014)*

I don't know whether he got as many student videos and letters as he led us to believe, but reasons abound for skepticism about his goals and motivations being solely about feeding athletes.

To be fair, some well-covered student protests and boycotts happened around that time in reaction to school lunch changes. As one *New York Times* article (Yee, 2012) enumerated, schools outside Pittsburgh, Milwaukee, and Newark, New Jersey, had each seen boycotts. (I wouldn't characterize that as a mass movement, but it's not isolated. A nephew of mine had the same complaint at the time, and he lived in South Carolina.) The article also mentioned a somewhat viral video made in Western Kansas.

That video, "We Are Hungry" (blk5348, 2012), a parody of the popular song "We Are Young" by the band Fun, has many hallmarks of a teenager-produced video I might have seen in my high school teaching days. The students—from Wallace County High School in Sharon Springs, Kansas—ham it up, with a slightly awkward teenager air, lip-synching lyrics like these, from the video's description on YouTube:

Give me some seconds
I, I need to get some food today
My friends are at the corner store
Getting junk so they don't waste away
My lover ate her 2 grams of meat
Just about to starve
My bread was taken by some school bully
Askin' bout s'more
...
So by the time you go to practice
And you feel like falling down
I'll carry you home
[Chorus:]
Tonight
We are hungry
Set the policy on fire
It can burn brighter
Than the sun

Except, it turns out that the students didn't write those lyrics. Apparently their English teacher, Linda O'Connor, wrote the lyrics for them (Wang, 2012). That doesn't sound typical for a "student-produced video"; why produce such an elaborate video if it wasn't for an assignment? And if it was for an assignment, surely the teacher wouldn't do the work for the kids. Strangely, too, an entire class of elementary-aged students dressed and backpacked for a school day, seemingly, feature in the video crawling along the ground. And there's a real ambulance with two real EMTs dressed for a workday featured in the video. Do you know how much an ambulance ride costs?! Indeed, it turns out that the English teacher along with the school's art teacher, Brenda Kirkham, were the video's masterminds. O'Connor listed herself as the video's "Writer and co-producer" on her LinkedIn profile (as of mid-November 2021). The video's star, wearing an "I [heart] Beef" t-shirt and lip-synching to a suspiciously professional-sounding soundtrack (which couldn't have been cheap), was Callahan Grund. Then a junior living on his family's cow-calf operation, Grund "is still highly involved today" (in late 2021) with that ranch and now is the executive director of a cattle disease tracing organization (U.S. CattleTrace, 2021). I can't find evidence that the teachers were directly related to the beef industry, but Sharon Springs is, according to Grund, "a very small farming and ranching community" in the western part of Kansas (USA Today Staff, 2012), so it's not inconceivable.

If the situation weren't suspicious enough, the video's YouTube description suggests that anyone wanting to "help repeal the new guidelines" should visit the Facebook page for Nutrition Nannies (www.facebook.com/NutritionNannies/; accessed November 15, 2021)—in the right-wing sense of "nanny state." And just who put together this Nutrition Nannies page? Representative Steve King, conservative Republican from Iowa, and Representative Tim Huelskamp, a conservative Republican from Kansas; it says so in the page's information section. The two representatives had just three days before introduced their No Hungry Kids Act (H.R. 6418, 2012) that called for lifting calorie maximums in the school lunch program. The *exact same day* as the "We Are Hungry" video was posted on YouTube, they also first posted to their Nutrition Nannies Facebook page. The school in the video, Wallace County High School, it might not surprise you to learn, was in Huelskamp's congressional district. And of course both Kansas and Iowa have gigantic beef industry interests. Also, if those factors weren't enough, the two congressmen were railing against the Obama Administration's Agriculture Secretary, Tom Vilsack. *The Hill*, reporting on the exact day the video launched, quoted King saying

> *The misguided nanny state, as advanced by Michelle Obama's 'Healthy and Hunger Free Kids Act,' was interpreted by Secretary*

> *[Tom] Vilsack to be a directive that, because some kids are over-*
> *weight, he would put every child on a diet. Parents know that*
> *their kids deserve all of the healthy and nutritious food they want.*
> *(Kasperowicz, 2012)*

I wonder if King's attempts to target Tom Vilsack, to tarnish him as an
elitist who didn't respect parents and wanted everyone's kids "on a diet,"
had anything to do with King at the same time running against Vilsack's
wife, Christie Vilsack, in a congressional race?

It also seems odd that, as reported on Tuesday, September 18, "The
parody video was also sent to Kansas Republican Rep. Tim Huelskamp last
week" (R. Johnson, 2012), meaning the week of September 10–14, several
days before the students (or whoever) even uploaded it to YouTube. They
sent it first to a congressman before uploading it for everyone to see?
So how, exactly, did they send it to Representative Huelskamp, if not as a
YouTube link? As anyone who's ever sent something to a congressperson
will know, it can take weeks for an unsolicited message to get through
and get a response, much less a mailed videotape or a huge video-
sized attachment to an email. Maybe the video was solicited, though.
I personally wouldn't think it impossible that an industry or a politician
would coordinate having a video produced by friendly teachers, using
cattlemen's children and local ambulance services, to both help the area's
and its voters' main industry and to score points against a political rival
just before an election. I can't prove that's what happened, but it would
require a lot of very timely coincidences to have occurred—and just a
couple of weeks into a new school year when the nutrition requirements
had just started. Are we to believe this grassroots groundswell occurred
spontaneously and got the attention of mass media organically in just a
couple of weeks?

Thinking back to North Dakota's senator, John Hoeven, perhaps he
didn't exaggerate the hue and cry from students when he released his
version of a similar bill the next year. Maybe it was popular parent
support? One North Dakota mom, Katie Pinke, blogged that she had
contacted Hoeven's office about the need to change the USDA regulations. Her linebacker son—according to an Associated Press story (Hill,
2012) conveniently published *the exact day* that Representatives King and
Huelskamp introduced their legislation—was then a 6-foot-5-inch high
school freshman and "needs more than 4,700 calories daily to maintain
his weight." As Pinke (2013) blogged,

> *We have disposable income and can adjust to afford to have him*
> *bring extra food to school.*

> But for the 67% of children nationwide that qualify for the free
> and reduced lunch program, they are going hungry because of the
> ONE SIZE FITS ALL calorie restrictions. (As written)

That language sounds awfully familiar. It's the same language and arguments made by Amanda Radke (2012) in a meat industry magazine, except about her sister Kaley, a volleyball player who was then starting her sophomore year.

> Kaley is lucky she has parents to help her put these lunches together,
> and that our family's income can support the decision not to eat the
> new school lunches. However, many kids don't come from this kind
> of household and, for too many, the school lunch is their only solid
> meal of the day. Filling them up with grains, fruits and vegetables
> while skipping the nourishing whole milk and animal proteins is a
> shame.

Pretty similar, I know. A blogger and a meat industry magazine writer using the same basic template for their argument, carefully noting that their family takes personal responsibility, but they just want plenty of meat for those kids who can't? Turns out, though, that Pinke also worked at the time (and still, as of this writing) as a writer for AgWeek, a media company owned by the conservative Forum Communications, focused on crops and livestock in the Northern Plains states. Apparently talking points have been shared, and—while, again, I can't prove these events aren't massive coincidences—the connections to the meat industry provide the only clear common denominators for all these students, parents, and politicians. Well, that and their rhetorical approach and their attempts to make what seems like industry coordination seem grassroots and viral instead.

In the end, without having to pass Hoeven's Sensible School Lunch Act, the USDA agreed to make permanent the changes he requested. The meat and grain limits were already temporarily halted, but he wanted them enshrined in the National School Lunch Program regulations. Ultimately, though, the *calorie* restrictions that athletes and parents complained about went unchanged. The USDA only lifted the cap on protein and grain servings. In other words, the only thing accomplished was what the meat and grain industries wanted: the "flexibility" to not have any restrictions on their products. Linebackers still had to make do with their 850-calorie maximum lunches. If they dropped the issue after getting just meat restrictions removed, were they really concerned about linebackers after all? Oh, or their poorer peers without parents who could afford to pack them a huge lunch?

The parents, students, and congress people also never disclosed that those hungry linebackers could always have gotten as many calories as they wanted from fruits and vegetables—seconds, thirds, and more if the school district was happy to give it to them. The regulations already allowed going over on calories with bananas, apples, and the salad bar. I suppose the meat industry wouldn't want to give too much airtime to the produce industry, though; they want all those "flexible" calories to come from meat and grain.

Amidst all the conservatives' advocacy, no one answered who they thought might determine the "needs" of individual kids if they just opened the school lunch program to endless calories. Would the cafeteria ladies do it? The food gets portioned, either ahead of time or as kids move through the cafeteria line, not doled out to each kid based on weight or sizing the child up. Doris the lunch lady isn't going to give twice as much to Chad the linebacker and half a portion to Milton the couch potato. My son—now in high school—plays football, and I don't want school lunches to grow to 3000 calories each just to suit him. He'd weigh 300-pounds by the end of the season! (That might suit some of his teammates, but he's not a lineman.) Let him eat the peanut butter sandwiches the coaches put out—that the lunch ladies make, bless them—before and after practice. Instead, what this unlimited meat campaign did was leave it up to the discretion of food service directors to set whatever portion they want for meats and grains as long as it's still within the calorie maximum. Students could continue to get disproportionate amounts of calories from carbohydrates and fats, all to the betterment of agricultural interests in the states.

If we dig deeper, what actually provoked student resistance to the new meals was largely the unfortunate implementation of the HHFKA ideas. Honestly, those tasked with "selling" the policy to stakeholders could have done a better job articulating what success would really require—namely fundamental shifts in how nutrition professionals plan for, purchase, and prepare meals—and more importantly, fully funding those changes. Instead, cafeterias decided to rein in calories not by cooking healthier fare, serving clean proteins and fresh vegetables, scratch-cooked and taste-tested with students, but by buying the same processed, boxed, manufactured carnival fare foods in smaller sizes. It's as if many school nutrition professionals and manufacturers decided, "Shrink, don't rethink!" Listen to what the kids in the New York Times story (Yee, 2012) about the new school lunches were truly saying:

> The set lunch that cost $2.50 last year now costs $2.60. The cafeteria still offers pizza, French fries and chicken nuggets, but all of the servings have shrunk. And the packaged baby carrots and apples

that each student must take before leaving the lunch line usually end up in the trash, said Brandon Faris, a boycott organizer.

"Everybody in the school's like, 'Have you seen the lunch prices? It's ridiculous!'" said Brandon.... "The portion of the meal went down; the price should also go down." (paras. 9 and10)

Or consider this from the "We Are Hungry" video's star:

We had chicken nuggets one day. Last year we got six and this year we only got three," says Callahan Grund, a 16-year-old football player .... "We had pork cutlets the other day and that was really small compared to last year. (para. 4)

Naturally, if you try to reduce calories but make the same food, the amount of food must be reduced. School lunchrooms were making the same food when they needed to start making different food—like non-nugget chicken or non-cutlet pork chops. It's hard to turn around a huge industry, though, particularly when you're not given the money, equipment, labor, or training to do it.

5

A Canary in the Mine: School Food Reform in England

Some preamble might ease an otherwise jarring shift from my focus thus far on the United States to this chapter's focus on England. As I noted in Chapter 2, England and the United States have quite similar food cultures, and the two have similar histories of school meals. Both countries share neoliberal and neoconservative political dominances, and their political tastes often eerily coincide; the United States elected a center-left Clinton and England elected a center-left Blair; the United States elected a far-right Reagan or Trump at the same time England elected a far-right Thatcher or Boris Johnson. Most importantly for my purposes, though, England has preceded the United States in their healthier school food reforms by several years. It provides the United States with an opportunity to look into a possible future, at what could happen, if we follow similar reform paths to theirs. England's example has both templates to follow and warnings to heed—a true "canary in the mine." So with that, let me take you now "across the pond" to view recent school food reforms in England.

M. B. Weaver-Hightower, *Unpacking School Lunch*, https://doi.org/10.1007/978-3-030-97288-2_5

* * *

In 2005, the British public—of course excepting schoolchildren, "dinner ladies," and school administrators—were shocked to discover that years of deregulation and neglect had eviscerated school meals' quality. Canteens were run down, cooks were deskilled, and, most importantly, the food was generally reheated or deep fried, highly processed food loaded with fat, salt, sugar, and calories. Fried potatoes with every meal, whether as "chips" or as pressed smiley faces, "fizzy drinks" and chocolates peddled by the school itself, and hardly a vegetable in sight. And then there were these greasy, unnaturally spiral-extruded poultry novelties invented by the modern, mechanized food industry: "Turkey Twizzlers."

The whistleblower about this dire state of school meals was TV celebrity chef Jamie Oliver, famous for his BBC cooking show, *The Naked Chef*. (Not to worry, hygiene enthusiasts, he didn't actually cook naked.) Oliver exposed the failings of British school feeding in his eponymous *Jamie's School Dinners* (Gilbert & Walker, 2005), which aired between February 23 and March 16, 2005. The four-episode documentary series followed the jocular chef into the kitchens of Nora Sands, a brash, resistant, long-serving head dinner lady. Using a common storyline, where viewers wonder whether Jamie can succeed against long odds and staunch resistance, the series makers lead us through gut-wrenching discoveries of poor food, ridiculously low funding (at the time just 37 pence per child, or about 55 US cents), and lack of training and equipment for preparing food from scratch (Leggott & Hochssherf, 2010). Along the way we also witness Jamie having to fight Nora, fight his wife, fight unhappy pupils robbed of their chips, and struggle to develop menus and training. In the end, Jamie wins Nora over, develops some menus, and gets some dinner ladies trained in a cooking "bootcamp."

Jamie's School Dinners was wildly popular and had a substantial impact. As a TV show, it garnered around 5 million viewers each week and got a follow-up show contracted. It also won two 2006 BAFTA awards—the UK equivalent to the Academy Awards and Emmys combined—one for Best Factual Series and one the Richard Dimbleby

Award (remember that name) for Oliver as outstanding presenter in a factual series.

Whatever popular and critical success it had, the series also had a considerable policy impact, catalyzing radical transformations in school meals even when decades of grassroots advocacy had not. A widely publicized meeting with then-Prime Minister Tony Blair and follow-ups with other government ministers garnered considerable resources from the English government:

- Blair committed £280,000,000 (about US$420 million) to improve school dinners, most of it focused on more money for fresh ingredients;
- The School Food Trust was established with an initial £60 million (US$90 million) grant, with the mission to develop nutrition guidelines and help schools improve (see Weaver-Hightower, 2011);
- Nutrient-based nutrition standards were mandated for government schools by 2009;
- Separate funds were established for training school chefs, buying kitchen equipment, and improving dining facilities; and
- Cooking was promised to be added to the National Curriculum for 11- to 14-year-olds by 2011.

Quite an impressive list of progressive changes, particularly for an issue the public hardly noticed prior to the show. Not everything got fixed, and not everything was easy, but school food became a front-page issue and a policy priority.

Again, I pair England with the US's school food because England provides a good corollary to the United States. First, England shares the United States' foodways in most respects, being addicted to junk food and seeing the effects in its waistlines; England has only slightly less prevalence of overweight and obesity than the United States (World Health Organization, 2017). The two countries also share a history of conservative resistance and backtracking in school food policy, as I discussed for the United States in earlier chapters. Most importantly, though, England shows what can happen to progressive successes—some the kind I advocate for in the final chapter—when the modernization of conservatism gets its hands on them. England, then, serves as a canary in the mine, as this chapter's title suggests, providing a warning for vigilance of conservative resistance techniques as they emerge and evolve. England's example, indeed, forecasts important changes in how conservatives strategize and structure policy, and we can learn much about other policy areas from considering school food.

School Food on the Ground

In 2010, five years after Jamie Oliver's quest began, I visited two schools in London to see what had happened to school dinners. I found a great many laudable aspects, but complications and dissatisfactions had cropped up that show the deep complexity of school food politics.

Middlebridge Secondary

The first school I visited was Middlebridge (a pseudonym), an imposing, blocky secondary school west of the city center, ringed with a razor fence, prickly greenery, and CCTV cameras. The students seemed locked into the building because, well, they were. Middlebridge doesn't let their students off campus, partly for safety reasons and partly because of food issues raised in recent years; shops on the nearby high street were spilling over with fast and junk foods.

Inside the school, though, a markedly healthier (though not totally healthy) food environment was evident. As I entered, teachers of various descriptions walked past with trays loaded with salads, a rice dish, and more. One student came through with nothing but a large slice of pizza and some bottled water. Lindy, an administrator, greeted me at the office like a whirlwind. She breezed us into the cafeteria, calling the older blond cafeteria worker "darling" and introducing me. The kitchen was right there, no walls separating it, with an approximately 12-foot steam table and warming lamps. On the far left was the pizza I had seen in the young man's hands. Tin pans of baked beans warmed on the table, too, and some students requested beans poured onto their pizza! They had "jacket potatoes" and a pan or two of condiments for them. Then, on the steam table's right side, they had the more traditional dinners. On offer were lamb biryani (an Indian dish comprising lamb, basmati rice, and curried vegetables) and a vegetarian quiche with a tomato baked on top. Farthest right was a heat lamp with several dishes of "apple pie" (really cake squares with apple slices in them) covered in yellow custard—when served together called a "pudding," a catch-all name for dessert.

Perpendicular to the steam table were open coolers with drinks (mostly water and some watery juices) and grab-and-go boxed sandwiches and wraps, much like you'd find in any grocery or convenience store around the country. A thick column separated the kitchen and cashier areas, and this had fruit on one side and a tray of cherry-topped cakes with white icing on the other.

I had the biryani, the "apple pie," and a bottled water with a sports top on it from the cooler (see Fig. 5.1). Lunch was served on china plates with real metal silverware. Lindy flew ahead of me, warning students that

Fig. 5.1 Lunch at Middlebridge School

she was "jumping the queue." She mentioned to the cashier checking out students that she would "come back to you later." I don't know if she ever did, but I never paid for my lunch. Had I paid for it, it would have cost just £2 (about US$3); my lamb biriyani from a takeaway in central London two nights later was about £15, and that was without a pudding.

Lindy explained over lunch that about three years prior, they grew dissatisfied with the catering company running their kitchens. The staff wanted healthier food, but the company wanted to keep the profitable junk food. The company, in the middle of term, "with almost no notice," canceled their contract, leaving the school without a lunch service. For a few weeks, then, they had to make do by setting up a pasta bar in the back of the lunchroom—still there that day, staffed by two dinner ladies serving paper cups of pasta. In the end, they decided that the easiest thing would be to train the dinner ladies they already had to cook. They "upskilled" them.

Their head cook, Judy, an older, bespectacled woman looking flush from hard work and steam, came out to talk with me. She's been working in foodservice "18 or 19 year," though for "a service," so she was not employed directly by the school. She works six days a week, five at the school and then one day on the weekend at a nursing home. The teachers I sat with and Judy kept stressing what a difference it made that the food was being made fresh. The meat was fresh. The vegetables were fresh. Lindy said that this one change was probably the biggest difference, and this was driving many teachers to eat the school dinner now. Teachers eating, in turn, was helping behavior in the cafeteria because they were now more present and visible.

I asked Judy about Jamie Oliver. She laughed, rolling her eyes, and said "Don't bring him up!" She continued, "He did a good thing getting parents and students to think about this. But some of the things just went too far." Her main example was salt. She wanted to use salt in her food to season it, but the nutritional rules prohibited it. "How can I not put salt in food?" She says it's understandable not to give it to kids at the tables, but "the amount they'd get from having it in the food isn't going to hurt anyone." Here was one of many complications offered to me in producing a sellable school lunch. Flavor was hard to develop in the nutrient-based guidelines that followed the food reforms. If it doesn't have flavor, it doesn't sell as well. If it doesn't sell, then under the demands for self-sufficiency, the cafeteria can't survive.

Vista Primary

The next day, I showed up early to Vista, a working-class primary school in a southwestern borough of London. I walked past small children playing cacophonously in the asphalt courtyard, and I was led up— and up!—a narrow stairwell inside the gray, slender nineteenth-century building; it was designed so that the kitchen staff had to walk all the way up. Gasping at the last stair tread, I came in the kitchen doors to find Bernice, the head cook. She was a 60-year-old Ghanaian, wearing a blue hairnet and a blue striped apron over a white chef's top. She was on the phone when I walked in, her hand covered up to the forearm with brown cake batter, which she struggled to keep from touching the phone. She kept her hand that way for the first few minutes, and she started to suggest that I pitch in. It took me a few minutes to realize what was going on—that she wanted me to do some cooking—but when I did it felt exciting, a chance to understand viscerally the work of a "dinner lady." So I pulled on my plastic apron and hairnet, and I became honorary "dinner lady" for a day—though I didn't do the same work the other cooks and assistants did.

Several things were striking about the experience. Most notable was that fresh food was mandatory. The whole kitchen had one small commercial refrigerator with a freezer not much bigger than the one most people have at home. It had no place for frozen food that only required opening and reheating. Instead, the storage room had racks and racks of fresh vegetables and a refrigerator stocked with fresh meat from a local butcher. We made our entire menu from scratch, top to bottom—savory minced lamb with creamed potato, pasta Italienne, cheesy bubble and squeak, seasonal vegetables, salad, chocolate sponge with chocolate sauce, fruit yogurt, and fresh fruit platter (see Fig. 5.2). Here were the vivid results of Jamie Oliver's "Feed Me Better" campaign: fresh food prepared by trained cooks, not frozen food reheated by unskilled workers.

Fig. 5.2 Lunch at Vista Primary

Yet when I asked Bernice or her assistants about Jamie Oliver, the room's tone got hostile each time. Jane, a senior assistant, told me "Don't say his name around here." As Jamie himself found out in his *Return to School Dinners* (Hornby, 2006), the reputations of dinner ladies were ruined by his interventions and, worse, their jobs were endangered. The media widely cast them as ineffectual or indifferent after the series, and parents *en masse* stopped buying their children school dinners because the parents largely assumed that all cafeterias were serving unhealthy slop. What's more, the work became harder as fresh, from-scratch cooking became mandated, but the intensification didn't come with extra hours and pay. Ultimately, Jamie Oliver has a complicated and "ambiguous" standing (see Pike & Kelly, 2014) in the school kitchens he fought to improve.

I could see firsthand the results of such complications for Bernice. She was alone in the kitchen preparing lunch for over 300 students and adults for several hours each day; me being there was likely a help (even though she had to direct me often), but it's hard to imagine how she managed most days. Finally the rest of the assistants came in about an hour before service time, but by then most cooking was done—otherwise they never would have finished on time.

I heard grumblings elsewhere in the school, too. The principal invited me to sit down with the teaching assistants, who were charged with overseeing lunchtime and policing what students had in their lunchboxes. (Like many other schools, Vista had made a policy of banning "crisps," sweets, and sodas from packed lunches, too [e.g., Clark, 2010].) They told me that much of their time interacting with the children was spent chiding them over Flake chocolate bars rather than more positive relationship building. They didn't see what all the fuss over food was about, anyway.

A major complaint too, both among the kids and adults, was that the meals still didn't taste very good. At first I was stung by the critique, having spent my morning helping to make the food. Yet when I got a chance to taste it just before service, I honestly didn't like it much myself. Apparently healthier, fresher food does not guarantee an appealing product, and reformers saw the variability in appeal as a danger to the larger project of food reform.

Overall, though, whatever complaints the school's adults had, it's hard to ignore the school food reforms' successes. Fresh food was now being made from scratch without deep frying, featuring more fruits and vegetables, and fewer sodas and sweets.

Even outside of what can be seen in particular schools, indications were strong that meal improvements sparked gains in what schools care more about: academic performance and behavior. Research by the School Food Trust, created directly because of *Jamie's School Dinners*, found, among other things, that students in schools that had made food changes were three times as likely to remain on-task as students in control schools (Storey et al., 2011). Installing breakfast clubs in impoverished schools showed impacts on behavior and academic achievement (School Food Trust, 2008). Other researchers, too, have found notable impacts of food reforms. Oxford and University of Essex researchers, Belot and James (2011), for instance, compared the schools from Jamie Oliver's series to a congruent control sample and found impressive effects:

We identify positive effects of the "Feed Me Better Campaign" on Key Stage 2 test scores in English and Sciences. The effects are quite substantial: our estimates show that the campaign increased the percentage of pupils reaching level 4 by 3 to 6 percentage points in English, and the percentage of pupils reaching level 5 by 3 to 8 percentage points in Science. Also, we find that the rate of absenteeism falls by about .80 percentage point, which is about 15% of the average rate of absenteeism. (p. 17)

In addition to academics and related behaviors, school meal changes influence children's eating habits, for school meal "take-up" (buying meals) increased each year after the initial post-Jamie Oliver dip, all the way through to 2012 (Nelson et al., 2012) when funding for the research was stopped. Students were also consuming more fruits and vegetables than before in both primary (School Food Trust, 2009) and secondary schools (Nicholas et al., 2013).

Those I spoke to at the School Food Trust in London and in Sheffield were immensely (and rightly) proud of their work with schools, and the research was backing them up that food was an important aspect of the school day. Yet there was also a palpable sense of worry in the air. National elections were on the horizon, and they were resigning themselves to the Conservatives—the party who had resisted the school food reforms—emerging victorious. As it turned out, the staff's fears were well-founded.

Conservative Re-emergence

In May 2010, following two years of suffering from a worldwide economic malaise under the Labour Party prime minister, Gordon Brown, Britain elected only the second post-World War II "hung parliament"—where no party had majority in the House of Commons. The Conservative Party, though, had the advantage, being only 20 seats short of majority. The centrist Liberal-Democrats, propelled by its leader Nick Clegg's phenomenal rise in popularity after strong debate performances, had newly acquired parliamentary seats. The party with whom the "Lib-Dems" formed a coalition would determine the country's direction. They ultimately cast their lot with the Conservatives. While differing substantially from their coalition partners, the Conservative's platform would dominate the Coalition's educational policies, including in school food.

Entering office deeply mired in the 2008 global economic crisis, the Coalition set a course of austerity measures and other neoliberal reforms, focused putatively on eliminating the UK's mounting national debt. The resulting changes were swift and looked like the 1980s' New Right reforms under Margaret Thatcher. Spend less on social programs. Increase privatization of government functions and resources. Cut regulation. Weaken unions.

For school food, some effects were immediate. Labour's plans to extend free school meals to 500,000 more students were scrapped (Ritchie, 2010). The Coalition also converted the School Lunch Grant, an £80 million-per-year fund specifically created to help schools meet meals' direct costs, into a general grant that schools could do anything with. Given the constant financial crisis of schools, many would no longer focus these funds on meal services.

In late September 2010, the School Food Trust was put on a list of government-funded service organizations that the new government intended to stop funding. As a quasi-governmental charity, the Trust could continue by raising its own funds, but with few government connections and the possibility of regulations going away (see below), the conversion was difficult and required charging fees for what had previously been free services to schools. By March 2013, the last government funding for the renamed Children's Food Trust was cut off, and with it died much infrastructure for collecting statistics on school meal take up and other research and consulting (Walker, 2013).

Perhaps most destructively—at least the most fought over—the Coalition government dropped the hard-won school food nutrition regulations for "academy schools." Under the Conservative party's incoming Secretary for Education, Michael Gove, the Coalition developed a law, the Academies Act 2010, to allow any public-sector school to become an "academy school." That meant the school could still receive public funding but not remain under the control of its local education authority

(LEA; think of these like school districts in the US), thus with significant freedom of curriculum, staff pay, and working conditions. Many academies were sponsored by private or religious organizations, and many had specialized curricula, like technology, the arts, and so on. (These resemble "charter schools" in the United States.) Such schools, originally created by the Blair Labour Government in 2000 to partner nongovernmental organizations with "failing" schools, were now being pushed by Gove and the Coalition as a way to innovate education. Gove also created "free schools," basically academies but started by parents and teachers rather than having to go through local administrators. Seeing advantages in the almost total regulatory freedom afforded academies and free schools under the Conservatives, the number of academies dramatically increased. Around 200 academies existed when the Coalition took over in 2010, but by March of 2013, there were 2673, enrolling nearly half the school-aged population of England. As I write this in late 2021, England has 9752 academies and free schools—79.4% of secondary schools and 38.1% of elementary schools (Department for Education, 2013a, p. 2021)—now enrolling pupils in similar proportions.

Of greatest concern to school food reformers, Secretary Gove decreed early in his tenure that academies would *not* have to follow the national nutrition guidelines. Given the sheer numbers of academies, many saw this as a precursor to undermining or dismantling the nutritional rules, that large numbers of students would return to Turkey Twizzlers and the less healthy but highly profitable sodas and sweets. Secretary Gove, though, dismissed such arguments, steadfast in his claim that all academies were by their nature, supposedly, led by self-starting innovators who only had the best interests of children in mind. As Gove explained to a parliamentary committee hearing,

> …sometimes, if you have a bad situation, strong, central intervention is right. In the past the Labour Government said, "Literacy in this country is not good enough; we are going to have the National Strategies-direction from the centre." But as the architect for the National Strategies, Michael Barber…pointed out, strong central intervention gets you from bad to good, but you move from good to great not by strong central intervention but by trusting professionals to be creative.

... It has been claimed [that academies are selling junk food], but I have not seen, and I would be interested in, *any* evidence that *any* academy has introduced, as a result of those freedoms, lower quality food. All the evidence seems to me to point in the other direction: that schools that have academy freedoms have improved the quality of food they offer children.

... The automatic assumption of some statists is that, if you remove central control, things will automatically get worse: without the state there to intervene, people will automatically be wicked and evil and do the wrong thing. I do not believe that. Second point: schools that become academies are schools that already have strong leadership. Our belief is that they will demonstrate that strong leadership not just in the curriculum but in other areas. But I am not leaving it to chance. The School Food Trust has looked at improvements that have been made in school food, and they will be publishing a report shortly. As I mentioned..., I am going to be taking steps shortly to look at best practice to see how we can spread it. (Education Committee Minutes of Evidence, 2012; lightly edited for clarity)

One can see here several hallmark ideologies of neoliberal privatization advocates (Chapters 3 and 4), wrapped up in pleasant discourses about trust in professionals. Government, in Gove's neoliberal view, impedes innovation and creativity, and it should stay out of the way except in dire circumstance. Private interests inherently perform and innovate better.

Despite Gove's lofty rhetoric, for school food reformers, the Conservatives' takeover of government in 2010 was a period of intense challenge. Five years and hundreds of millions of pounds spent on reform to school food had been seemingly unraveled in about six months. Jamie Oliver's reaction was understandably impatient:

This mantra that we are not going to tell schools what to do just isn't good enough in the midst of the biggest fucking obesity epidemic ever. The public health of five million children shouldn't be left to luck or chance.... (Adams, 2012)

Of course, Oliver had seen school food without tight regulations when he started his campaign. He had every reason to believe that Secretary Gove was being naive in his unwavering faith in academy leadership.

The Education Secretary and the public would soon learn the truth about what academy schools were doing. In the meantime, though, Secretary Gove found a creative way to deflect the intense media criticism from Jamie Oliver and others (e.g., "Michael Gove doesn't...", 2012): Gove just started the whole process over.

The Independent School Food Review

On July 4th (my birthday) in 2012, Mr. Gove finally showed what he meant when he told the Parliamentary Education Committee (above) that he would start "taking steps shortly to look at best practice to see how we can spread it." He announced the creation of a new school food plan task force. Gove named two men to lead this new endeavor, Henry Dimbleby—son and grandson of some of the most famous journalists in modern English history, one of whose name adorned the BAFTA award Jamie Oliver won—and business partner John Vincent. The two were co-founders of LEON, a popular restaurant chain in London (which has since grown nationwide and expanded into Europe) that billed its victuals as "healthy fast food."

Originally, the media's storyline focused on the personalities involved. As always, Jamie Oliver, as the face of school meals reform, was contacted for comment, and journalists highlighted mostly his exclusion from the process. Headlines proclaimed, "Chef Wars!" (Garner, 2012). Oliver complained that

> Now is not the time for more costly reports. Now is the time for action and that doesn't seem to be what we get from Mr Gove when it comes to school food and food education. This just delays action for another year or more. ... I'm fairly confident that the gentlemen from LEON will end up pushing for the same things that I, and many others, have been pushing for years, but the question is, will Mr Gove listen? Will he finally do anything about the problems in school food? ... Will this

be just another report by good people which is destined to be ignored? I hope not but I fear it will. ("School food campaign update", 2012)

Oliver's concerns mirrored those of other groups, including the major professional organization for school food professionals in the UK, the Local Area Caterers' Association (LACA; Lyall, 2013). The worries were clear: Was this a delaying tactic on answering the academies question? Was this just political spectacle (Edelman, 1988; Smith, 2004), giving the public the impression that action was happening? Would the money spent on the new plan only buy what others had already found and worked so hard to accomplish? What could two fast-food restauranteurs find out that eight years of dedicated work by multiple organizations working closely with schools could not?

Partly the answers to critics' questions come from understanding the political philosophy behind Conservative policies. Gove and the Conservatives had been unapologetic in their crusade to install a neoliberal reality (see Chapter 3) in England's schools. To fit the classic definition of neoliberalism, again, each initiative would (a) focus on free-market emulation, (b) privilege consumer choice, (c) reward personal responsibility, (d) reward entrepreneurship, and (e) remove government involvement except to enforce contracts. Basically, private business is good, government is bad. You can see these philosophies in Secretary Gove's defense of exempting academies, above, and the creation of an "independent" School Food Plan.

Consider the emulation of free markets and consumer choice. Neoliberal dogma holds that any sector operates better when subjected to the disciplines of a free market. This logic undergirds the push for academies and for open enrollment in any school parents want; if schools compete, they will supposedly operate more smartly and come up with innovative solutions to problems. Yet schools don't operate exactly like markets. If a company goes out of business, it's sad, but if a school fails, the students suffer irreparable harm. School cafeterias do not operate exactly like fast-food restaurants, either. Yes, they share fast production and cost efficiency, but students don't have unlimited choices in a school. They either eat the school meal, bring food from home, or leave campus to eat, often from a fast-food restaurant. If they can't afford a packed lunch and cannot leave campus, students must eat whatever the school feeds them. Students are basically a captive audience, subjected to a monopoly at the individual level. The professionals who run the dinner service face constraints that private restaurants do not. School cafeterias cannot raise prices at will, get better ingredients, or do other things that exceed their tight budgets.

Still, tapping Dimbleby and Vincent, fast-food innovators, had a public perception allure. The thinking was surely they would know how to make healthy food quickly for a moderate price; they do it in their restaurants. LEON also built their brand on a perception of health-iness and sustainability, both things that have also driven the school food reforms. For the healthiness, LEON menus (2013) were better than some other restaurants, but much of its food wouldn't have met the nutrient-based nutritional standards for school food (School Food Trust, 2008). Many of their dishes were over the calorie limits (except for the salads), and few can meet the limits on sodium. The Garlic Chicken Wrap, for instance—the lowest calorie non-salad menu item—met calorie limits (without any sides) but it has too much sodium by 1000 mgs, this difference representing two-thirds of children's entire recommended daily consumption of sodium (Agriculture et al., 2010, p. 21). How easily could LEON compete if they had to use half the salt? Of course, they don't have the same price constraints as school nutri-tion programs, either; just a bowl of soup from LEON, on special for £3.30 in the spring of 2013, costs more than a full meal at school. A burger would set you back £6; the cost of just one LEON side with your burger—£2—could buy an entire school dinner at the time.

Many assumed from the review's beginning that it would likely result in exempting academies from the nutrition standards, which Gove wanted all along. While touting the new School Food Plan as "inde-pendent" on the website masthead and its promotional material—likely meant to convey "better" since it was not being done by government workers—the LEON owners were hardly independent of government influence. Mr. Gove hired them because he knew what he would get. We know this in part because they discussed it on the luxurious Marrakesh holiday Gove and his family took with Henry Dimbleby in early April, just months before hiring them on. There, apparently, the Secretary was lavished with liquor and likely outlined his hopes for the inquiry (Preece, 2012). The two also dined together at Dimbleby's home after their vacation.

Dimbleby and Vincent, moreover, were not just humble restaurateurs who happened to make a hit with LEON, whatever the homespun marketing of their chain (see http://leon.co). In fact, the two learned deeply the neoliberal worldview through their previous work in venture capitalism and corporate raiding. The two met when they worked for Bain Capital, the firm made (in)famous during the 2012 US Presidential election as the company that Republican nominee Mitt Romney fronted. Bain Capital made its livelihood taking on struggling companies and subjecting them to the rigors of the neoliberal marketplace. Mostly Bain saddled companies they bought with the debt Bain used to buy them. If the companies succeeded, they shared the profits; if they failed, Bain profited from selling the assets (Taibbi, 2012). With that pedigree and those high-level connections, Mr. Gove could be relatively sure that choosing LEON's owners would get the predicted result.

But what was in it for LEON's founders? According to Dimbleby, in an interview with the *Daily Mail*, "This is not a job that is going to make us money. It will take us away from LEON, and we are very nervous about that. The only reason to do it is to make a difference" (Preece, 2012). While I trust their altruistic motive, it's hardly the "only" reason to have done the review. The undertaking represented an unparalleled advertising opportunity, particularly for a relatively small but popular chain that, at the time, was only beginning to venture outside London. They had 13 restaurants when they were chosen; they have more than 70 restaurants as I write this in 2021, along with grocery items, cookbooks, and homewares sold both in their restaurants, online, and in other major retailers. Not only were the print and television stories about their work on the School Food Plan free, but the LEON name was prominently displayed on every page of the official government website and in every news feature. The Government funded the creation of this media for them, including some high-production-value videos that were on the School Food Plan website and YouTube. The Government also funded workshops around the country, providing more exposure for the pair. These well-covered events showed Vincent and Dimbleby as engaged, caring, and even philanthropic. The pro-social feelings and free advertising, then, were great reasons for the two to head the review. It was also a win for neoliberal reforms: present the market as kind and socially just, and show that business will ultimately take care of its customers so that government doesn't have to.

One might also look to the information gathering and production during the School Food Review as a source of both political spectacle and tension within its neoliberal context. In neoliberal philosophy, having at least the veneer of democracy—what Edelman called "political spectacle" (Edelman, 1988)—and the wide dissemination of certain kinds of information has become more important. It firstly, theoretically, ensures the rationality of consumer choice fundamental to neoliberalism. If you don't have sufficient information, you can't make good choices, and the market subsequently becomes distorted. Secondly, the public must have the sense that the process was open and democratic, for participation—even if only an illusion of influence—can "manufacture consent" among the public (Chomsky, 1999).

Regarding the School Food Review, specifically, throughout the website (http://www.schoolfoodplan.com) were pleas to share stories and media of what was working well in cafeterias; they wanted as many people as possible to "get involved" and focus on positives. To facilitate this, the School Food Plan group created links to the most popular social networking sites—Facebook, Twitter, and YouTube—where various stakeholders could upload photos, videos, and comments about school food successes. "Regional events" were also held in seven cities, where parents, caterers, and school personnel could do workshop activities to discuss successes and lingering issues. The result was a stack of best practices cards done during an activity that the review could use to create suggestions (Department for Education, 2013c). Finally, they met with "experts," like representatives of the Children's Food Trust, the Food for Life Partnership, and School Food Matters, and created a "big plan" that the experts agreed on as "the vision for the future" (Department for Education, 2013b).

The appearance of transparency and input seemingly won over many to the review's sincerity and to its architects. As Morag Lyall wrote in *Educatering*, a trade magazine for British school food professionals, in her feature titled "Are We Eating Our Words About the School Food Plan?":

> Six months later, and the disbelievers are starting to thaw out. One of the reasons for this could be down to the openness in which John and Henry are conducting their review. In November, the School Food Plan website was launched, providing information on the purpose of the review, with regular updates on their findings and opportunities for people to get involved. ...

> On heading to the news page of the website, every week an itinerary of John and Henry's visits are posted, so that you can see which schools they visited or which panels they sat on. By October, they were able to present an update to the All Parliamentary Group for School Food and they have recently formed a panel of experts, including LACA national chair Anne Bull, to act as a sounding board for their ideas and recommendations.

> John and Henry have also been able to speak to those working 'on the ground' in school kitchens. They were invited to the EDUcatering Excellence Awards to meet a variety of people, from foodservice suppliers to school caterers, while they regularly visit primary and secondary schools in England and, recently, Scotland to speak to pupils about the food they like to eat and what they dislike.

The production of information by polling those "on the ground"—and being seen producing it—can effectively "thaw out" critics and instill a sense of legitimacy. Never mind that many of these same voices had already been heard in earlier attempts to reform school food.

Yet this production of knowledge during the review may yet have more purposes down the road. Such knowledge government and businesses alike can use to craft messages in the language of those from whom they seek consent. And—who knows?—a couple of clever fast-food restaurateurs might have used some of this Government-funded information gathered about children's preferences and best practices to refine their own business' menus and processes.

Though too easy to have the knee-jerk reaction of regarding businesses cynically, as if they have solely self-interested motives, one must keep an open mind, trying to see the complexity of human motivation. On one level, these men naturally want to do right by children. Their country and their fellow citizens stand to benefit, and service of this sort naturally feeds on a sense of patriotism and duty. At the same time, creating a School Food Plan suits well their business interests, too. It was the biggest taxpayer- and charity-funded boost to their restaurant chain that they could have hoped for. Analysts must keep both these things in mind simultaneously.

So what did Mr. Gove get from this move to start a review that would then create a new School Food Plan? Certainly he could bask in the glow of Vincent and Dimbleby's successes; it reflected well upon him to have tapped such proactive and diplomatic gentlemen who have "thawed out" so many critics. He needed the distraction, too, as he was at the time embroiled in a scandal over revelations that low-quality meat and prepared meals were using horse meat as filler (e.g., Pike & Kelly, 2014), including in some school dinners (Richardson, 2013). Mr. Gove also gained superb political cover against his conservative colleagues to finally accept some more progressive parts of his critics' plans, even making it appear the ideas were his. Early in 2013 he announced that cooking lessons would finally become mandatory under the National Curriculum (Duell & Levy, 2013). Of course, Jamie Oliver had been pushing for cooking to join the mandatory curriculum for years—remember Tony Blair had promised it—even creating his own commercial lessons, *Jamie's Home Cooking Skills*, that were being used in schools around England. Dimbleby and Vincent also recommended restricting packed lunches and students leaving campus during lunch time (Duell, 2013), but those didn't make its way into the final plan except as a possibility for schools to consider. Others had requested all of this before the School Food Plan, but now Mr. Gove could look visionary for accepting it from his preferred representatives.

One central question remained unanswered. What about academies? Would the government allow them to disregard the standards? What about the claims that the academies would surely do right with their newfound freedoms? Those with long memories were rightly skeptical.

Forgotten Histories

Forgotten in the privatization reforms of 2010 through the School Food Plan's launch in 2013, particularly the debate over academies forgoing the standards, was just how England's school meals service had gotten so bad originally, particularly given the many progressive successes in its history (Berger, 1990; Earl, 2018; Evans & Harper, 2009; Gustafsson, 2004; Lalli, 2021; Morgan & Sonnino, 2008; Pike & Kelly, 2014; School Meals Review Panel, 2005). Here's a quick tour. The Education (Provision of Meals) Act of 1906 was the first organized governmental school meals provision in England, though many voluntary agencies had already been feeding children, much like in the United States (see Chapter 2). Also like the United States later, a main argument for school meals provision was concern about British soldiers' fitness, particularly following major losses incurred during the Boer Wars in South Africa. The 1906 Act was not a mandate to provide meals, but it allowed LEAs to use taxes for them.

The post-World War II Education Act of 1944 dramatically changed schools in England, including restructuring LEAs, increasing the school leaving age and establishing a new secondary education system. It also changed school meal provision dramatically by mandating that all LEAs provide a fixed price meal to every child who wanted one. Schools around the country had to expand or create meal services, and many began to hire nutritionists and professional staff to accomplish the expansion. A system of cafeterias also sprang up in both primary and secondary schools nationwide to meet the needs. By 1947, the government paid 100% of school meals to those LEAs who met the conditions for poor children. The long-term goal was to provide meals free to all students, but by 1952 the education ministry conceded that this was unlikely to ever happen, and prices for paying children began to climb thereafter (Berger, 1990).

Both Labour and Conservative governments of the late 1960s through the 1980s unraveled the school meals service. In 1968, Harold Wilson's Labour government withdrew free milk from secondary schools, and the Education (Milk) Act 1971, championed by then-Secretary of Education Margaret ("Milk Snatcher") Thatcher, further withdrew free milk from students over age seven. The Education (No. 2) Act of 1980, Thatcher's major education privatization reform as Prime Minister, did the most to send the service into entropy, mainly by removing the requirement that every school serves meals. The Act left only two compulsory tasks for LEAs: (a) provide some kind of food for students on welfare and (b) have a place for students to eat lunches brought from home. In the 1980 Act's wake, kitchens closed, jobs were lost, and free meals took on renewed stigma, for often only poor children were given meals. The Social Security Act 1986 added the price of school dinners to welfare checks rather than directly giving the meals, giving families a choice of whether to purchase school dinners; this resulted in hundreds of thousands of children not taking a daily meal. Further dismantling the service, the Local Government Act of 1988 instituted "compulsory competitive tendering," forcing LEAs to award meals contracts to the lowest bidder, the intention being to show the inefficiencies of public services compared to private industry. The quality of meals—especially given that nutritional requirements were completely removed—declined precipitously as private caterers, who replaced unionized employees of local governments, sought to maximize profit. The school food service environment stayed much the same for years—losing student take-up and declining in nutritional standards—until 2000 saw some restoration of nutrition standards through the Education (Nutrition Standards for School Lunches) Regulations, and until *Jamie's School Dinners* in 2005.

With this history of New Right neoliberal reform as evidence, how could politicians and policymakers see reason to believe that a new round of neoliberal reform in the twenty-first century would do any better? Indeed, they were about to receive more evidence that their sanguine approach to the wonders of the unregulated free market was flawed.

The Truth of the Academies Situation

So why would Mr. Gove have had so much faith in individual schools sticking to—or, as he argued, exceeding—national food guidelines? Why would school heads, under constant financial strain and largely uninterested in food or tired of meeting its restraints, bother to voluntarily meet nutrition standards? *Not* meeting the standards suited schools' immediate fiscal needs much better.

Proof came soon before launching the new School Food Plan. The Government had commissioned the School Food Trust to conduct research on food in academies, and their findings confirmed many critics' worries. As the qualitative study showed, "while some academies are making good efforts to maintain compliance with some of the food-based standards, others are doing no better (and in many instances worse) than secondary schools nationally" (School Food Trust, 2012a). By "worse," they meant that the other, quantitative research (School Food Trust, 2012c) found that schools were almost twice as likely to serve "desserts, cakes and biscuits including confectionery" in academies five days a week than were the schools subject to the nutrition standards—47% vs. 25%. Further, what academy pupils were actually taking (not just what was *available*), included more condiments, more food and drinks prohibited by the standards, more starchy foods cooked in oil, less dairy products, and less healthier food options. In consequence, pupils in the academies were taking more calories and fat, and they were taking less vitamin C and calcium, than the students in regular, "maintained" schools.

In a telephone survey of academy school heads (School Food Trust, 2012b), many admitted providing snacks prohibited under the national standards (but not prohibited for them) and that these weren't restricted to older children or to vending machines. Partly academy leaders often didn't see food provision as an important part of their mission; a third of the heads said that providing food was "a burden" and a fifth saw it as "mainly a commercial service." As I have said elsewhere (Weaver-Hightower, 2011), school leaders just don't often take school food seriously, so why should we expect that they would focus on it without standards? It's also clear that academy leaders—for understandable reasons—can't or don't keep up with research on successful practices in school food (School Food Trust, 2012a). So how could the government expect academies to have the necessary knowledge to serve good food without standards? Dimbleby and Vincent found exactly that in researching the School Food Plan. In an update to parliament, they reported that

Baldly, the schools we visit tend to fall into three camps: those that appreciate the importance of good food, and are doing a wonderful job of incorporating it into school life; those that have a growing feeling that it is important but don't know how to go about changing things; and those for whom it is long way down their priority list. It is clear that different schools will require different solutions. (https://media.education.gov.uk/assets/files/pdf/u/appgbriefing.pdf [accessed 6 March 2013])

So despite Mr. Gove's faith, clearly his contention that academies would prove paragons of virtue in school food was untrue. As the School Food Trust concluded, "in the absence of standards, competing priorities will quickly lead to compromise and a deterioration in the nutritional quality of the school meals service" (School Food Trust, 2012b). It happened in the past, and it was happening again.

A Surprising "New" Policy: The School Food Plan

Undeterred by what was truly happening in academies, the School Food Plan was released on July 12, 2013, just a few days past a year since Gove announced its process (the School Food *Review*). Despite initial fears of standards rollbacks, the plan Dimbleby and Vincent developed aligned well with extant policies prevalent in England's school nutrition industry. It was remarkably similar, in fact, to what was already happening and what had already been called for by child and hunger advocates. So similar was it that some received it, with clear astonishment, as Mr. Gove's "remarkable socialist masterplan"—said admiringly—and "filled with unexpected ironies" (Butler, 2013) given that a Conservative government produced it.

So what did the Plan call for? Dimbleby and Vincent's (2013) Plan expressed a vision of

Flavourful, fresh food
Served by friendly, fulfilled cooks
In a financially-sound school kitchens [sic]. (p. 25)

To carry it out, they set out 17 "actions" and divided these into responsibilities for head teachers—basically equivalent to principals in the US—for government, and for organizations and activists.

For head teachers—"the only people who can truly lead the revolution in school food" (p. 10)—the plan presented a checklist of actions to reform school eating. "Give children what they care about," they said, like good food and water, a pleasant environment to eat in, allowance for their social lives, a good price and discounts, and develop the "brand" of school food and dining areas. One can see here the business sensibility from Dimbleby and Vincent's background, but the School Food Trust had been working on dining environment (2008a) and marketing school food programs (2009a) for years already and had many of the same recommendations. And the Trust already had the infrastructure in place to help schools and their heads before Gove shut them down, only to replace them with basically the same thing in the School Food Plan.

Actions the Plan delegated to "us and others"—the Plan's expert panel and other organizations dedicated to school food—included sharing "what works well" for school caterers on the website and improving the image of school food, letting the public know that school dinners had improved drastically since *Jamie's School Dinners*. Cooks needed assistance too, they said, by including them in catering sector events and improving their skills. Finally, the Plan promised to help small and rural schools, especially, that can find procurement and economies of scale difficult with their small student populations. To help rural schools, the Plan promised to create a Small School Taskforce and to write personally to LEAs to help them understand meals service finances.

For the Government, the Plan lays out 10 actions, which Gove had apparently already approved before releasing it. The approved actions included:

1. making cooking lessons mandatory for children ages 5–14;
2. introducing food-based standards to replace the nutrient-based standards (discussed below);
3. providing seed money to increase meal take-up (that is, pupils buying meals);
4. setting up "financially self-sufficient" breakfast clubs;

5. joining with the London Mayor's Office (led by then-mayor and soon-to-be Prime Minister Boris Johnson) to set up "flagship boroughs" in London to demonstrate impacts of large-scale school food provision;
6. investigating expanding free school meals;
7. training head teachers in food and nutrition;
8. using Public Health England to promote healthy diets in schools;
9. having Ofsted's (the Office for Standards in Education, Children's Services and Skills) school inspectors include "behaviour and culture in the dining hall" in their inspections; and
10. measuring the plan's success using five metrics: take-up of lunches, nutritional quality, workforce morale, number of schools winning a quality award, and percentage of 16-year-olds who can cook five savory dishes.

The Plan also makes one recommendation that Gove had not approved, that all primary school children should receive meals free. Apparently the Government had no money dedicated to that. They suggested starting with the locations with the highest percentage of children already eligible for free meals, somewhat like the US Community Eligibility Provision.

And what about the main sticking point, that Gove had originally planned to let academies forgo food standards? In the end, the School Food Plan hits a middle ground, saving face for Mr. Gove and others who wanted academies exempt from regulations. Any academy school chartered before 2010 had to meet the food standards already, and the School Food Plan required *new* academies created after June 2014 to follow them, too. That just left academies started between 2010 and 2014 unaccountable to the standards, but the Plan noted (p. 99) that many had already agreed to voluntarily comply. This compromise—to give schools a year to be created without being subject to the standards— helped Gove save face. It also meant nearly 4000 schools weren't subject to the standards, about 16% of English schools. By the final published tally on March 31, 2016 (School Food Plan, 2016b), only 1420 of those 4000 academies and free schools had volunteered to adhere to the standards. Thus roughly 2476 schools remained on their own to sell whatever food they wanted—about 10% of all English schools.

Why, many had asked when the review was first announced, was the Government starting over on a new review (p. 92)? It proved a prescient question. Much of what the "new" School Food Plan policy laid out was little changed from what had gone before. The startup funding for breakfast clubs and meal take-up was new, though focus on those was not, and adding food and nutrition to educational leader training was new. Ofsted inspections were supposedly new, but inspectors had been commenting on school food for years as part of healthy environment inspections, even without specific mandates (Clark, 2010). Flagship boroughs were little different from the thousands of schools that had already been demonstrating the impact of school meals from the School Foods Trust era. Metrics had already been established and reported by the School Food Trust, and many had already been researching universal free school meals.

It can hardly surprise anyone that the School Food Plan's tenets were so similar, honestly. Many in the School Food Plan's expert panel were the same people who had been leading the previous work, too. And in the end, the new nutrition standards (the *Requirements for School Food Regulations 2014*) went back to food-based standards, replacing the nutrient-based standards enacted by 2009, which, in turn, had replaced food-based standards from 2006 (the post-Jamie Oliver policy). As Table 5.1 shows, the School Food Plan standards just tweaked the 2006 interim food standards (School Food Trust, 2008b), making no change to 17 of 27 of the original food-based standards and resuming two standards eliminated in the shift from the 2006 to the 2009 final standards. The new Plan combined some food group and slightly revised category names, but these were surface changes. As it was for US school food policy described in Chapter 2, the English School Food Plan standards were what I term a *palimpsest policy*, with many original intents and rules still visible beneath policy tinkering made later.

The Plan's actual ideas and actions were arguably and ironically the least important aspects of the policy, though, and this, I argue, explains why progressives should study this policy event. The changes were minimal. More crucial was the change in rationale, language, and policy techniques, which I turn to next.

Table 5.1 Comparison of England's 2006 interim food-based standards, 2007 final food-based standards, and 2014 food-based standards

2006 Food/food group	2006 Interim food-based standards[a]	2007 Final food-based standards[a]	Nutrient-based (2009–2013)	2014 School Food Plan foods-based standards[b]	2014 Food/food group
Fruit and vegetables	1) At least two portions per day per pupil 2) At least one vegetable or salad and at least one fruit	No change		1) No change 2) No change 3) A dessert containing at least 50% fruit two or more times a week 4) At least three different fruits and three different veg each week	Fruit and vegetables
Meat, fish, and other non-dairy protein	Must provide a food from this group daily	Standard eliminated		Standard resumed For vegetarians, non-dairy protein three or more days a week	Meat, fish, eggs, beans, and other non-dairy protein
Red Meat	Must be provided twice a week for primary schools and three times for secondary	Standard eliminated		No change	
Fish	Must be provided once a week for primary schools and twice for secondary	Standard eliminated		No change	
Oily fish (e.g., salmon, mackerel)	At least once every three weeks	No change		No change	
Meat products (processed; e.g., hot dogs, meat pies, burgers, nuggets)	No more than one serving from each of four categories over two weeks (total of 4)	No change		No more than once each week in primary and twice a week in secondary (no categories)	
Starchy food	1) Must be provided daily 2) Starchy foods cooked in fat/oil no more than three times a week 3) Each day a starchy food cooked in fat/oil provided, one not cooked in fat/oil must be provided	First standard eliminated; last two standards no change		1) No change 2) No change 3) Standard eliminated 4) Three or more different foods each week 5) At least one wholegrain variety weekly	Starchy food
Bread	Must be provided daily (no added fat or oil)	No change		No change	

(continued)

Table 5.1 (continued)

2006 Food/food group	2006 Interim food-based standards[a]	2007 Final food-based standards[a]	Nutrient-based (2009–2013)	2014 School Food Plan foods-based standards[b]	2014 Food/food group
Milk and dairy	Should be available daily	Standard eliminated		Standard resumed; Lower fat milk must be available for drinking at least once a day	Milk and dairy
Deep-fried food	No more than two in a single week	No change		No change (battered or breadcrumb-coated added to definition)	Foods high in fat, sugar, and salt
Salt and condiments	1) No added salt in recipes or at tables. 2) Condiments in packets only, not more than 10g or 1 teaspoon.	No change		1) Salt allowed in recipes but not available after cooked (on tables or as packets) 2) No change	
Snacks	1) No crisps 2) Nuts, seeds, veg, and fruit must have no added salt, sugar, or fat 3) Dried fruit may have up to 0.5% veg oil for glazing 4) Savory crackers must be served with fruit, veg, or dairy	No change		1) No change 2) No change 3) Standard eliminated 4) No change	
Confectionery (e.g., chocolate bars, chocolate cookies, cereal bars)	Not allowed	No change		No change	
Cakes and biscuits	Allowed but must not contain confectionery	No change		No change	
Drinking water	Free, fresh water available at all times	No change		No change	Healthier drinks
Healthier drinks	Only permits water; skim, low-fat, or lactose-reduced milk, fruit or veg juice; plant milks (calcium enriched); yogurt drinks; combination drinks [those mixed with water or milk]; flavored milk; tea, coffee, and low-calorie hot chocolate.	No change		No change (greater specificity for "combination drinks")	

[a]School Food Trust (2008), pp. 2.2–2.4
[b]School Food Plan (2015)

Neoliberal Technologies of Policy Shifting

Despite the new School Food Plan's surprisingly progressive(ish) outcomes, which Dimbleby and Vincent restored rather than created, the policy process exhibited important signs of a new policy regime in British school food. It demonstrated important neoliberal technologies of governance. Some progressive reforms made it past conservative attempts to squelch it precisely *because* progressive reformers learned to speak the language of neoliberalism that Gove had set before them. Theirs was a hybrid understanding: progressive intentions could jibe—creatively— with the needs of capital and government. In this section, then, I explore how the School Food Plan both creates and illustrates new governance forms, new approaches to installing conservative ideologies into school food programs.

First was an agreement to focus on making the program "self-sufficient" rather than dependent upon government. "Take-up" was the mantra, appearing 126 times in the report, 25th most frequent of all words. For the LEON leaders, having students buy meals was central. They described it as "the means *and* the end" in the title of their Chapter 3 (p. 41), "the means, because it would make the service economically viable; the end, because eating a school dinner is so much better than the alternatives" (p. 48). Profitability, or even just breaking even, became the goal under the School Food Plan. Clearly the Coalition's neoliberal, austerity ideology had taken hold. It became unthinkable, literally, that the Government would pay the full cost of meals any longer.

To their credit, Dimbleby and Vincent do mute the profit motive in the Plan. Their selling point to business-minded members of parliament and Mr. Gove was that increasing take-up to just over 50%, from the then-43%, would make the program self-sustaining. Getting beyond that, to 60% or even 70%, would create opportunities for further investment in school meals:

> That money could be used in many different ways to reinforce the food culture of the school. It could help finance breakfast clubs, or buy even better ingredients, or bring down the price of school meals so that even

more children can enjoy them. It could be used to fund an extension to free school meals, or to support cooking and growing clubs. In short, high take-up would create a virtuous circle, enabling schools to do a range of things that their present financial predicament just won't allow them to do. (p. 49)

While the "virtuous circle" metaphor has a pleasant sound, the under-lying, unstated message signals that cafeterias would soon be on their own to make the finances work. After some initial help, yes, but clearly the Coalition Government wanted no part of continuing to pay for meals into perpetuity. The breakfast club grants, for instance, were to become "self-sustaining" after just two years of seed funding.

Passing the work, responsibility, and blame to lower levels of gover-nance has become a neoliberal pastime in recent decades. I found it a critical part of creating Australian educational policy for boys in my previous work (Weaver-Hightower, 2008), for example. The idea works simply: identify or agree with an important problem, pose a costly or time-intensive solution, and then leave it to state governments, local governments, or even individual schools to enact it. In a regulatory system, this shields neoliberal governments from both the complexity of overseeing compliance and protects them from blame if things don't work out. While the School Food Plan had actions allotted to the govern-ment and organizations, most were general roles to help school governors get started: seed money, technical assistance, setting easier to follow stan-dards, mandating cooking in the curriculum. The government work was to "introduce" (action 2), "kick-start" (action 3), and "set up" (actions 4, 5, and 10). Far from taking a "statist" approach that Gove criticized, the School Food Plan took a more venture capitalist approach. Oh, and a couple of ongoing roles for the technical/managerial class: inspections (action 9) and measuring "success" (action 10).

Old neoconservative and authoritarian populist claims about deficit families make their morally judgy ways into the Plan, as well. In the Plan's Chapter 10, on hunger and poverty, they say "It is clear that some children are not getting fed adequately at home. These children come from poor—and often chaotic—families" (p. 114). Later in that same chapter, when discussing families' income percentage spent on food,

Dimbleby and Vincent say, "Whatever the underlying trend, there are undoubtedly families whose food budgets are stretched, as well as some that are too dysfunctional to feed their children well." They seem to say that some—the stretched—are deserving while some—the dysfunctional—are undeserving (see Katz, 1990). Such moral evaluation lies beneath many school food debates in England (Earl, 2018; Pike & Kelly, 2014), blaming the individual fat body and negligent parents for failing to maximize information and opportunities to align and maintain their own health within acceptable bounds. Such arguments elide the sense that social, political, and economic forces constrain the lives of poor peoples and the food insecure. Overlooking these constraints explains why the School Food Plan authors would believe simply giving startup funds would prove sufficient. Armed with information and a start, they seem to have thought, surely children and their parents would make their own morally "correct" and economically rational choices in food. If they don't, they're irredeemable—might as well call them "looters" and "moochers" like in Ayn Rand's novels—and have only themselves to blame if they can't or won't conform.

Indeed, the School Food Plan presents the challenges of school food as primarily an information problem. Schools needed to teach students to cook and to choose healthy school dinners, and the Plan authors explicitly hope that students will take such lessons home to their families. Head teachers needed training in food and nutrition, too. Cooks needed more training and connection with their larger profession. Many actions focused on providing more information, whether as standards, as checklists, as "what works well" best practices, or as marketing. The centrality of information in the neoliberal ideal cannot be overstated, even though information alone usually pales in its effect on structural inequality. Additionally, "best practices" become a substitute for regulation and rigorous research, focused on the production of technical-administrative knowledge rather than vigilance over social justice and governmental responsibility.

A policy technology neoliberal governments have employed with vigor since the 1980s—though the approach was invented much earlier (Congressional Research Service, 2020, Appendix A)—was using block grants rather than categorical grants, or what the British refer to as *ring-fenced funding*. *Ring-fencing* means to have specific requirements for what recipients can spend funds on, whereas non-ring-fenced funding (or a *block grant*) arrives as a lump sum that the recipient can spend as they see fit. Neoliberal proponents see removing ring-fencing as a way to save the national government money, avoid duplication from overlapping programs, reduce bureaucracy, and allow local governments to innovate. Opponents see it as a way for the national government to avoid paying more if program expenses rise or eligibility increases, forcing localities to do more with no additional funding.

The removal of ring-fencing—going instead to block grants—returned as a major dynamic within school food policymaking in England when the Conservative–Lib-Dem Coalition won government in 2010. In particular, the Coalition Government decided in 2011 to end the ring-fenced School Lunch Grant, which had been used by schools since 2008 to help pay for ingredients, labor costs, equipment, and nutrient analysis required by the food standards. The Coalition instead lumped that money into the Dedicated Schools Grant, a block grant, with which schools could do anything, lunch-related or not. Naturally, in austere times, many schools diverted those funds to other priorities.

The School Food Plan creates an evolution in this general neoliberal funding approach. Rather than suggesting LEAs use block grant funding in a particular way, the School Food Plan takes the approach of short-term ring-fenced funding as startup expenses, with the expectation that local innovators, fueled by "what works well" from others, will find ways to become self-sustaining. In this way, the Government avoids even the burdens of continuing block grants.

The School Food Plan I also consider an exemplar of what Stephen Ball (2010) calls education policy heterarchies. This new governance form involves opening both policymaking and implementation to nongovernmental agencies, think tanks, philanthropists, private sector businesses, charities, consultants, trusts, social entrepreneurs, and so on. As Ball explains,

> tasks and services previously undertaken by the state are now being done by various 'others', in various kinds of relationship among themselves and to the state and to the remaining more traditional organisations of the public sector, although in many cases the working methods of

these public sector organisations have also been fundamentally reworked, typically by the deployment of market forms (competition, choice and performance-related funding). (p. 155)

Government thus mitigates costs, risks, effort, and responsibility by leveraging relationships with these many policy players. Ball asserts that the state does *not* give up their role steering policy; rather, heterarchies help the state achieve "political ends by different means" (p. 158). Governments parcel out work—and to varying extents, power—to multiple locations and actors. This "deconcentration and dispersal of policy locations" works to bring new policy actors into the process while it excludes others, often slyly disempowering policymakers' old enemies and entrenched interests and "'short-circuit[ing]' existing policy blockages" (p. 158).

Consider how the School Food Plan formed a heterarchy. The review for it was posed as "independent," but it involved allied leaders in Dimbleby and Vincent, who Secretary Gove already trusted to develop a certain outcome. The two LEON owners donated their time along with money from their philanthropic foundation. The review process sought input, information (particularly best practices), and agreement from state school personnel, nonprofit organizations, and experts from academia and business. Also, the review was funded using a combination of public and private funds from individuals, charities, and corporations, allowing Gove and the Government to deflect criticism of the costs and demonstrate that private interests selflessly shared public concerns. Implementation, finally, was distributed similarly, to private companies and nonprofit organizations. The Plan group used nonprofit organizations for proxy metrics to measure performance (like the number of schools getting awards from the Food for Life Partnership); they hired a public relations firm to handle the policy's dissemination and marketing (Mattinson, 2013); they developed a "public–private alliance" led by the professional group for school nutrition, LACA, to help train cooks (action 14); and they distributed promotion, head teacher training, and inspection duties to other non-Department for Education government entities including Ofsted, the National College for Teaching and Leadership, and Public Health England, the latter two having since ceased to exist.

Creating a heterarchy like this, with functions and responsibilities parceled out between public and private interests, those with profit motives and those with mission-driven motives, fits well the neoliberal vision of running government operations privately. In this neoliberal ideal, the market and altruism come together to tackle problems without either burdening or, worse, empowering the state. Indeed, this kind of governance feels like a neoliberal dream, for the government not only regulates but gets to forward business interests by giving private enterprises grants, connections, access to information, and publicity.

From the perspective of accountability to citizens, though, heterarchies can prove both progressive and regressive. Heterarchies—defined as having scales, values, and power relations among entities that shift depending on the circumstance (Crumley, 1995)—can allow some people and organizations access to power and a way to utilize their expertise. Their diffuse nature, though, can make heterarchies difficult to track and difficult to seek redress from. Primarily, of course, private organizations and philanthropists have no obligation to act democratically, so citizens cannot vote them out or seek rights from them. Further, in cases like the School Food Plan, so many entities were involved that citizens would have to air any grievances they had to numerous venues. Policymakers could shift blame around, and points of failure could seem ambiguous at best. Part of heterarchies' appeal, their nimbleness to change amidst contextual shifts rather than being stuck in settled hierarchies, also means conversely that citizens may not know who is responsible for particular parts of a plan.

One could speculate, of course, that the School Food Plan was intended from the first as political spectacle (Edelman, 1988) rather than thick democracy. It provided Secretary Gove and the conservative-dominated Coalition Government a means to more quietly—and with a thawing smile—undo a highly popular, high-interest government undertaking in school food. The public had previously been largely galvanized around needing government intervention in school dinners. Gove found a way to recast that intervention into a highly distributed, cheaper, and—perhaps most importantly—temporary solution. Even better, he and his designates got praise from all sides, largely because he didn't simply and immediately eliminate eight years of progressive gains, but instead he imposed a short timeline and made them someone else's problems. Ultimately, most of the School Food Plan's functions had already been undertaken by the School Food Trust. The government had an existing infrastructure for school food reform, but Gove dismantled it and then just recreated it using largely private means. He and the LEON founders took the ideas and best practices—already known by school food professionals from years of work—and repackaged them as if private interests had solved the problem. Gove, in other words, recast previously progressive demands as neoliberal successes.

Conclusion

Some readers might wonder, finally, with nearly eight years gone by since its release, what has happened to England's School Food Plan? Perhaps having read the preceding analysis, its status won't surprise you.

Michael Gove, architect of the review and Plan, left the Secretary for Education role in a cabinet reshuffle by then-prime minister David Cameron, roughly a year after the Plan's release. He was chief whip for the House of Commons for a year thereafter and has had a variety of both higher and lower roles since. After the 2015 general election, Cameron promoted him to Justice Secretary and Lord Chancellor—basically second in charge behind the Prime Minister. He then twice competed for the role of party leader (to in effect become prime minister) after the "Brexit" vote that led the UK to leave the European Union. Gove lost in these attempts, to Teresa May in 2016 and then Boris Johnson in 2019. As of this writing, he is the Secretary of State for Leveling Up, Housing and Communities ("Leveling Up" was Boris Johnson's British equivalent to Trump's "Make America Great Again" slogan). Gove now sits seventh in line behind the prime minister. I suppose one should be careful when playing the game of thrones.

Henry Dimbleby and John Vincent won MBEs (Member of the Order of the British Empire) from the Queen in 2015 for their work on the Plan. In 2017 Dimbleby left LEON, and in 2019 Michael Gove, then Environment Secretary, appointed him to lead the National Food Strategy independent review—a kind of School Food Plan for the entire food system post-Brexit. Vincent now oversees the rapid expansion of LEON.

And what about the Plan itself? Technically, the School Food Plan remains England's national policy for school feeding. After publication, an office was established to support implementation, and Myles Bremner, former CEO of the charity Garden Organic, was made the National Director. The funding ran out for the School Food Plan Office in 2015, though Bremner was awarded more about £162,000 (roughly US$220,000) to his personal company, Bremner & Bremner, to run it for another eight months. The Office formally closed on March 31, 2016. Importantly, this dedicated workforce on implementing the plan left without any formal evaluation of the Plan's impact (Phillips, 2016), though the website's dashboard for each action does include "Snippets of success" with anecdotal evidence and lists of their activities. From April 2016, the School Food Plan Office's and Expert Panel's efforts were handed off to a newly created School Food Plan Alliance to serve as the Plan's "on-going champions." The announcement carefully emphasized that this Alliance was "independent of any government funding" (School Food Plan, 2016a). In other words, Alliance members became unpaid volunteers taking on the work they or others used to do for livable salaries.

As of this writing, the website for the School Food Plan remains accessible, including the Plan itself, the school food standards, and various resources for schools, inspectors, governors, and head teachers. The "What Works Well" Recipe Hub has transformed from an interactive website into a PDF file. The last updated page I could find on the entire website was added in 2016. As for the Alliance, it has a small Internet presence (the announcement of its formation on schoolfoodplan.com seems like its only official website), but it still holds meetings and has an active Twitter feed. Periodically the group releases statements, as when the Conservatives under Teresa May unsuccessfully attempted to stop providing universally free infant school meals to four- to seven-year-olds, the School Food Plan's signature accomplishment (School Food Plan

Alliance, 2017), or when COVID-19 prompted them to release a school food checklist (2020) to help kitchens reopen. As the initial Alliance co-chairs noted in an interview with LACA (Foad, 2016), "We don't have the funding or a budget. We've got a commitment from all members of the alliance that they will do what they can to … let people know about all the good things that are taking place."

Government has thus, in summary, largely retreated from school food reform. The Plan was, as I said, a way to make reform temporary, to let it fade away or become an issue for others to deal with as their voluntary energies allowed. Most recent evidence suggest that this has created a decline in quality and adherence to the school food standards. The Bite Back 2030 campaign (2021), a youth-focused movement on food quality issues founded by Jamie Oliver, heard in student focus groups around England that most students' schools were not following the standards, that candy was again being sold by schools, that vegetarian options were scarce or monotonously repeated, that water was often hard to access, and that pricing meant that students on free meals had restricted choices. Not exactly what the School Food Plan had in mind. Yet no one seemed to be responsible for making sure that good food practices were happening anymore. I argue that was the design all along.

This chapter, a case study of what England has done these last 15 years to reform school food, holds many lessons for those who might attempt progressive reform. Like the US example detailed in previous chapters, England owns a history of conservative resistance to progressive policy. The history, both long-term and more immediate, shows cycles of gains in access to and healthiness of meals set against conservative attempts to limit or end access and contain the complexity and burdens they believe standards represent. England shows most clearly, I believe, the ability to backslide and the creativity of conservative governance to adapt to its contexts, undermine progressive victories, and capture and recast progressive policy under neoliberal and neoconservative ideologies. They never stop. Struggle for reform goes on and on. I'll give more evidence later in the Coda, which provides an update on English school meals in response to the COVID-19 pandemic.

Snack Five: Plain Cheese Sandwiches and Shame

We seem obsessed in the United States with making sure that kids and their families pay for their school meals. "There's no such thing as a free lunch," some say, almost as a badge of pride for themselves and a moral judgement of others. But what do you do when parents just don't pay for their kids' lunches?

In the parlance of nutrition professionals, as I said in Snack Three, so-called *unpaid meal charge policies*, or just *charge policies*, have remained a huge issue for many years. "It's been a longstanding issue in schools, one that's gone on for decades," according to Obama Administration USDA Undersecretary Kevin Concannon (Siegel, 2017). To the public, though, the practice has become known as *lunch shaming*. It's defined as using publicly visible consequences when students have a negative balance on their lunch accounts. It makes them stand out from their peers as being poor, whether they actually are or not. For some students, that consequence comes in the form of a letter handed out in class. For some they must work in the cafeteria, such as cleaning tables in front of their peers. For some it might involve having their meal thrown away when the cashier realizes the student has an unpaid balance. For some it might involve staff writing with a marker "I need lunch money" on the student's arm. In many places, though, the visible consequence comes in the form of a plain cheese sandwich rather than the regular meal that day.

For some school food operations, to be fair, unpaid meals can present a huge problem. Firstly, USDA regulations mandate that cafeterias have an unpaid meal charges policy and attempt to collect on these accounts, but cafeterias cannot use any federal funds to pay off delinquent accounts. Collecting the money thus falls to cafeterias themselves or to school districts, many of which can't afford to simply write off the losses. That is especially the case in economically underprivileged areas where the combination of struggling parents and struggling school budgets can make for wildly unsustainable finances. In 2010 most school districts (89.4% of them) had losses of less than 1% of their annual revenue, but in nearly 1% of districts the losses were more than 10% of their annual revenue—an astounding amount; 10% of districts lie between those two poles (May et al., 2014, p. 149). The School Nutrition Association (2019) reported that the median amount owed has grown 70% in recent years, from $2000 in 2014 to $3400 in 2019.

Lunch shaming as a practice came to wide public attention in 2014. In January, workers at Uintah Elementary School in Salt Lake City, Utah, threw away the meals of some 40 children with unpaid balances once they got to the cash register (Schencker, 2014), an event that made national and international news. Then at the end of March a second grader at Desert Cove Elementary in Phoenix, Arizona, came home with "LUNCH MONEY" stamped on his wrist in black ink (Griffin, 2017). This story, too, went viral. Soon the web was full of stories of "lunch shaming."

I think it shook people to think of elementary school children slouched in the cafeteria, their faces sunken and tear streaked, while an adult stands by having branded them or thrown away their food. It strikes those reading such tales as incompatible with how US culture treats its children, its most vulnerable population. Are we as a nation so stingy? Do we think it builds character to work off a debt your parent made? Some apparently answer "Yes." Take Republican former Representative Jack Kingston's comments in late 2013 while he was campaigning to become a US senator:

> But one of the things I've talked to the secretary of agriculture about: Why don't you have the kids pay a dime, pay a nickel to instill in them that there is, in fact, no such thing as a free lunch? Or maybe sweep the floor of the cafeteria—and yes, I understand that that would be an administrative problem, and I understand that it would probably lose you money. But think what we would gain as a society in getting people—getting the myth out of their head that there is such a thing as a free lunch. (Terkel, 2014)

Thankfully most people don't have that same belief system, where child labor replaces generosity—or, as conservative former House Speaker Newt Gingrich suggested, where child labor helps bust up unions (Haberman, 2011). Forcing poor children to work seems particularly heartless in a Dickensian way.

Private generosity has thus far been the major solution to the problems of unpaid lunch debts. Around the United States, nonprofits, businesses, and individuals charitably paid off lunch debts to ensure that kids wouldn't face punishment, shame, or hunger. In Washington State, an 8-year-old raised more than $4000 to pay off his classmates' school lunch debts (Haskins, 2020). When the school district in Warwick, Rhode Island, announced that students with unpaid debt could only eat "sun butter and jelly" sandwiches until their accounts were paid, the Internet outrage was swift, as was the outpouring of donations. The founder of Chobani yogurt donated more than $47,000 to clear the debts. One can find thousands of examples just like this (just do an internet search). Indeed, more than half of districts (55.4%) cite charitable contributions as a major source of pay down (School Nutrition Association, 2019); school district general funds were listed as a major source by 36.2% of districts. Teachers in my graduate classes assure me that their schools frequently ask them to donate to the cause out of their own modest salaries. Yet charity cannot serve as a long-term solution. Kind-hearted kids and businesses will only patiently and generously solve this problem for government institutions so many times.

To my mind, and as I'll argue in Chapter 6, one permanent solution stands out. The School Nutrition Association (n.d.) says it best in their talking points document for unpaid school charges: "School meals are as important to learning as textbooks and pencils—ideally, we would have funding to serve all students free meals so this would not be an issue." Agreed. Why shouldn't lunch be as free as all the other services schools provide?

6

Rethinking School Food: Innovative Programs and a Progressive Vision

Trying to alter the trajectory of a food culture can prove incredibly difficult. Even with the best of intentions, and with science and some political will on one's side, resistance can be fierce.

Take just a small example that happened to me. In 2011, knowing that I was researching food issues, my then-dean asked if I would convene a task force on wellness issues for our college's newly renovated building. A progressive former minister, he was concerned about the faculty's holistic health, the planet's health, and the example we were setting for teacher trainees. So he asked if some others and I could suggest ideas for creating a new building environment that encouraged healthiness, including physical fitness, healthy food options, and environmental sustainability. Wanting to put my research to the test, I agreed.

So, over the course of a couple of months, I invited participation, did some research and outreach around the university, and spoke with administrators and staff from diverse departments. I was surprised both at the welcome cooperation of some and the vitriolic resistance of others. The biggest issue by far was vending machines.

© The Author(s), under exclusive license to Springer Nature
Switzerland AG 2022
M. B. Weaver-Hightower, *Unpacking School Lunch*,
https://doi.org/10.1007/978-3-030-97288-2_6

The task force and I agreed that we wanted only healthy vending choices. If the schools in the area couldn't have full-sugar sodas and high-sugar, high-fat, high-salt snacks, then why should we sell such things to prospective teachers during their training? Were we going to talk with them about teaching the health benefits of fruits, vegetables, and grains in class, but then chat with them at the candy machine during break? Were we to ignore the brain and behavior research we preached in class, just so long as the College was making some money from candy bars? Even beyond the mixed messages (read: hypocrisy), looking around we could clearly see that faculty waistlines were growing. Those of us struggling to maintain or get to a healthy weight—myself included—could use a respite from the constant presence of Snickers and Doritos taunting us as we walked the halls. In this one building, we thought, surely we could escape the obesogenic world around us.

As a committee, we descended upon the director of food services for the campus, and he told us that it was possible to do a "health*ier*" (but not "healthy") vending machine in our building. The director clearly wasn't excited about it given that sales for those machines were nowhere close to sales in the "regular" machines (a difference of several hundred dollars a year per machine), but he was willing to let us do it. The vending at the new Wellness Center was of this healthier variety, so we could just use that same plan. The beverage machines would have only water—though including "vitamin" waters despite objections—and the food machine would have only the yellow and green designations of the campus-wide stoplight nutrition system, meaning these were healthier options for occasional consumption. No "red" foods for us.

The reactions were in some cases startlingly fierce, and they started concurrently with the task force, even before the machines were installed and stocked. Previously mild-mannered colleagues occasionally got red in the face and accused me of being the "food police." "My students," they would claim, were here late at night or on weekends, and they don't have time to eat on the way to campus from their schools or offices or jobs. Besides, "We're all adults!" they would end with, and "We should be able to eat whatever we want." I would always try to stay calm and assure them that they could, in fact, eat whatever they want; we just weren't going to sell it to them. And I would go into my spiel about practicing what we preach and so on. Clearly, though, they took it personally, as if I was saying that what they like to eat—what was in the regular vending machines—was no good. For some it might have been a class issue (Bourdieu, 1984), having been told much of their lives that their food was "less than" and should be replaced with someone else's food. For some, it was also likely an issue of psychological control; they might feel powerless at work or with their partners and children, but a Reese's was all theirs—no one could stop them, and it was damn yummy to boot! And of course, their resistance originated in deep philosophical and political beliefs: to control food choices seems fascist, whereas they believed sincerely in the libertarian tenets of contemporary American politics. And here was, from their perspective, a known liberal telling them that what they wanted to eat was no good and, worse, I was having it banned.

Of course, we weren't actually telling anyone what to do or preventing them from eating what they wanted. If they wanted an Almond Joy and a Dr. Pepper, they only had to walk to the adjoining building, which was even connected, so they didn't have to brave the frigid North Dakota winters. What we were trying to do, instead, was take a principled stand (a largely symbolic one given the proximity of other junk food) to show that different possibilities exist. It would at least prompt people to think about their choices, and maybe even compare the food environment we were constructing—and *all* food environments are *constructed* by someone—to ones they encountered elsewhere.

Renovations to the building finished, and we moved into our beautiful new workplace. All went relatively well with the first year the healthier machines were in place. Some grumbling occurred, but mostly people just coped with the changes, and no one revolted. Then, at the end of the year, I went on sabbatical (during which I began writing this book).

When I returned, the water machine remained a water machine, but the granola bars, nuts, pita chips, and healthier snacks had been mostly squeezed out by Snickers, Pop-Tarts, Doritos, Twix, and barbecue-flavored Lay's potato chips. All the past few months' research, meetings, pacifying, and work had been thrown out to earn a few more dollars. Even the stoplight labeling scheme had disappeared, and students, faculty, and staff were left to guess from the packaging what they were about to do to their diets by feeding their hard-earned dollars into the machine.

As this anecdote suggests, and as evidence from England in Chapter 5 showed, changes in a food culture can entail fierce uphill battles, and food reforms can backslide. Even so, I have come to believe that, if we want to ensure kids' and adults' long-term health and knowledge about food choices, we must make major changes to schools' cultures, the food available to students, and policymaking in and outside of education. We simply must turn around problems of obesity, diet-related disease, food insecurity, and malnutrition. If not, the potential effects on our entire society, *but particularly vulnerable populations in our society*, are simply too grave to accept. Reforming our food environments in schools thus presents both a logistical and a moral challenge. (That is what politics seeks out!).

Good news, though: Numerous people already spend much of their time rethinking and reforming school food. We can learn much from what these people have done, including new ways of doing things, new ways of collaborating, and new ways of thinking about food and even education writ large. This chapter tells just a few of those many stories. I shift, in other words, from the critical scholar's task of "bearing witness to negativity" of educational domination and exploitation (Apple, 2009, p. 31), to "spaces in which counter-hegemonic actions can happen or are now going on." I've chosen these few case studies because they highlight a politically progressive vision of school feeding, one that envisions more access, more culturally plural choices, more education about food, and more nutritionally sound menus.

Though some may be disappointed to hear it, I don't think a single best program exists, no panacea for feeding kids to simply "scale up," if you'll pardon the corporate jargon. No package or guidebook can simply be distributed to each school for easy implementation. Even national transformation with money and policy behind it can prove hard to pull off, as England's example shows. That's because, firstly, food systems are vastly complicated. Think back to Chapter 2's discussion of school food policy ecologies. That diagram, though broad and complicated, nevertheless represents only a sliver of the entire food system. Even if the cafeteria starts serving better food to more students, huge questions remain for society that schools must play a part in addressing. How can the next generation make wise decisions at grocery stores, bodegas, airports, or gas stations? How much should students know about agriculture, whether to facilitate shopping choices or to grow their own food? What do kids need to know to intelligently participate in the democratic process that creates our food policies?

Secondly, individual communities' ecologies are complex, as well. We could hardly get practices from the highly progressive communities of Berkeley, California, to work in the highly conservative communities of Berkeley County, South Carolina, and vice versa. To attempt to do so would create clashes of food beliefs, food histories, class relations, race and religion, and more. That's not to say that we should leave everything to local schools to decide for themselves, as conservatives might argue, but rather we should value distinctiveness and diverse and local foodways. In this chapter, I provide ideas—maybe some inspiration or hope—for what possibilities are being played out elsewhere. Any community can do better, I believe, but that might look different from place to place. Community members, working together have great insights into what has a chance to work and what tinkering would fit their context.

Reconceptualizing School Food: Innovative Programs

Let's be radical for a moment. What if we threw out the supposedly sacrosanct ideas of the past—"the way things have always been done"—and thought anew about what's possible? Cast the sporks and trays off the table and start again. What priorities would we have? What could we remake in creative ways? What productive potentials could we find if we simply think differently?

One thing that has hampered the Healthy Hunger-Free Kids Act (HHFKA) from 2010 was that too many school cafeterias didn't think differently *enough*, or they lacked the resources to fulfill the scratch-cooked, fresh food vision at the core of those reforms. Many schools and food distributors simply tried to layer the new regulations onto the reheated carnival fare they were already serving. Smaller portions of hamburgers and fries or reengineered whole wheat crusts on the industrially produced pizza rather than creating larger dishes of chicken stir-fry or jambalayas or fresh rolls. Who could blame cafeterias, though? It's not like they were suddenly given new facilities, adequate equipment, enough workers, or sufficient training. They got six cents extra per meal through the HHFKA. Historic, yes, but not sufficient. If a cafeteria served 1000 kids a day, that's $60 extra. That amount would barely cover an extra minimum wage worker, much less the extra cost of fresh vegetables.

So no, as progressive as the HHFKA was about modernizing the nutrition of school meals in the US, it was hardly a "rethinking." That should give us pause, to realize that even an incremental, but still historically significant, change could provoke such hot debate and fierce action. It makes one wonder if a grander rethinking is folly to imagine.

I, for one, have hope that school meals can indeed become more progressive, more equitable, healthier, and more environmentally sustainable. Sure, some will complain. Some will stand in the way and seek to claw back any gains. Democracy just works that way. It's a tiresome struggle. But it's worth it to ensure that children benefit the most they can from schools. My kids, your kids, and everyone else's kids.

Thankfully, we have people across the United States and the world who not only have that hope but who work at rethinking and remaking school food right now. These hundreds of dedicated food service directors, parent groups, principals, and students do amazing, hard, hot, sometimes dirty work to change the food systems in their schools. Below I profile just a sampling of the many possibilities for doable school food reform.

Alice Waters and the Edible Schoolyard Project

Perhaps the most popular current idea for progressive reforms actually recovers an old idea: school gardens. Naturally many US schools had gardens right from the beginning of community schooling in the nineteenth century, growing food for the local teacher, to supplement student meals, and to teach agricultural practices (for a history of England, see Earl & Thomson, 2021). Formalizing the school garden, though, began in the late 1890s and into the US's involvement in World War I (1917–1919). The "victory gardens" of both World Wars had their roots in the school garden, particularly the United States School Garden Army (Hayden-Smith, 2007), a Department of the Interior program focused on ensuring that citizens didn't starve on the home front while food was being redirected to military endeavors overseas. Figure 6.1 shows a poster and frontispiece that graced many USSGA gardening manuals, with Uncle Sam leading the wartime child troops into the fields to help the war effort. During the same era, progressive educators like John Dewey (Ralston, 2011) and Maria Montessori (2004) were extolling school gardens' virtues for learning and for reconnecting (particularly urban) children to nature. With both the government and education-ists on board, the school garden took off across the country, reaching millions of children and tens of thousands of teachers (Hayden-Smith, 2007). Eventually the wartime fervor waned and, though some school gardens were still operating around the country (e.g., Mader, 2010), it would take nearly 75 years before gardens regained their early twentieth century popularity.

In recent years, school gardens have returned as a major cultural and educational force. Even the White House, led by Michelle Obama, created a garden as inspiration for citizens to eat healthier, as a source for the White House kitchen, and as a learning opportunity for local schools (Obama, 2012).

The new gardening movement is perhaps best represented by the Edible Schoolyard created by Alice Waters, a celebrated chef, owner of the famed Chez Panisse restaurant, and a former schoolteacher. Her renown has once again come to the fore within the school garden move-ment for converting Berkeley, California's, public Martin Luther King Jr. Middle School hardscaping into a learning garden. This work began in 1995, and, in the years since, Edible Schoolyard projects have sprung up in nearly 5700 schools worldwide, and they have trained more than 1000 educators in the program's practices and philosophy (Edible Schoolyard Project, 2019).

Fig. 6.1 "Follow the Pied Piper. Join the United States School Garden Army" by Maginel Wright Barney, circa 1919. Public domain image from http://hdl.loc.gov/loc.pnp/ppmsca.53320

As Waters (2008) explains and illustrates in her book, *Edible Schoolyard: A Universal Idea*, and on the Edible Schoolyard Project website (edibleschoolyard.org), the garden at MLK Middle School has grown in size and complexity over the years, adding various trees and plants and even chickens, but the basic mission has remained. They show MLK's students how to work in the organic garden tradition, how to try new and different foods, how to prepare and eat simple and fresh recipes, how to work with garden and kitchen tools, and how the natural systems work together to grow food. Even more, though, they take it as their mission "to awaken every American child's senses toward a new relationship with food, one in which deliciousness comes first and good health and well being [sic] are happy results" (p. 38).

Teachers at the school also use the garden as a laboratory of sorts for science lessons, English lessons, and art lessons. Students, for instance, write about their food memories and journal for language arts, and they discuss plant structure or decomposition in science.

As for impact on the things that matter to policymakers, parents, and the public, the Edible Schoolyard has seen gains for students in schools that have more developed garden initiatives. An evaluation commissioned from University of California Berkeley researchers (Rauzon et al., 2010) found that, in more developed school garden programs, students' nutrition knowledge scores were higher, younger students preferred a larger variety of fruits and vegetables, middle-school students had positive attitudes about fresh foods and the environment, and students' produce consumption increased.

As Waters puts it, though, something ineffable happens in the school garden that lesson plans and evaluations can't contain.

> All you have to do to be convinced is come see for yourself—come watch children from all walks of life making salads with ten different kinds of lettuce, or patting together Indian samosas from potatoes and onions and garlic they've dug with their own fingers. All it takes is the kind of walk I make a few times a year, from my restaurant down to the Edible Schoolyard for yet another look at kids covered in red raspberry juice, foraging among the vines, or elbow-deep in the dirt, planting amaranth seedlings, or laughing and talking around a kitchen table while they shell peas for their friends. (p. 41)

In an education policy era centered on standardization, testing-based accountability, and technological utopianism, basic tasks like working in dirt with one's hands might sound fanciful and without any metrics to make them countable. I would argue, though, that wonder and experience are key educational goals. We discount them, because we can't count them, at our peril.

Doug Davis and the Burlington, Vermont, School District

School gardens like the Edible Schoolyard can prove a wonderful teaching tool, but their relatively small scale can hardly supply all the food needed for even a single school, much less an entire district. Farm-to-school programs fulfill this role instead, linking districts serving two meals a day to hundreds or thousands of children with larger scale producers at local farms.

Nationally, farm-to-school activities have blossomed over the past two decades. The US Department of Agriculture's (USDA, 2021b) census of farm-to-school activities during the 2018–2019 school year found that 65% of US school food authorities participated in at least one farm-to-school activity, and 46% participated in seven or more activities. While more than half (57%) had been doing farm-to-school for less than three years, this still represents a huge growth. Partly that might come from increased visibility of school gardens and farm-to-school successes, but greater resources have become available, too—like a USDA $5 million grant fund—and schools now get more and better technical support from organizations, researchers, and farmers themselves.

A leader in the farm-to-school movement among nutrition professionals is Doug Davis, the nutrition director for the schools in Burlington, Vermont. Hearing the many things that he and his staff and community organizations have done leaves a deep impression. It shows creativity, dedication, generosity, business acumen, and good old fashioned people organizing skills.

Just consider the many activities Davis and his colleagues (2011) described undertaking:

- Creating a Vermont Junior Iron Chef Competition that publicized their efforts, connected more farmers, gave away a culinary school scholarship, and raised over $10,000 for the local school food projects each year.
- Running taste tests with students before any food gets added to the school menu, to make sure the students like the foods and would eat them again.
- Creating and selling note cards—instead of selling candy and wrapping paper from a fundraiser company that would take half the profit—and using the money to fund the farm-to-school program's purchases of local apples and cheese.
- Contracting with a local artisan bakery to use their bread in school meals for no extra cost, by developing a community supported agriculture (CSA)-like bread subscription service for district employees.
- Contracting with a local free-range poultry farm to get their unused chicken drumsticks for the same price the district was paying for processed patties and nuggets.
- Utilizing the member workers from a local food co-op, who volunteered so they could get food discounts, to process produce, like local butternut squash, roasted root vegetables to replace fries, and salad bar ingredients.
- Developing regular field trips to local farms, where the farmers lead students in "touring farms, harvesting, tasting, working, and asking any and every question they could think of" (p. 179).
- Bringing farmers to schools to work with students in classrooms and having students host community dinners they have made from the farm-to-school products.

This impressive list demonstrates well why so many call farm-to-school programs "win–win" arrangements. In creating these activities, more than putting local food on a lunch tray can occur. Such programs can, like they do in Burlington, create community relationships and cohesion, benefit local economies, help farmers develop reliable and anticipatable markets for their products, and provide new learning opportunities for students. Oh, and remember that children now eat fresher, more local foods, sometimes even trying things they might not otherwise give a chance.

Tony Geraci and the Baltimore, Maryland, School District

While Burlington, Vermont, with a population of about 3500 students in 2020, can do a great many things because of its modest size, reforms in large cities can have different challenges because of their huge scale. Tony Geraci faced this in seeking to reform school food in the Baltimore City Public School system of more than 83,000 students. As featured in the film, *Cafeteria Man* (Chisolm, 2011), Geraci set out to transform the child nutrition program in Baltimore to make it healthier, fresher, more local, and a source of opportunity for kids and farmers.

A centerpiece of his reforms was aiding the creation of Great Kids Farm, 33 acres of garden beds, greenhouses full of herbs and micro greens, beehives, a barn full of animals, and chicken coops, all surrounded by urban environs. Students come and taste the plants, smell them, roll them around in their fingers, wash them in a big tub. The students also pack CSA boxes for community members, an effort that funds the farm, along with restaurant sales and grants (Gustafson, 2012, pp. 104–109). Schools around the city also established individual school gardens with support from the district. Geraci threw his support behind Hoop Village in Baltimore, an urban agriculture initiative that built hoop houses—portable greenhouses—to grow fresh produce and create jobs for low-income teens (Associated Press, 2010). To make school food into a learning opportunity, Geraci visited classrooms and helped in preparing a community dinner where the kids made the food from the Great Kids Farm and the school's own garden.

A central tenet of Geraci's reforms was local procurement—buying from local and regional farms rather than sourcing products from distributors across the United States, as USDA foods usually are. As he says in the documentary, "There are more chickens in Maryland than people! Why am I buying chickens from Arkansas? It doesn't make any sense."

Most controversial of his reforms was instituting Meatless Mondays. Each Monday Baltimore schools would serve meatless, plant-based dishes to children, with entrees like cheese quesadillas, vegetarian chili, or vegetarian lasagna. Geraci didn't invent the idea; indeed Meatless Tuesdays (a terrible missed opportunity for alliteration) were popular during World War I as a means—along with school gardens—of saving food for the war effort (Avey, 2013). As he says in the documentary, it wasn't intended to shame the meat industry, but rather to "have a conversation" about how we eat. Expectedly, the meat industry disliked Geraci's Meatless Monday campaign, so they—and other conservative commentators—wrote scathing critiques across the media (Barclay, 2009). The main thrust was that they were shocked that the cafeterias would deny protein to school kids—conveniently overlooking the high protein present in the beans being served and that the other four days each week featured meat. Despite the pushback, the idea has spread to school systems around the country, including all New York City public schools, Los Angeles Unified School District schools, and more.

Geraci also launched an after-school supper program to help feed students in high-poverty elementary and middle schools in Baltimore for free. The program utilized culinary students from five high schools to prepare roughly 2000 meals a week in exchange for credits toward their chef certification (Green, 2010). The program still exists today, in 2021, and has expanded to all schools for after-school program students.

Naturally Geraci couldn't accomplish everything he wanted to do. Chief among his wish list was a central kitchen that could prepare and distribute fresh local food to the many schools in Baltimore that had ill-equipped kitchens. Though media coverage differed on the reason this couldn't happen, it was a blow to his plans to remove pre-plated, reheated meals and an endless parade of pizza and fries. Geraci left his position after just over two years, and he has come under frequent criticism for the things left undone or exaggerated (e.g., Anft, 2010; Woldow, 2012). Yet Geraci went on to helm the school food program in Memphis, Tennessee, from 2011 to 2015, where he successfully recreated many of Baltimore's successes. This time, though, Memphis already had a state-of-the-art central kitchen to make his ideas possible (Chisolm, 2012).

I highlight Geraci's efforts here not because of the man himself, though I personally find him a compelling character. Rather, his efforts show what large city districts can do to reform their food programs in progressive ways. His story also highlights the internal and external politics, bureaucracy, and indecision that can stand in the way. Certainly not every nutrition director can have the energy and fortitude to take on City Hall. Yet examples like Geraci's—and Ann Cooper's in Boulder, Colorado, and Bertrand Weber's in Minneapolis, Minnesota, and so many more—prove that cities can do better, even despite frequent difficulties of poverty, red tape, and lack of green space.

STAR (Service to All Relations) School, Flagstaff, Arizona

The STAR (Service to All Relations) School is a charter school 25 miles from Flagstaff, Arizona, near the Navajo Nation. It serves almost entirely Native American (Navajo, Hopi, and Apache) students from preschool to eighth grade, with an 82% free and reduced lunch rate. It is a small, rural school in an arid region, ten miles from the nearest utility lines. This context makes its dedication to progressive school food provision particularly unique.

People tend first to comment on STAR School's energy and water independence. It is the first completely "off the grid" public school in the United States. Solar panels and wind turbines provide all the power needed for its several buildings, and its architecture takes advantage of natural heating and lighting. The school also has its own well and filtration, along with various rain and snow capture systems, that provide safe drinking water and gardening water in an area otherwise plagued by high levels of mining-related arsenic and uranium in the groundwater. STAR School thus serves as a demonstration project for sustainable living in an area where many residents have no electricity, running water, or sewage lines, and where conditions prove difficult for modern consumption habits and for agriculture. As the school's materials emphasize, though, indigenous peoples have lived in the area and thrived for centuries.

In addition to the great activity described above, I have, of course, included the STAR School here because of its efforts in school food. The campus construction features food preparation, with greenhouses abutting classroom buildings and a traditional Navajo stove. The curriculum includes holistic food education, as well. Take for example the activities described and illustrated in a booklet the culinary instructor produced (Montour, 2015), titled *Nizhónígo Íiná: Cooking with Navajo Traditional Foods.*

> We incorporate Navajo traditional foods into our breakfast and lunch weekly menus. By volunteering our time to help with cleaning, irrigating, planting and harvesting at our local Navajo farms we have built a strong relationship with our Navajo farmers. After trying a new recipe and are happy with our taste-testing process, the students use the recipes presented in this cookbook by preparing traditional meals for parents and elders once a month.

STAR's students help with the planting of and making recipes with blue and white Navajo corn, onions, various squashes and melons, greenhouse-grown lettuce, and chilis. From these they create blue corn tortillas, three sisters soup, Navajo squash blossom soup, and pumpkin pie. Students learn the cultural and nutritional values of seasoning with juniper ash, a traditional Navajo ingredient. They connected with health professionals from Indian Health Services as well as community elders, who told them stories of life on their lands decades ago.

A core value at STAR School, indeed, involves "honoring our place," which deeply relates to their food practices. As its website notes (2019), the school focuses on self-sufficiency and self-determination in food matters: "Even though our area is quite arid—and farming and gardening is challenging—indigenous people have lived in this area for many centuries, and have successfully supported their families and communities, without food being brought, from anywhere else." STAR School provides a curriculum, then, that focuses on using native plants from the area, capitalizing on local farming knowledge, and service projects that provide nutritious food to area residents. They have committed to "providing fresh vegetables in the school breakfast and lunch program, as much as possible from local farms and gardens, and involving students in the preparation of food—so that they will try eating various vegetables, and locally-grown [sic] sheep." The food system they have created takes seriously their name, to provide Service To All Relations, including serving their culture, their neighbors, and their ecosystem.

The STAR School project sits within a larger national and worldwide movement toward indigenous food sovereignty. While in general the term *food sovereignty* means a group of people making their own decisions about food policies and practices, Grey and Patel (2015) note that *indigenous* food sovereignty means much more. Considering Native American food sovereignty, "a 'right to define agricultural policy' is indistinguishable from a right to *be* Indigenous, in any substantive sense of the term" (p. 439, emphasis original). Indigenous food sovereignty, they argue, belongs within the larger project of decolonization, of reclaiming the foodways that imperialism and industrial capitalism has long sought to exploit, destroy, or replace. Of course, indigenous food sovereignty looks different by place and by tribal nations (e.g., Rawal, 2020). Such a perspective also fits well with the STAR School's aims for self-determination and cultural preservation for local tribes. Whereas boarding schools and other schools in the United States (and elsewhere) have long sought to assimilate Native students and force them to forget or hide their cultures (Lomawaima & McCarty, 2006), the STAR School counts among the many Native schools attempting to revive and strengthen cultural practices and languages for today's Native students.

The STAR School has been rightly celebrated for its many programs to make the school a model of sustainability, health, and cultural integration. In 2012, Scholastic Parent and Child magazine named it among the 25 "Coolest Schools in America" (Editors, 2012), and the US Department of Education gave it a Green Ribbon designation for sustainability practices. In 2015 the education website Noodle.com named it one of the 41 most innovative schools in America. Perhaps most exciting, because the STAR School participated in the USDA Farm-to-School program to connect with their area's indigenous farmers, five of their students were invited to Washington, DC, to help Michelle Obama harvest the White House Garden (Theobald, 2014).

What Does a Progressive Vision of School Food Look Like?

While no one person can claim to have *the* solution to a system so vast and complex as US school food, I do see several themes emerging from the many programs and people—like those above and many more—who work to make schools and kids healthier. I also have learned a great deal (as I hope readers now have) about how those of us who call ourselves politically progressive differ from those in previous chapters who have a conservative vision of school food. Rather than simply declare ourselves as against some group or some ideology, though, I believe it is critically important to declare what progressives stand *for*. "What do we want, and when do we want it?" as the chant goes. Thus this final section of the final full chapter (though a Coda follows), I attempt that important work by laying out a specifically progressive vision of school feeding. It's only my view, of course, and other ideas deserve consideration, but these collate common ideas I see in the literature and in practice that could provide a mainspring for change. Here then I present 15 maxims, if you will, that define progressive school food reform.

Give Every Child Food for Free

So many of the progressive things school food could do would be made vastly easier if we just made food a free part of the school day for every child. Poppendieck (2010) makes a persuasive case for giving all kids free lunches at school; it would save money, feed more children, and remove stigma and shaming. Further, numerous projects around the country—which have been well evaluated—show that the Community Eligibility Provision, which gives all students in poorer districts free meals, works well (e.g., Bartfeld et al., 2020; Gordon & Ruffini, 2021; Hecht et al., 2020; Schwartz & Rothbart, 2020; Trapp, 2018). During the COVID-19 pandemic most students in the United States have gotten food free, and, despite conservative warnings, society has not collapsed.

So what would this cost? I find Poppendieck's (2010) calculations relatively persuasive. Her "back-of-the-envelope" figuring put the cost to switch to universal free meals at about 100–120% of current funding added again (p. 288). US federal school food programs cost around $18 billion each year from 2016 to 2019 (U. S. Department of Agriculture, 2021a), so we're talking about an investment of between $18 billion and $21.6 billion. That's a lot of money, but consider the tradeoffs. Investing in healthy meals for kids can prevent costs in other areas, like the healthcare expenses involved in treating obesity, heart disease, and other food-related maladies. Investing in free food also makes hundreds of millions of dollars in administrative work go away, including 20 million or so free and reduced-price meal applications that workers must evaluate and store, along with the 3% of those (about 600,000) that someone must carefully verify. Cafeteria lines would shorten because meals would count the same way at the register (which wouldn't even be a *cash* register anymore). No more scarring from lunch shaming because no kid would have an account to go into arrears on, no chance someone snatches their tray, and no more plain cheese sandwiches. Schools could save the millions of dollars they spend on software to enforce the shaming system and spend it on food instead. And parents could save the fees they pay to keep an account topped up for other things that kids need more, like college savings, clothes, and better food at home.

Naturally the federal budget would require trimming elsewhere, but surely we can find places our money goes that we might value more elsewhere, like feeding kids. As a fun experiment, try looking through one of the periodic debt-reduction options reports released by the non-partisan Congressional Budget Office (CBO) for things the United States could do differently and thus afford universally free school food. The most recent (CBO, 2020), for example, shows that a paltry 5% budget reduction for the US Department of Defense—already larger than the budgets of China, India, Russia, the UK, Saudi Arabia, France, Germany, Japan, South Korea, Italy, and Australia *combined* (Stockholm International Peace Research Institute, 2021)—could pay for universal free school meals almost twice over (CBO, p. 41). Or charging a tiny 0.1% tax on stock market transactions, like stocks, bonds, and derivatives—currently not federally taxed—could pay for free school meals for every child nearly four times over (p. 86).

What if good food were a basic right? The adults in society make children go to school, with the belief that educating everyone provides a societal good. Most public schools transport students to school, not charging them to board the bus. We supply textbooks free, rather than renting them on a sliding scale. We let students see counselors and nurses without running their insurance cards and paying a co-pay first. We give kids a free seat to sit on in class, and they can use the bathrooms without paying a dime to open the stall. Why is feeding children different? Why is food somehow seen as a welfare giveaway with moral ramifications and worthy of recriminations? In a progressive vision of school meals, feeding is part of the *infrastructure* of schooling and should be as free as the rest of the facility.

School Food Should Provide for Physical Health

Food and water are basic human necessities; indeed they are a human right, enshrined in the Universal Declaration of Human Rights (United Nations General Assembly, 1948) and the Convention on the Rights of the Child (United Nations General Assembly, 1989). Every student should be able to partake of school meals that help them grow, be strong, develop muscles and organs and bones that function well, and keep them energetic and attentive during the school day. No one would dispute the ability of food to impact the body's functioning, whether for good or ill. A progressive view of school food holds that food should maximize the good and minimize the ill. This can look different for different children, so schools should accommodate children with allergies or metabolic disorders (diabetes, phenylketonuria) to every extent possible. School nutrition professionals can aid by labeling foods and educating kids with these food-related problems. All children, though, should have food that is maximally healthy rather than just maximally convenient. A healthy body has flow-on effects in so many ways. Providing for children's physical health should put them in the best position for academic achievement, as well.

School Food Should Aid Social Learning

The meal as social setting, and manners at the table, have had a major impact on the development of civilization and nations, installing self-restraint in the place of human's animalistic natures (Elias, 2000). Though some progressives might recoil from the imposition of culture, which always carries with it questions of *whose* culture gets imposed, one cannot deny that particular practices have power in a culture. This is true of literacy practices (Delpit, 1995), and it's true in manners around meals. If one knows how to use cutlery or make conversation "properly" in a place, one has more access to the culture of power.

In many cultures teachers and students share school meals, eating together. In Sweden, where all students receive meals free, they call this the *pedagogic meal*, where children get to see how adults behave in and think about meal situations and various foods (Osowski et al., 2013). No matter the location, students always learn what adults care about from meals, whether adults have high expectations or don't care much about what or how kids eat. I've been a high school teacher myself, so I know that some students—probably all adolescents—don't want their teachers around during their lunch, and many teachers don't like a rare break during the day being taken up eating with students. Pedagogic meals in the United States would thus prove a hard sell. Yet we give up something else of value for these breaks kids and teachers get from one another, like the ability to instill social learning.

I like how Lalli (2020) defines *social learning* in school meals as "coming to understand the different discourses that emerge from teaching staff, non-teaching staff and pupils about how to behave appropriately when eating with other people" (p. 27). The proposition that different discourses, multiple discourses, about eating exist and can come to the fore during a meal excites me most about this definition. If educators utilize the meal to provide skills in how to eat with others in the culture of power *and* in other diverse cultures, school meals can provide a truly educative setting. Adults can learn about children's eating cultures (Ludvigsen & Scott, 2009) and family meal customs (e.g., Backett-Milburn et al., 2010), while the children do the same in turn. Teachers thus learn and form bonds of understanding about their students, and they can encourage students to try new things. New ingredients and many cultures' cuisines and practices can be incorporated into the school meal.

School Food Should Provide Pleasure

The Center for Ecoliteracy (2013) poses a challenge to how we should think about the student experience in school lunches: What if we thought about school food as an opportunity during the school day for students to have pleasure? Not just feeding the hungry. Not just giving them an adequate "fueling" for the day. Pleasure! It's a radical way for most American educators to think about lunch periods, I would venture.

Food has so much potential for pleasure. Humans derive pleasure from the look, taste, and smell of food. We appreciate its temperature and texture. We sense overlapping basic tastes, like sweet, bitter, salty, sour, and umami—and perhaps others (Beauchamp, 2019). Many if not most humans take pleasure from participating in growing, harvesting, or shopping for, preparing, cooking, and serving food. We like to sample. We like to talk and write about food, photograph it, create recipes, collect and use family recipes, follow TikTok trends, watch people cook it on television or on a hibachi grill or campfire in front of us. Schools should allow children to bring such pleasures into the school and the cafeteria, and adults should try to look beyond just the nutrients of food toward the pleasure it can provide. And not just treats but a well-rounded sense of the many pleasures food can bring.

Make as Much Real Food as Possible

Michael Pollan (2008) often gets quoted for his food rule that one should eat "real food." He means things "your great-grandmother would recognize" as food, and not highly processed, engineered "foodlike" products. Food-like things that kids enjoy consuming fill grocery stores, vending machines, and school cafeterias: Flamin' Hot Cheetos, Go-GURT, Fruit by the Foot, pudding cups, breakfast bars, nuggets made from a chicken version of "pink slime," and on and on. Yes, such items have been reformulated to meet the food standards, and their makers have convinced the FDA and USDA to accept their processes and ingredients, but their nutritional profile and institutional approval don't make them into "real" food. And don't let manufacturers fool you into equating all processing; cutting and freezing are not the same as ammonium hydroxide treatment, the addition of purely chemical colorants and flavors, the introduction of anti-foaming or anti-caking agents, or replacing lost nutrients with fortifying sprays and powders. Tang orange-flavored drink powder is not oranges, even if it meets one's vitamin C needs for a day.

So many dynamics make serving real food challenging for schools. Real food requires safe storage and processing, which requires space, labor, and equipment. It's harder to keep fresh. Food safety challenges and responsibilities fall to cafeterias rather than to manufacturers. All true, but real food has bodily effects and pleasures that empower children, educators, and parents. Excessive processing generally takes away nutrients from food, and eating from pre-packaged meals and fast-food outlets deskills the populace, removing the knowledge needed to maintain one's food sovereignty (Vileisis, 2008). Providing real food—and not just for the sake of foodieness (Earl, 2018)—helps ensure so many other progressive ideals I've listed.

Real food isn't as hard to produce as many argue, either. Kate Adamick (2012), a consultant and trainer for scratch cooking in school foodservice, notes that cooking from scratch being cost-prohibitive remains a pervasive myth. Yet she shows through a series of worksheets how cafeterias waste both time and money in cooking from frozen and from cans. With careful audits of their practices, some planning, and the improvement of cooking skills, school cafeterias can actually save money with scratch cooking. They can use dried beans instead of canned, lower the number of entrees, stop individually wrapping items, get fresh rather than processed commodities, improve time efficiencies, and use real plates and cutlery.

Yet real food requires more rethinking than just the logistics. I suggest that US school food rethink its strange dependency on the "food crediting" system. Though the USDA standards are nominally food-based (just like England has returned to, as I discussed in Chapter 5), the USDA uses a complex system of *nutrient-based* standards to define what counts within a particular food group. That's how pizza came to count as a serving of vegetables, as I noted in Snack Two. If some manufactured Frankenfood meets a general nutrient profile, it can count as a substitute for real food with a similar profile.

I argue we need to close this loophole process that turns our food-based system into effectively a nutrient-based system. In that way, schools and districts will be encouraged to plan menus based on the real food groups—not potassium levels but bananas, not selenium and zinc levels but beef. Using traditional definitions of food, the definitions our great-grandmothers (and great-grandfathers!) had, might help prevent the endless cycle of just reformulating or fortifying the same old high-calorie carnival fare. Cafeterias could focus instead on providing larger portions of nutrient-rich fresh foods that provide a better nutritional payoff for their calories.

Remove as Much Branding as Possible

Another plus of serving real rather than highly processed food comes from less branding (name-brand fruit like Cuties might be an exception [Jordan, 2012]). Otherwise, advertising bombards children all day long (Institute of Medicine, 2006), and more and more schools willingly join in. While corporations might rationalize their work in schools in philan-thropic language, as Molnar and Bonninger (2020) explain, marketing in schools actually miseducates and is anti-democratic:

> If the methods of modern mass marketing threaten the self-control and judgment of adults, deploying them against children is particularly insid-ious. No one can seriously suggest that children are rational consumers who have the same power, information, and freedom that adults are said to have to freely enter into contracts for goods and services. Advertising to children is, then, a kind of immoral war on childhood, waged for the profit of adults who should be childhood's guardians. Furthermore, when advertising is conducted in schools, the immorality is compounded because the power of the state is twisted to the service of special interests, the ethical standing of educators is compromised, and the orientation of the school is shifted toward mis-educative experiences. (p. 9)

This moral equation of schools being guardians of children, exposing them *solely* to truth and modeling justice and democracy, stands as incompatible with, for instance, posting ads and branded vending machines that suggest Powerade will make one a better athlete or that Coke will make one a well-liked hipster. The era of computers or tablets provided to every child only amplifies such dangers. Who knows what ads they see or data they leave behind while they "google" information for reports, use ad-supported learning games, and enter their assignments into "free" learning management systems and cloud storage?

Among Siegel's (2019) wishes for school food reform, particularly, was getting rid of copycat foods, and I agree this is a priority. Barely changing the formulation and packaging of highly processed food amounts to little better than deception, serving corporate interests by setting kids up for brand loyalty. Educators, though, should focus on health loyalty. The lunchroom shouldn't cement customers for Pop-Tarts and Uncrustables. Lunch ladies and gentlemen shouldn't don caps and aprons with the Dominos logo, nor should they deliver their pizzas (even if they count as "vegetables").

Disrupt and Ultimately End All Forms of Food Shaming

In Snack Five, I described a practice long used to try to get parents to pay their child's food bill, the dreaded plain cheese sandwich. As I said there, the cheese sandwich marks kids as different, as perhaps too poor to pay for their food. Let's be honest with ourselves: As many in the public agree, it's a shaming practice, one intentionally wielded to get kids to bug their parents into paying the bill. We must remember to regard the kids eating lunch *as children*, though, as innocents deserving their own fresh chance at dignity and protection, rather than as proxies for their parents. We should not punish children to somehow discipline the adults in their lives. So we shouldn't shame children by giving them a cheese sandwich or making them clean tables or marking them with hand stamps when their parents haven't paid the lunch bill. And we shouldn't imagine, much less say out loud, that third graders will become permanent wards of the state if we give them a lunch.

Stigmatizing free meals was prohibited by the original National School Lunch Act. It has always been illegal, but it has been a long, long road toward ending practices that call attention to those who can't pay full price. I remember as an elementary school student in the 1970s the kids with free lunches having a different colored punch ticket for their meals. I remember in middle school having separate lines for free and reduced meals and for paid meals. School nutrition operations have made great strides in ending such practices, but more remains to be done. Again, the easiest—even if not the cheapest—solution to interrupt shaming would be to make food free, just like nearly every other aspect of school.

Yet food shaming involves more than just the administrative response to a child's lunch account. Shaming can happen among children, between children and adults, and between educators and parents, whether in the cafeteria, in the curriculum, or in letters home or at the classroom door. Commenting on how "unhealthy" someone's lunch seems, making snide comments about their portion sizes (whether too big or too small), complaining about the smell or look of someone's food, or even expressing disgust about an ethnic dish, can sting the recipient, creating embarrassment, long-term self-esteem issues, or eating avoidance. Food shaming in the worst cases can become a feature of bullying. Shaming someone for what they choose to eat or what they can afford to eat can harm children as much or more than singling them out for their lunch balance. Educators and nutrition professionals must learn to recognize such shaming behaviors and interrupt them so that everyone feels safe and valued in the school.

School Food Always Teaches, so Schools Should Act Purposefully on What Kids Learn

A progressive vision of school food sees mealtimes as learning times, not simply bodily maintenance. As a nutritionist from Greenville County, South Carolina, said about lengthening their lunch period (a rare direction), "When children come to the cafeteria, they are not coming to lunch, it is not a break in the day, they are coming to a nutrition lab where they are learning to make healthy choices" ("New healthier school lunches …," 2013).

Furthermore, learning in the cafeteria, from a progressive vantage point, revolves around more than just nutrition. Of course what we eat matters, but why and how we eat matters, too. As Trapp (2018) notes, nourishment involves more than nutrients. She suggests that nourishment must include "the capacity to: *fill* (quell hunger and fill the stomach), *invigorate* (provide nutrients), and *gratify* (satisfy social, emotional, and/or psychological preferences and needs)" (p. 2; emphasis original). As noted above, school meals present opportunities for social learning, to explore ourselves and others and the relationships we forge around food. Many relationships forged on food are about family bonding, tradition, and culture.

Food carves out powerful windows into history, too. The US's food history has been shaped by sharing, innovation, technological advances, and more. Its food history also has some not so positive traditions, like colonization and exploitation, slavery, racism, cultural appropriation, land theft, stripping food cultures to "Americanize". children or remove their ruralness (House, 2021). US governments have used food policy to starve enemies and those on the margins. General William T. Sherman, by himself, was responsible for policies to starve the Confederate civilian population into submission at the Civil War's end, then later he was a major architect of slaughtering the buffalo to subdue Native American tribes (Smits, 1994). Longtime Federal Bureau of Investigation (FBI) director, J. Edgar Hoover, utilized the FBI's resources under his illegal COINTELPRO program to undermine trust in the Black Panther Party's free breakfast program (Lateef & Androff, 2017). The list could go on. Students can discuss these issues, not to feel guilty or angry about this history, but to pay homage to where our food cultures have originated and to pledge that weaponizing food and agriculture doesn't happen in the future.

Any subject taught in school can study food. Take as an example my discipline as a high school teacher, English. As Franzen and Peters (2019) illustrate in their book, *Say Yes to Pears*, food literacy can provide gateways to skills learned in the English classroom, whether connecting students to stories, getting students to write about food and family, helping them think deeply about food in literature, or learning how to host guests and discuss one's learning. Any class—history, writing, reading, science, art, math, agriculture, culinary—can use Franzen and Peters' examples (see also Editors of Rethinking Schools, 2006) as a springboard for incorporating crucial food issues into the curriculum.

School Food and Food Education Falls Under the Responsibility of More Than the Cafeteria

To truly seize breakfasts, lunches, and snacks as learning opportunities, we must expand who takes responsibility for school foodscapes. Learning about and from food requires more than leaving it up to the cafeteria staff. Administrators and teachers must shift to thinking about food as a learning challenge, not simply a logistical or managerial one.

Indeed, the responsibility for school food must go beyond the schoolhouse doors, as well. As Dolby (2020) argues, preservice teacher education needs to include attention to the role of school lunch in students' lives, which means that professors of education must consider such aspects, as well. Politicians and policymakers should think about school food carefully, and not just to prove their ideological bona fides to voters and donors, but to actually solve challenges and make the program solvent, accessible, ecologically friendly, and nutritious. Chefs, as our most knowledgeable fellow citizens about food preparation, have been heavily involved in school food, and should continue their involvement. Jamie Oliver has waded into school feeding issues, of course, but so have *Top Chef*'s Tom Colicchio and daytime host Rachael Ray. They and thousands of other chefs have stepped into school kitchens and district offices to help make positive changes. Parents should think about and act on school food, as well, not just complaining when something goes wrong, but lending ideas and time to help cafeterias do the complex, under-resourced job they face every day. And parents can lend time and brainpower to politicians, as well, helping them know what values the public truly hold. The film *Two Angry Moms* (Kalafa, 2007), for instance, shows what dedicated parents can accomplish by working from the ground up to reform school food. Many, many other examples are out there to learn from.

Connect Students with Natural Experiences

Most researchers and advocates working on school food have focused our attentions on school gardens. As Earl and Thompson (2021) note, four discourses have been prevalent about school gardens: (a) healthy eating, foodieness, obesity; (b) hunger and poverty; (c) well-being, resilience, sustainability; and (d) access to nature (p. 91). I think we too often overlook the last of these, the value of getting kids in contact with the natural world. Many students, particularly in urban areas or even industrialized agriculture areas, can find real nature—wild nature—hard to access. School gardens can serve as little natural oases in children's lives, even if only a row of paper cups is on the classroom windowsill.

We can expand these opportunities beyond just gardens, though. Ranches, grasslands, forests, rivers, mountains, streams, and oceans also provide places for humans to gather and grow their food, too. All can be locations where students explore natural ecological processes, the ethics of eating animal products and caring for our fellow animals, and the important connections people have to places (e.g., Gruenewald, 2003). In such natural places students can be outside with sun, wind, snow, rain, and dust on their skin; can touch, taste, and smell the natural world; can get dirty, wet, sweaty, and stinky; and can learn about interconnections both biological and social. A progressive vision looks for ways to remove alienation from the natural world and to remove the economic and logistical barriers kids face in accessing natural spaces.

Consider the Social Justice Implications of Food and Food Education

Statistics from the USDA show again and again that access to good quality food has not been equal for all communities. As a 2020 report (Coleman-Jensen et al., 2021) shows, the national average for food insecurity was 10.5% of people. As any average does, though, this number hides communities significantly more likely to have higher food insecurity: any household with children, single-parent households, those with incomes below 185% of the poverty threshold, and households headed by Black and Hispanic peoples. Providing school food to kids makes a major difference for these vulnerable families and communities, and without it families would struggle more, economically, socially, and politically.

Researchers know that food-related health disparities have social determinants, as well. Diseases related to diet, including diabetes, hypertension, heart disease, and obesity, occur more prevalently in low socioeconomic communities and communities of color (Weinstein et al., 2017, Chapter 2). School food reformers must attend to those disparities that cafeteria cultures may originate, reproduce, or ameliorate.

In communities of color and working-class communities, including Native American reservations and urban and rural schools, food justice or lack thereof feeds the school-to-prison pipeline, Nocella and colleagues (2017) show convincingly. The lack of access to healthy, fresh food within a reasonable distance; exposure to greater amounts of environmental toxins; and the lack of green spaces and garden access can compound inequities in poor quality or highly processed school food. For students who come to school hungry, with toxic exposure, or "sugared up" on convenience store food, learning and behavior suffer. Educators, administrators, and police resource officers in schools can see such behavior as a disruption or even a threat, and overly punitive responses can funnel children into the criminal justice system. Food should thus feature in conversations about avoiding the criminalization of poor kids and kids of color.

Gender has long been as a major factor in food justice concerns, too (Counihan & Kaplan, 1998). Who makes the food? Who chooses what gets served? Who grows or hunts the food? These ask core questions about the division of labor that put the largest burden of work and care on women. The modern food economy, particularly school food, often exploits women's labor to ensure that food remains cheap. Women's professionalism and employment are, furthermore, usually first to get eliminated when manufacturing supersedes scratch cooking (Gaddis, 2019). Gender influences body image, too, and that has deep connections to food's place in the cafeteria and curriculum.

Religion and culture, too, play a complicated role in school food justice. Certainly communities should preserve local food and food customs. That pertains to Native American communities, as I said above, and it equally pertains to areas within majority cultures. I wouldn't want grits removed from Southern schools any more than I want wild rice removed from reservation schools in the Northern Plains. That said, we must expand the food understandings and preferences of children in all schools; food and eating instills social skills and knowledges necessary for an increasingly diverse and globalized world. It also means including, say, halal meat periodically to meet the needs of Muslim students, having a fish option on Fridays for Catholic students, incorporating kosher foods for Jewish students, and more.

Outstanding programs in school food reform promote layers of benefits for multiple stakeholders, purposefully including all members of a community, both inside and outside schools. Take for example the Drew Farm in Detroit, Michigan (Roden, 2014), a two-acre farm housed at Drew Transition Center, a public special education school teaching 18- to 26-year-olds with physical and cognitive impairments and who have aged out of traditional schools. Students run the farm, and they learn valuable skills in growing and preparing food, which could lead to lives of fulfilling work and independence. Drew Farm also produces 20,000 pounds of fresh, organic produce for the City's school lunch program, and it serves as a site for field trips and family events to learn about food. Drew Farm thus creates a virtuous cycle of help from student to student to community, with an eye to justice for everyone involved.

What I'm really saying, at its heart, is that we must reframe our focus on school lunch, leaving behind the "charitable" model and refocusing on the social justice aspects of school food as citizenship and human rights. It's a shift from the politics of welfare and division toward the politics of rights, dignity, and unity. As Welsh and MacRae (1998) pose the differences in views:

> Charity can be destructive in the way it depoliticizes hunger and poverty, and in the way it divides us as full participants in society: the donor and the recipient; the powerful and the powerless; the independent and the dependent; the altruistic and the grateful; the competent and the inadequate; the winners and the losers; the proud and the shamed; those who define the conditions or rules and those who conform (Curtin and

Heldke, 1992, p. 304-310). Instead, projects must embody strategies reflecting a more comprehensive view that defines food security work to include a focus on income, an attention to food system issues and a recognition of the social and cultural importance of food and food work.

If we continue looking at school lunches and breakfasts as charity, in other words, we miss many of the important underlying causes of food insecurity and its precursors. Worse, we drive wedges between ourselves as humans and citizens.

Consider the Environmental Implications of School Food

We live in an era of climate crisis, with food systems contributing mightily to our planetary degradation. As the EAT-*Lancet* Commission outlines (Willett et al., 2019),

> Food production is the largest cause of global environmental change. Agriculture occupies about 40% of global land, and food production is responsible for up to 30% of global greenhouse-gas emissions and 70% of freshwater use. Conversion of natural ecosystems to croplands and pastures is the largest factor causing species to be threatened with extinction. Overuse and misuse of nitrogen and phosphorus causes eutrophication and dead zones in lakes and coastal zones. Environmental burden from food production also includes marine systems. About 60% of world fish stocks are fully fished, more than 30% overfished, and catch by global marine fisheries has been declining since 1996. In addition, the rapidly expanding aquaculture sector can negatively affect coastal habitats, freshwater, and terrestrial systems (related to the area directly used for aquaculture and feed production). (p. 449)

Schools play a substantial part in food-related impacts on environmental sustainability. Clearly a school food system that grows, transports, cooks, and serves several billion meals each year will have a major ecological footprint. Any progressive school food reform must thus find ways to reduce the use of resources, reuse things that can have a second life, and recycle materials to avoid waste and pollution.

To what extent do our school cafeterias focus on sustainability and environmental care? For some school nutrition professionals, these core values guide their practice (Arnold, 2019). But as an overall system, reliant on manufactured products, school food operations use tremendous amounts of freezing and refrigeration, boxes and packaging made of paper, plastic containers and cutlery, ground transportation, water not for consumption and other environmental costs. Schools also serve menus heavy on dairy and meat, products with significantly higher carbon footprints and environmental damage than fruits and vegetables (Kraus-Polk & Hamerschlag, 2021).

Just as Poore and Nemecek (2018) argue that food producers must communicate their environmental impacts to consumers, a progressive view of school food suggests school nutrition providers—industry and cafeterias—should do the same. How much packaging have they sent to landfills? How much water do they use? How much refrigerant? In a democracy, communicating impact makes an industry accountable to citizens, allowing those citizens to vote for what they truly want for their children and the world.

In school food, the perhaps dull-sounding topic of procurement—the power to buy—stands as perhaps the most direct route to creating a more environmentally friendly system (Morgan & Sonnino, 2008). Just moving toward plant-based foods rather than meat as the center of the plate can make a huge difference in the ecological costs of school lunches, not to mention their healthiness. And make no mistake, schools have a tremendous ability to shape food's production. If large districts or entire states wielded their purchasing power to reward animal-friendly and low-greenhouse gas-emitting producers, the carbon and water footprints of schools would improve tremendously (Kraus-Polk & Hamerschlag, 2021).

Kids Should Stay Deeply Involved

Adults have a way of assuming they know what kids will like without ever asking them. I have read so many times over the years excuses like "Healthy food doesn't do any good if it's only thrown away" or the related "Kids won't eat healthy food." Sure, kids do craft food cultures and subcultures just for themselves, sometimes proudly rejecting "healthy" or "adult" food (Best, 2017; Ludvigsen & Scott, 2009). That tells just half the story, though.

A recent review of experimental research seeking to change children's eating behavior (DeCosta et al., 2017) showed that some approaches succeed in influencing children's food preferences and intake while some don't. Not surprisingly, attempts to control kids' food practices tended to backfire, whether through restricting foods or offering incentives or rewards. School gardens, which usually include tasting and cooking sessions, showed positive effects. So did providing a variety of fruits and vegetables for free. Using well-known "spokes-characters" was effective in pushing changes, too; I'd advocate limiting that to fresh foods rather than allowing more branding for manufactured foods. The point remains, though, that children's eating habits—and adults'—are malleable and influenceable. Food manufacturers and marketers know this well, but schools and parents can find ways to capitalize on progressive influences, too.

That doesn't mean the adults involved should act covertly (Ogden et al., 2006) in their attempts to change food systems and preferences. Kids should participate in the process; they should be counted among those "responsible" for food and food education that I discussed above. Indeed, they already *are* a part. Many young people already advocate and protest and lead, just like the kids in the film *Lunch Line* (Park & Graziano, 2011) who traveled to help lobby Congresspeople and show what youth can do; just like the kids in New Orleans who started Rethink (formerly Kids Rethink New Orleans Schools) with school lunch as a major platform for improvement (McNulty, 2008). Young people can help start and maintain gardens, kitchens, and food distribution charities; they've been doing it. Kids can at least taste test foods, giving new recipes an honest chance, and kids can give their opinions to adults who promise to take them seriously. Whatever the task, a progressive vision includes children and young adults as partners and thought leaders.

Make Food and Food Education as Local as Possible, but with National Standards (No Conservative Opt-Outs)

School cafeterias cannot practically serve solely local, organic food, at least not within the current food system the United States has created. Policies and practices have made meeting all food needs with local food impossible. The geographic dispersion and specialization of our agriculture, combined with the diversity modern eaters expect and the power of cultural conventions against public-sector feeding being taken seriously (Morgan & Sonnino, 2008), make such a hope (currently) unrealistic. Grand Forks, North Dakota, for instance, might be surrounded by some of the richest soil in North America, but sugar beets for processing into table sugar fill that soil. Plus, Grand Forks' growing season lasts so short a time that fresh vegetables would be impossible half the year, and a few months you'd have to eat them from canning jars. I mean, there's a reason lutefisk became popular there! So the United States' school food system can't rely on solely local food, but we can do better one step at a time. Doug Davis's example above, and to a much smaller degree school gardens, show how clever sourcing can snowball into a more local, more place-conscious and seasonal system.

I also believe that food *education* can prosper from local focus. Children can learn a great deal from seeing the foods made, shared, and sold in their communities. Who does the growing, harvesting, and cooking? Whose food is here, and what history does it hold? Whose food is not here, and why? How can we build links to new foods and heritages in the community? I personally find the history of grits fascinating (e.g., Murray, 2018; Neal & Perry, 1991; Woodward, 1978), a food that meant a great deal to my father and to our Southern upbringing. I feel closer to my roots by finding "real" grits, boiling them for a long time, slathering them in butter and salt or eating them with shrimp, and sharing a bowl with my kids. Educators can profitably capture joy and interest by bringing such connections to food into the classroom, while still ensuring that people who weren't born locally can also bring their foods to those who were.

Even considering the benefits of a local lens, I am mindful that conservatives I've profiled throughout this book often use "the local" (and "flexibility") as a rationale for ending nutritional regulations, ending subsidies for low-income students, or maybe even ending school lunch provision altogether. So my urging of local food and food education comes with a caveat that as nations and societies we must maintain access and quality that represents the vast majority's will, protecting the vulnerable against the possible tyranny of the local. That means we need national nutritional standards and requirements, too.

Provide Supports for Making Programs Sustainable (Less About Grants and Superstars)

Attention to school food tends to often follow controversies and stunts. Mrs. Q, the pseudonym of teacher Sarah Wu, got attention for a year of eating and photographing lousy-looking Chicago school food every day (Wu, 2011). Jamie Oliver came to the United States to try replicating his food revolution over a couple of television seasons (Smith, 2010); by the time the second season limped toward an ending, he was retreating without much headway. As I noted in Snack Five, lunch shaming required wide media coverage before more than just school nutrition professionals paid attention. Yet the hard work of school food reform cannot rely on stunts and controversies for motivation; reform requires patience, persistence, and vigilance.

School food reformers must take care to create sustainable programs, ones that don't rely on X Prizes and short-term grants, and ones that don't require the visionary leadership of a single star. The US food system, particularly its *school* food system, needs some serious reforms and serious resources to get it there. Government involvement, corporate involvement, and public involvement all have a place in making these necessary changes happen.

Conclusion

I believe, ultimately, a progressive vision like the one I've outlined in this chapter contains the seeds of a better future for kids, for our society, and for the planet. We have choices to make—political choices. We can follow a path where kids learn the hardscrabble view that everyone must fend for themselves, that you pay or starve, and that what's best is what's good for industries and manufacturers. I think we have a better path to follow, though, one that puts our money behind our rhetoric of caring about children. It's a path that sees community, togetherness, health, sharing, the future of our planet, and public interest as the most important values. It's time for a grander rethinking of school food—and schooling itself. We don't have to just give out smaller portions, whether of chicken nuggets or of justice. We can choose real food and real democracy and real health instead.

CODA: COVID and Beyond

The years 2020 and 2021 changed the world drastically—for how long and in what ways I can only imagine in late 2021, while I write this. The COVID-19 global pandemic has ended millions of lives, disrupted economies and employment, and seen the fabric of life altered by quarantines, masks, stringent sanitizing, shortages of essentials, and social distancing. As with other spaces where people come together, schools had to change their standard procedures, too. Many schools closed their doors and abruptly switched to online learning. While many schools eventually returned for in-person days behind masks and plexiglass, many closed buildings the entire school year and stayed virtual. Sports seasons were truncated or abandoned. Proms and graduations were canceled.

A sea-change event like a pandemic casts in high relief how a society functions. Is health care adequate? Is it fair? How well does government function in a crisis? How well and how quickly does the technological and social infrastructure adapt and function? Is the populace well educated enough to understand the peril and how to avoid it? What would we do without schools and teachers for extended periods?

M. B. Weaver-Hightower, *Unpacking School Lunch*, https://doi.org/10.1007/978-3-030-97288-2

Fig. 1 USDA Lunch distribution point in San Antonio, Texas, during the COVID-19 pandemic, April 9, 2020. Public domain image from https://www.flickr.com/photo.gne?short=2iNFV1S [accessed October 29, 2021]

As you might have guessed, school *food* became a crucial topic early into the COVID-19 pandemic. As a key social support system, school breakfasts and lunches ensured that millions of children avoided hunger as their families lost jobs and even lives to the virus. Suddenly, lunch ladies and lunch gentlemen became "essential workers," who needed to continue working despite the threat of contagion. Principals, teachers, and cafeteria workers hopped aboard busses to deliver meals to housebound students, or they created safe pickup spots, as in Fig. 1, for families to collect meals (Mitchell, 2020). Menus had to be suited to being reheated or left out, and the weekend food many schools supplied had to be easy to prepare, particularly for children of essential workers who might have to heat the food themselves.

Not unexpectedly, money became a consideration. With millions suddenly unemployed in a few weeks, how would school food programs pay for these new meals and how would they handle screening for financial need? The Trump Department of Agriculture extended free meals reimbursements at the beginning of COVID-19 lockdowns in March 2020—technically, waivers of rules for eligibility and where schools must serve meals—including allowing parents to pick up meals without their children present. The Trump Administration, in line with conservative principles, wanted to end these rules for the 2020–2021 school year's start, even though the United States was still in the pandemic's grip. They extended the waivers only at the last moment, only until December, and only under pressure from mayors across the United States and from bipartisan members of Congress (Taylor, 2020). (Perhaps they wanted to avoid the poor publicity of snatching school lunches away with a November election looming?).

After that election, which Trump lost, the incoming Biden USDA renewed the waivers, including for universal free meals past the December cutoff the Trump administration left, and even extended it through the entire 2021–2022 academic year (Blad, 2021a). Advocates have been pressuring the Biden administration to make meals universally free going forward (Blad, 2021b).

Thus during the COVID-19 pandemic school food has had another moment in the public consciousness. While many dynamics described in this book held true—conservative resistance to extending food benefits and focusing on nutritional minimums over food quality and experience, for example—many previously hidden aspects of school food gained new appreciation. Many in the general public had not realized the extent of school food's reach to millions of kids. Pandemic-era school food showed itself as an indispensable safety net for *all* children, not just the chronically poor but also for the acutely distressed, too. No matter how secure they had believed their own communities, people saw just down the street the social and economic importance of feeding every kid for free. They got a chance to see the dedication of the school nutrition labor force, along with how little they earn. And many middle-class progressive parents began to realize the need to have their children eat the school lunches (Sole-Smith, 2021), as an act of political solidarity to maintain program sustainability.

The pandemic also proved that school lunch does, in fact, operate much like a business, even if not focused on the profit motive. Just as most other businesses during the COVID-19 pandemic, shortages of food, labor, and supplies, compounded by delivery slowdowns, eventually snarled school feeding programs beginning in September of 2021. Cafeterias were forced to shop at consumer warehouse stores, and the shortage of plastic cutlery forced some districts to serve only finger food (Ngo, 2021). The mass return to in-person schooling in Fall 2021 suddenly put cafeterias back in full operation, and the already thinly stretched supply chain proved unprepared. At crisis moments like that, though, one does marvel at the complex logistical task feeding children represents in normal times. It also highlights how beholden cafeterias have become to boxed, reheatable food like chicken nuggets and to environmentally unsustainable practices like using plastic utensils, trays, and cups. The program's security is thus at stake if we don't future-proof it based on the pandemic experience.

As I write this, the futures of school lunch and breakfast programs are being rethought and rewritten worldwide, not just in the United States. That holds true for England, too.

Marcus Rashford, and the Cycle Starts Again in England

During the early days of COVID lockdowns in 2020, school meals reemerged as front-page news in Britain despite conservative's best attempts to wash the government's hands of it a few years earlier, as I explained in Chapter 5. The hero of school dinners this time was a soccer player, Manchester United and England national team forward, Marcus Rashford (a fellow proud member of the Marcus club!).

Like Jamie Oliver, Rashford was able to parley his fame into attention to a problem inherent in shutting down schools to prevent coronavirus spread: millions of children depend on the meals they get at school to stave off food insecurity. Rashford knew this problem well because he experienced it growing up, with his family using food pantries, school meals, and the kindness of neighbors and coaches to get by. On the night before English schools shut down for the first time during the pandemic, he tweeted:

Guys, across the UK there are over 32,000 schools. Tomorrow all of these will close. Many of the children attending these schools rely on free meals, so I've spent the last few days talking to organisations to understand how this deficit is going to be filled. (Rashford [@MarcusRashford], 2020)

Pairing with the charity FareShare, the country's charitable food redistribution network, Rashford called for donations and set about volunteering himself to get meals distributed. Because of his high profile as a national sporting hero, the public response was quick and generous. By April, Rashford announced that £20 million had been raised, enough to provide meals to three million people (Plant, 2020).

By June of 2020, the Conservative Government, headed by Boris Johnson, had decided that they would end the food voucher scheme created near the beginning of the pandemic. That scheme had electronic vouchers worth £15 each week distributed to families eligible for free school meals so that they could buy food at grocery stores to replace school meals. But the scheme was weeks in getting started, wasn't valid at more affordable supermarkets like Aldi and Lidl, and—perhaps most importantly—stopped during school holidays (Wittaker, 2020), leading to much public concern over "holiday hunger" (Lalli, 2021). Johnson and the Conservatives decided not to continue it during the summer break either.

Rashford acted quickly, penning an open letter to the Government to reconsider this decision (M. Rashford, 2020). He decried the conservative rhetoric that had followed the public outcry—"some have placed blame on parents for having children they 'can't afford'" and he got a tweet from an MP reminding him that the existing benefits system should be enough. He urged those conservative critics, "find your humanity" and extend the vouchers over the summer break. He pleaded, "The government has taken a 'whatever it takes' approach to the economy—I'm asking you today to extend that same thinking to protecting all vulnerable children across England." With the public firmly on his side and the Conservatives faced with having to defend in Parliament taking meals away during a pandemic, Johnson and the government made a "U-turn" and extended summer meals funding the day after the letter's publication.

Perhaps the Conservatives thought that the issue had gone away and that people weren't paying attention anymore, for by October they were again attempting to shut down the free school meals scheme, once again ending payments over the Easter school holidays. Conservative MPs tweeted at Rashford that "extending freebies are a sticking plaster [a band-aid] not a solution." They suggested that the meals provision "increases dependency." They came up with technical sounding problems like trying to prevent "destroying the currency with excessive QE [quantitative easing]" (Weale, 2020). These value-laden phrases should sound familiar from my Chapter 4 on conservative rhetoric. The Conservative majority voted 322 to 261 on October 21, 2020—still deep into the pandemic's unemployment crisis—to end the scheme.

Rashford was there to whip up a backlash again, and for a second time, Johnson and the Conservatives were forced to reverse course. This time they extended school meals provision with a £170 million winter grant scheme, but they developed a plan to prioritize food parcels being distributed rather than cash benefits. While a parcel distribution scheme has advantages, like being able to check on students when they pick them up and being able to ensure the food's nutritional quality (Department for Education, 2021), it ran into problems that demonstrate downsides of contracting government work to those with profit motives. Compass Group, the world's largest food distribution company, which is headquartered in England—and not incidentally a purveyor of the Turkey Twizzlers that irked Jamie Oliver—was given millions of pounds to provide 10-day meal parcels to children, the equivalent of £30 each fortnight, equal to the previous food vouchers. In an apparent attempt to extract profit from the scheme, the food parcels provided were meager, some estimated to contain about £5 worth of food and some food past its expiration dates (Blackall, 2021). Compass apologized and agreed to cover the parcels' costs—not exactly generous given that Compass had also taken nearly £100 million in government furlough payments during the pandemic (Jolly, 2021). (How's that for "quantitative easing"?!).

This food parcel scandal was replicated in the United States during the pandemic. The Trump Administration felt that private companies should become the beneficiaries of providing food relief, secure in their neoliberal belief that private companies would act "innovatively" rather than being tied down in bureaucracy. Trump's USDA created the Farmers to Families Food Box program, hiring hundreds of private companies to buy surplus food from restaurants, cruise ships, and schools that were closed for the pandemic, and to take it to food banks that were being overwhelmed by pandemic-driven demand. As in England, many private companies showed that they were no more innovative than those who had spent their lives in government feeding the hungry. Indeed, despite costing $4 billion, six times the USDA's normal emergency food aid budget, problems were rife:

> Some of the companies charged the government more than double the program average while delivery to food banks was sometimes late. When the government contracted new vendors, some food banks relying on the program stopped receiving food at all. At the same time, the contractors delivered to churches or daycare centers that lacked adequate refrigeration.
>
> …
>
> While food bank operators are thankful for the large volumes of fresh food from the food box program—and they stress that aid is still needed—many say far more families could have been fed by sticking to existing programs with proven quality and oversight. (Walljasper, 2021, paras. 5, 10)

The food box problem exposed in both the United States and England that trying to extract a profit from humanitarian aid and to start from scratch rather than relying on *government's* already robust logistical infrastructure exposes the neoliberal ideal as largely a fantasy.

In Marcus Rashford's battle with the Conservative Government in England, we see again the dynamic I have documented throughout *Unpacking School Lunch*: conservative resistance and undermining of school meals provision. One shudders to think what would have happened if a high profile athlete with diplomatic skills and persistence beyond his then 23 years had not taken up this charge. As a Guardian opinion essay put it,

we should not lose sight of the simple fact that he [Rashford] should not
have had to do any of this. It is not the responsibility of a footballer,
especially one in his early 20s, to ensure that the poorest children in
England do not go hungry during the school holidays. Rashford's job is
to score goals for Manchester United, not to force a government to care
about poor children. That he has done it says a lot about him—and much
about the Britain of 2020. (Olusoga & Olusoga, 2020, para. 9)

Indeed, how governments have reacted to the COVID-19 pandemic says
a great deal about the moral, economic, and logistical state of their countries. Most citizens have shown great compassion for the humanity of
those in need, many of whom never would have imagined suddenly
needing welfare. Yet there have also been new realizations of just how
bad some already had it before virus lockdowns and layoffs. That has
sparked new energy and participation among some who hope that the
world won't simply go back to "normal" as it was before COVID when
the pandemic ends. Will governments listen? Will they find ways to
resist conservative backsliding and resistance? Or will we resume carnival
fare school meals? We have a chance and an insight at this moment of
great disruption, with social and economic inequalities laid bare for all
to see, to think differently. We can reconceptualize school meals as free
to everyone, as healthy, as a wise investment, and as the right thing to
do. Do we have the courage?

To Conclude

As I wrap up the work of nearly fifteen years researching school food,
swaddled here between the covers of a book, some lessons stand out.
Unpacking School Lunch does not simply detail the specificities of school
lunch policy in one place and time. The specifics illustrate some *general*
principles. In case I have been opaque throughout this book, let me
cement these general principles into sentences.

- The decisions made about food work much like any other educational
  decision, whether curriculum, teaching, economic, funding, or so on.
  Such decisions reflect deeply held philosophical, cultural, religious,

political, and human commitments that decision makers have, and reformers must interrogate these decisions to find who benefits.

- The key stakes of school food politics are getting to define the basic terms of our lives, like *food, welfare, water, vegetables, fairness, adequacy, standards,* and even *education.*
- The recipients of school food suffer the same stereotypes and perspectives that recipients of other social policies do. They either get held as "worthy" or "unworthy" depending on the beholder.
- Gains are not permanent, nor are losses. The movement toward progressive educational policy must be struggled for, defended, and maintained. The "losing" side rarely simply "sees the light" and jumps on board. Would you?
- Thousands of dedicated folks work hard every day to make the future brighter, more secure, and more just for kids using food. Often they go above and beyond their job descriptions, using their creativity, knowledge, brawn, and caring to stretch meager resources.
- School food should be free for every student, just like the other indispensable parts of school. It would solve many problems if we stopped treating food differently, as a domain wrapped up in welfare and morality.
- The way we do meals at school represents just one way—a choice we made up long ago and continue to mostly reiterate each day. Change might not prove easy, but we can create a new way that represents who we are today or want to become in the future.

It's up to us—all of us—to bravely and democratically make the political choices that define what schools will serve to our children. We must do so with a clarity of vision about what those choices mean, not comforted that the status quo will be just fine. The COVID-19 pandemic will surely not be our last test, but we do have a unique opportunity to build a different way from the ashes of COVID. Will we seize it? Will our longing for "normality" at any price make us forget the pain of these years of tumult? Or will we remember what happened when everything in our society went downhill and change course to avoid future calamities? Our children need us to do this important work.

References

Abdouramane, A. (2016, April 27). How the shame of 'free-free' inspired my push for universal free lunch. *Chalkbeat*. https://ny.chalkbeat.org/2016/4/27/21098156/first-person-how-the-shame-of-free-free-inspired-my-push-for-universal-free-lunch

Adamick, K. (2012). *Lunch money: Serving healthy school food in a sick economy.* Cook for America.

Adams, T. (2012, April 21). Jamie Oliver: "Tell me Mr Gove, Mr Lansley. How can we stop Britain being the most unhealthy country in Europe?" *The Guardian.* https://www.theguardian.com/lifeandstyle/2012/apr/22/jamie-oliver-obesity-interview

Agricultural Marketing Service. (2014). *Fiscal year 2013 AMS purchases summary.* USDA. Retrieved February 16, 2014, from http://www.ams.usda.gov/AMSv1.0/ams.fetchTemplateData.do?template=TemplateJ&page=CPDAnnualPurchaseSummary

American Conservative Union. (2014). *CPAC 2014—U.S. representative Paul Ryan (R-WI)* [Video]. https://youtu.be/fiwnUaGZOdk

Anderson, J. E. (2014). *Public policymaking: An introduction* (8th ed.). Cengage Learning.

© The Editor(s) (if applicable) and The Author(s), under exclusive license to Springer Nature Switzerland AG 2022
M. B. Weaver-Hightower, *Unpacking School Lunch*,
https://doi.org/10.1007/978-3-030-97288-2

Anderson, M. L., Gallagher, J., & Ramirez Ritchie, E. (2018). School meal quality and academic performance. *Journal of Public Economics, 168*, 81–93.

Anft, M. (2010, July 10). Hard to swallow: School lunch guru Tony Geraci steps out amid dashed expectations. *Urbanite, 73*, 25, 27.

Anspach, N. M. (2021). Trumping the equality norm? Presidential tweets and revealed racial attitudes. *New Media & Society, 23*(9), 2691–2707.

Anyon, J. (2005). What counts as educational policy? Notes toward a new paradigm. *Harvard Educational Review, 75*(1), 65–88.

Apple, M. W. (1990). The text and cultural politics. *The Journal of Educational Thought, 24*(3A), 17–33.

Apple, M. W. (1995). *Education and power* (2nd ed.). Routledge.

Apple, M. W. (1996). *Cultural politics and education.* Teachers College Press.

Apple, M. W. (2000). *Official knowledge: Democratic education in a conservative age* (2nd ed.). Routledge.

Apple, M. W. (2002). Interrupting the right: On doing critical educational work in conservative times. *Symploke, 10*(1), 133–152.

Apple, M. W. (2006). *Educating the "right" way: Markets, standards, God, and inequality* (2nd ed.). Routledge.

Apple, M. W. (2009). On the tasks of the critical scholar/activist in education. In R. Winkle-Wagner, D. Henderliter Ortloff, & C. Hunter (Eds.), *Bridging the gap between theory and practice in educational research: Methods at the margins* (pp. 21–34). Palgrave.

Arnold, A. (2019, October 17). School lunch is becoming more sustainable. *FoodCorps.* https://foodcorps.org/school-lunch-is-becoming-more-sustainable/

Associated Press. (2009, November 9). Industry pushes chocolate milk in schools. *Education Week.* http://www.edweek.org/ew/articles/2009/11/09/312330usgotchocolatemilk_ap.html

Associated Press. (2010, December 2). House Republicans stall school nutrition bill. *Education Week.*

Associated Press. (2010, January 7). Baltimore teens grow veggies in portable greenhouses. *Christian Science Monitor.* https://www.csmonitor.com/The-Culture/Gardening/2010/0107/Baltimore-teens-grow-veggies-in-portable-greenhouses

Associated Press. (2011, November 16). Tomato sauce on pizza is a vegetable, says Congress; GOP says healthier school lunches are too expensive. *NY Daily News.* https://www.nydailynews.com/life-style/health/tomato-sauce-pizza-vegetable-congress-gop-healthier-school-lunches-expensive-article-1.978339

Avey, T. (2013, August 16). Discover the history of Meatless Mondays. *The History Kitchen*. https://www.pbs.org/food/the-history-kitchen/history-mea tless-mondays/

Avila, J. (2012, March 7). Pink slime and you [Television broadcast]. *ABC World News*. https://web.archive.org/web/20120311235246/https:// abcnews.go.com/WNT/video/pink-slime-15873068

Backett-Milburn, K., Wills, W., Roberts, M.-L., & Lawton, J. (2010). Food and family practices: Teenagers, eating and domestic life in differing socio-economic circumstances. *Children's Geographies, 8*(3), 303–314.

Bailey-Davis, L., Virus, A., McCoy, T. A., Wojtanowski, A., Vander Veur, S. S., & Foster, G. D. (2013). Middle school student and parent perceptions of government-sponsored free school breakfast and consumption: A qualitative inquiry in an urban setting. *Journal of the Academy of Nutrition and Dietetics, 113*(2), 251–257.

Bakst, D., & Sheffield, R. (2017, January 4). *3 steps lawmakers could take to roll back government control of school lunches*. https://www.heritage.org/gov ernment-regulation/commentary/3-steps-lawmakers-could-take-roll-back-government-control-school

Ball, S. J. (1998). Big policies/small world: An introduction to international perspectives in education policy. *Comparative Education, 34*(2), 119–130.

Ball, S. J. (2010). New states, new governance and new education policy. In M. W. Apple, S. J. Ball, & L. A. Gandin (Eds.), *The Routledge international handbook of the sociology of education* (pp. 155–166). Routledge.

Ban on sweet drinks in schools on hold. (2010, December 31). *News4JAX*. http://www.news4jax.com/print/26333658/detail.html

Barclay, E. (2009, October 27). Meatless Mondays draw industry ire. *The Atlantic*. https://www.theatlantic.com/health/archive/2009/10/meatless-mondays-draw-industry-ire/29092/

Barone, L. M. (2011, October 23). Schools exaggerate food allergy concerns. *Southtown Star*. http://southtownstar.suntimes.com/opinions/834 4879-474/schools-exaggerate-food-allergy-concerns.html

Bartfeld, J. S., Berger, L., & Men, F. (2020). Universal access to free school meals through the community eligibility provision is associated with better attendance for low-income elementary school students in Wisconsin. *Journal of the Academy of Nutrition and Dietetics, 120*(2), 210–218.

Bashinski, S. M., & Smilie, K. D. (2018). "Social consequences" of school lunch for students who receive special education services: A critical outlook. In S. Rice & A. G. Rud (Eds.), *Educational dimensions of school lunch* (pp. 135–155). Springer International Publishing.

Baskin, M. L., Ard, J., Franklin, F., & Allison, D. B. (2005). Prevalence of obesity in the United States. *Obesity Reviews, 6*(1), 5–7.

Bass, D. N. (2008, July 21). There is a free lunch—In schools. *Carolina Journal.* https://www.carolinajournal.com/news-article/there-is-a-free-lunch-in-schools/

Bass, D. N. (2010, September 10). Congress should shore up school lunch reliability. *Education Week.* https://www.edweek.org/policy-politics/opinion-congress-should-shore-up-school-lunch-reliability/2010/09

Baumgartner, F. R., & Jones, B. D. (2009). *Agendas and instability in American politics* (2nd ed., Vol. 1–Kindle e-book). University of Chicago Press.

Baumgartner, F. R., Berry, J. M., Hojnacki, M., Kimball, D. C., & Leech, B. L. (2009). *Lobbying and policy change: Who wins, who loses, and why* (ebook). University of Chicago Press.

Beauchamp, G. K. (2019). Basic taste: A perceptual concept. *Journal of Agricultural and Food Chemistry, 67*(50), 13860–13869.

Belasco, W. (2008). *Food: The key concepts.* Berg.

Belot, M., & James, J. (2011). Healthy school meals and educational outcomes. *Journal of Health Economics, 30*(3), 489–504.

Berger, M. (2004, June 6). Ronald Reagan dies at 93. *New York Times.* https://www.nytimes.com/2004/06/06/us/ronald-reagan-dies-at-93-fostered-cold-war-might-and-curbs-on-government.html

Berger, N. (1990). *The school meals service: From its beginnings to the present day.* Northcotte House.

Bernstein, B. (1977). *Class, codes and control (Volume 3: Towards a theory of educational transmissions)* (Revised ed.). Routledge & Kegan Paul.

Best, A. L. (2017). *Fast food kids: French fries, lunch lines, and social ties.* New York University Press.

Bisserbe, N. (2021, July 14). France's school lunches become battlegrounds in dispute over Islam's place in society; A push for broader rules on secularism leaves Muslim families feeling targeted. *Wall Street Journal.*

Bite Back 2030. (2021). *Spill the Beans campaign report: Students' voices on the School Food Standards.* https://biteback2030.com/sites/default/files/2021-11/Spill%20the%20Beans%20school%20report_Subbed-Digital_FINAL.pdf

Blackall, M. (2021, January 12). "What am I supposed to make with this!" Parents on schools' meagre food parcels. *The Guardian.* https://www.theguardian.com/education/2021/jan/12/what-am-i-supposed-to-make-with-this-uk-parents-on-schools-meagre-food-parcels

Blad, E. (2021a, April 20). Citing pandemic, USDA waives school meal regulations through June 2022. *Education Week.* https://www.edweek.org/leadership/citing-pandemic-usda-waives-school-meal-regulations-through-june-2022/2021a/04

Blad, E. (2021b, June 1). The pandemic brought universal free school meals. Will they stay? *Education Week.* https://www.edweek.org/leadership/the-pandemic-brought-universal-free-school-meals-will-they-stay/2021b/06

Blakemore, E. (2021, January 29). How the Black Panthers' breakfast program both inspired and threatened the government. *History Channel.* https://www.history.com/news/free-school-breakfast-black-panther-party

blk5348. (2012, September 17). *We are hungry* [Video]. https://youtu.be/2IB7NDUSBOo

Bonnett, K., Bromley, S., Jessop, B., & Ling, T. (1984). Authoritarian populism, two nations, and Thatcherism. *New Left Review, 147,* 32–60.

Bourdieu, P. (1977). *Outline of a theory of practice* (R. Nice, Trans.). Cambridge University Press.

Bourdieu, P. (1984). *Distinction: A social critique of the judgment of taste* (R. Nice, Trans.). Harvard University Press.

Boychuk, B., & Lopez, P. (2010, December 22). Head to head: Is the new school lunch law an example of government run amok? *The Sacramento Bee.* http://www.sacbee.com/2010/12/22/v-print/3274551/head-to-head-is-the-new-school.html

Brennan, P. (2014, March 6). Paul Ryan's moving story that explains the difference between hard work and dependency. *National Review.* https://www.nationalreview.com/corner/paul-ryans-moving-story-explains-difference-between-hard-work-and-dependency-patrick/

Burrows, S. (2012, February 23). DHHS defends school lunch inspections. *Carolina Journal.* https://www.carolinajournal.com/news-article/dhhs-defends-school-lunch-inspections/

Butler, P. (2013, July 12). School food: Michael Gove's remarkable socialist masterplan. *The Guardian.* https://www.theguardian.com/society/patrick-butler-cuts-blog/2013/jul/12/school-food-gove-remarkable-socialist-masterplan

Buzby, J. C., & Guthrie, J. T. (2002). *Plate waste in school nutrition programs: Final report to Congress* (E-FAN-02–009). Economic Research Service/USDA.

Buzby, J. C., Wells, H. F., & Hyman, J. (2014). *The estimated amount, value, and calories of postharvest food losses at the retail and consumer levels in the United States* (EIB-121). U. S. Department of Agriculture. https://www.ers.usda.gov/webdocs/publications/43833/43680_eib121.pdf

Cardello, H. (2010). To fight obesity, give industry a carrot. *The Atlantic.* http://www.theatlantic.com/food/archive/2010/04/to-fight-obesity-give-industry-a-carrot/39591/

Carter, P. (2012). Policy as palimpsest. *Policy & Politics, 40*(3), 423–443.

Caruso & Rosenthal. (2020). Meeting students where they eat: A qualitative study exploring k-12 student experiences of the school cafeteria. *Children, Youth and Environments, 30*(1), 101.

Cassar, E. M. (2018). Hunger and fullness: How high-poverty urban students experience school food policy. *Urban Education.*

Center for Ecoliteracy. (2013). *Rethinking school lunch: A planning framework from the Center for Ecoliteracy* (2nd ed.). Center for Ecoliteracy. www.ecolit eracy.org/sites/default/files/uploads/rethinking_school_lunch_guide.pdf

Center for Science in the Public Interest & Public Health Advocacy Institute. (2006). *Raw deal: School beverage contracts less lucrative than they seem.* Center for Science in the Public Interest. http://www.cspinet.org/beveragec ontracts.pdf

Center for Science in the Public Interest. (2007). *Sweet deals: School fundraising can be healthy and profitable.* http://www.cspnet.org/schoolfundraising.pdf

Center on Budget & Policy Priorities. (2021). *A quick guide to SNAP eligibility and benefits.* Center on Budget and Policy Priorities. https://www.cbpp.org/sites/default/files/atoms/files/11-18-08fa.pdf

Chaykin, D. (Director). (2012, May 14). *Weight of the nation* [TV Series]. HBO Documentaries.

Chicago Metropolitan Agency for Planning. (2021). *Lake view: Community data snapshot.* https://www.cmap.illinois.gov/documents/10180/126764/Lake+View.pdf

Chicago Public Schools. (2011). *Racial/ethnic report, 2010–2011.* Chicago Public Schools. https://www.cps.edu/globalassets/cps-pages/about/district-data/demographics/fy11_racial_ethnic_survey.xls

Chisolm, R. (2011). *Cafeteria man* [Film]. Recipe for Change Films.

Chisolm, R. (2012). *Cafeteria man—Memphis schools makeover* [Video]. https://vimeo.com/53221815

Chomsky, N. (1999). *Profits over people* (iBook ed.). Seven Stories Press.

Clark, L. (2010, November 13). The lunchbox police: Ofsted snooping on children's snacks and rating schools badly if they are unhealthy. *The Daily Mail.* https://www.dailymail.co.uk/news/article-1329309/Ofsted-snooping-childrens-snacks-rating-schools-badly-unhealthy.html

Clarke, J., & Newman, J. (1997). *The managerial state.* Sage.

Cohen, J. F. W., Hecht, A. A., McLoughlin, G. M., Turner, L., & Schwartz, M. B. (2021). Universal school meals and associations with student participation, attendance, academic performance, diet quality, food security, and body mass index: A systematic review. *Nutrients, 13*(3), 911.

Coleman-Jensen, A., Rabbitt, M. P., Gregory, C. A., & Singh, A. (2021). *Household food security in the United States in 2020* (ERR-298). U.S. Department of Agriculture, Economic Research Service. https://www.ers.usda.gov/webdocs/publications/102076/err-298.pdf?v=9105.3

Coles, A. D. (2000, April 1). The dairy dilemma. *Teacher Magazine, 11,* 16–17.

Colicchio, T. (2020, August 20). *How we feed our students* (No. 11). https://podcasts.apple.com/us/podcast/citizen-chef-with-tom-colicchio/id1513237410?i=1000488671702

Condon, E., Drilea, S., Lichtenstein, C., Mabli, J., Madden, E., & Niland, K. (2015). *Diet quality of American school children by National School lunch participation status: Data from the National Health and Nutrition Examination Survey, 2005–2010.* United States Department of Agriculture. http://www.fns.usda.gov/sites/default/files/ops/NHANES-NSLP05-10.pdf

Confessore, N. (2014, October 7). How school lunch became the latest political battleground. *The New York Times Magazine.* https://www.nytimes.com/2014/10/12/magazine/how-school-lunch-became-the-latest-political-battleground.html

Congressional Budget Office. (2020). *Options for reducing the deficit: 2021 to 2030.* Congressional Budget Office. https://www.cbo.gov/system/files/2020-12/56783-budget-options.pdf

Congressional Research Service. (2020). *Block grants: Perspectives and controversies* (No. R40486). Congressional Research Service. https://sgp.fas.org/crs/misc/R40486.pdf

Cook, G. (2010, July 4). The reason kids are getting fat. *Las Vegas Review-Journal.* http://www.lvrj.com/opinion/the-reason-kids-are-getting-fat-97758279.html

Cooper, A., & Holmes, L. M. (2006). *Lunch lessons: Changing the way we feed our children.* Collins.

Counihan, C. & Kaplan, S. L. (Eds.). (1998). *Food and gender: Identity and power.* Routledge.

Cox, C. (2012). *'Pink slime' will be a choice for schools.* ABC News Radio. http://abcnewsradioonline.com/health-news/pink-slime-will-be-a-choice-for-schools.html

Crosnoe, R. (2010). Obesity as an educational issue. *Teachers College Record.* http://www.tcrecord.org/Content.asp?ContentID=15924

Crumley, C. L. (1995). Heterarchy and the analysis of complex societies. *Archeological Papers of the American Anthropological Association, 6*(1), 1–5.

Davis, D., Hudson, D., & Members of the Burlington School Food Project. (2011). Going local: Burlington, Vermont's farm-to-school program. In

S. A. Robert & M. B. Weaver-Hightower (Eds.), *School food politics: The complex ecology of hunger and feeding in schools around the world* (pp. 162–182). Peter Lang.

DeCosta, P., Møller, P., Frøst, M. B., & Olsen, A. (2017). Changing children's eating behaviour—A review of experimental research. *Appetite, 113*, 327–357.

DeLeon, A. (2011). What's that nonhuman doing on your lunch tray? Disciplinary spaces, school cafeterias, and possibilities of resistance. In S. A. Robert & M. B. Weaver-Hightower (Eds.), *School food politics: The complex ecology of hunger and feeding in schools around the world* (pp. 173–190). Peter Lang.

Delpit, L. (1995). *Other people's children: Cultural conflict in the classroom.* The New Press.

Department for Education. (2013a). *Open academies, free schools, studio schools and UTCs and academy projects in development.* Department for Education. http://www.education.gov.uk/schools/leadership/typesofschools/academies/b00208569/open-academies

Department for Education. (2013b, February 1). *Expert group meet to discuss school food* [Video]. https://www.youtube.com/watch?v=TTHx_u71kC0

Department for Education. (2013c, February 21). *Leeds school food event* [Video]. https://www.youtube.com/watch?v=tmrKy1S67ps&list=UU4NkS_w8o50U6jw2oksEMxQ&index=2

Department for Education. (2021, October 5). *Guidance: Providing school meals during the coronavirus (COVID-19) outbreak.* Department for Education. https://www.gov.uk/government/publications/covid-19-free-school-meals-guidance/covid-19-free-school-meals-guidance-for-schools

Dietz, W. H. (1995). Does hunger cause obesity? *Pediatrics, 95*(5), 766–767.

Dimbleby, H., & Vincent, J. (2013). *The school food plan.* Department for Education. http://www.schoolfoodplan.com/wp-content/uploads/2013/07/School_Food_Plan_2013.pdf

Doering, C. (2013, April 10). Vilsack says he'll defend nutrition programs. *Des Moines Register.* http://www.desmoinesregister.com/article/20130410/BUSINESS01/304100073/-1/GROUPBLOGS/Vilsack-says-he-ll-defend-nutrition-programs?nclick_check=1

Dolby, N. (2015). Flint's story: Education and justice for animals. *Teachers College Record Online.* https://www.tcrecord.org/content.asp?contentid=17833

Dolby, N. (2020). Learning at noon. *Critical Education, 11*(8).

Drake, L. J., Woolnough, A., Burbano, C., & Bundy, Donald (Eds.). (2016). *Global school feeding sourcebook: Lessons from 14 countries.* Imperial College Press. https://documents.wfp.org/stellent/groups/public/documents/communications/wfp284904.pdf

Dreher, R. (2006). *Crunchy cons: How Birkenstocked Burkeans, gun-loving organic gardeners, evangelical free-range farmers, hip homeschooling mamas, right-wing nature lovers, and their diverse tribe of countercultural conservatives plan to save America (or at least the Republican Party).* Crown Forum.

Duell, M., & Levy, A. (2013, February 10). Packed lunches should be banned and all children should be taught how to cook in fight against obesity, say experts. *The Daily Mail.* https://www.dailymail.co.uk/news/article-2276402/Compulsory-cooking-lessons-proposed-pupils-drive-child-obesity.html

Earl, L. (2018). *Schools and food education in the 21st century.* Routledge.

Earl, L., & Thomson, P. (2021). *Why garden in schools?* Routledge.

Economic Research Service. (2021). *National School Lunch Program.* https://www.ers.usda.gov/topics/food-nutrition-assistance/child-nutrition-programs/national-school-lunch-program/

Edelman, M. (1988). *Constructing the political spectacle.* University of Chicago Press.

Edible Schoolyard Project. (2019). *The edible schoolyard project 2019 annual report.* https://edibleschoolyard.org/file/867325/download

Editors of Rethinking Schools. (2006). Special issue: Feeding the children: The politics of food in our schools and classrooms. *Rethinking Schools, 20*(4).

Editors. (2012). *The coolest schools in America.* Scholastic Parent & Child. http://www.scholastic.com/coolschools/

Education Committee Minutes of Evidence, HC 1786-ii, UK House of Commons, 2012–13 (2012). https://publications.parliament.uk/pa/cm201012/cmselect/cmeduc/1786ii/120424.htm

Eisner, E. W. (1992). Educational reform and the ecology of schooling. *Teachers College Record, 93*(4), 610–627.

ElBoghdady, D. (2011, November 16). USDA: Continuing to serve pizza to schoolchildren won't save much money. *Washington Post.* https://www.washingtonpost.com/business/economy/usda-continuing-to-serve-pizza-to-schoolchildren-wont-save-much-money/2011/11/16/gIQAeGPTSN_story.html

Elias, N. (2000). *The civilizing process: Sociogenetic and psychogenetic investigations* (E. Dunning, J. Goudsblom, & S. Mennell, Eds., E. Jephcott, Trans.; Rev. ed). Blackwell.

Evans, C. E. L., & Harper, C. E. (2009). A history and review of school meal standards in the UK. *Journal of Human Nutrition and Dietetics, 22*(2), 89–99.

Eyre, B. (2011, September 28). School food bans leave a bitter taste. *The Saskatoon Star Phoenix*. http://www.thestarphoenix.com/story_print.html?id=5468091&sponsor=

Fairclough, N. (1995). *Critical discourse analysis: The critical study of language*. Longman.

Fassler, J. (2019, February 7). ABC News called it "pink slime." Now, USDA says it can be labeled "ground beef." *The Counter*. https://thecounter.org/bpi-pink-slime-ground-beef-usda-reclassifed/

Fawcett-Atkinson, M. (2020, October 19). A national school lunch program would solve more than hunger, advocates say. *National Observer*. https://www.nationalobserver.com/2020/10/19/news/national-school-lunch-program-would-solve-more-hunger-advocates-say

Flegal, K. M., Carroll, M. D., Ogden, C. L., & Curtin, L. R. (2010). Prevalence and trends in obesity among US adults, 1999–2008. *JAMA, 303*(3), 235.

Foad, D. (2016). *School food plan alliance—The work goes on*. Local Area Caterers Association. https://laca.co.uk/news/school-food-plan-alliance-work-goes

Food Research & Action Center. (2019). *School breakfast scorecard: School year 2017–2018*. https://frac.org/wp-content/uploads/school-breakfast-scorecard-sy-2017-2018.pdf

Fox, L. E., & Burns, K. (2021). *The supplemental poverty measure: 2020* (No. P60–275). US Census Bureau. https://www.census.gov/content/dam/Census/library/publications/2021/demo/p60-275.pdf

Franc, M. G. (2010, July 19). The welfare script. *National Review*. https://www.nationalreview.com/2010/07/welfare-script-michael-g-franc/

Franzen, J., & Peters, B. (2019). *Say yes to pears: Food literacy in and beyond the English classroom*. National Council of Teachers of English.

Fryar, C. D., Carroll, M. D., & Afful, J. (2020a). *Prevalence of overweight, obesity, and severe obesity among children and adolescents aged 2–19 years: United States, 1963–1965 through 2017–2018*. Centers for Disease Control and Prevention. https://www.cdc.gov/nchs/data/hestat/obesity-child-17-18/obesity-child.htm

Fryar, C. D., Carroll, M. D., Ahluwalia, N., & Ogden, C. L. (2020b). *Fast food intake among children and adolescents in the United States, 2015–2018*

(No. 375; NCHS Data Brief). National Center for Health Statistics. https://www.cdc.gov/nchs/data/databriefs/db375-h.pdf

Fund, J. (2014). The "common calorie" revolt. *National Review.* http://www.nationalreview.com/article/389589/common-calorie-revolt-john-fund

Gaddis, J. E. (2019). *The labor of lunch: Why we need real food and real jobs in American public schools.* University of California Press.

Gaffigan, J. (2014). *Food: A love story.* Crown Archetype.

Garcia, N. (2011, July 15). Cafeteria workers to try "pay for performance" plan. *9News.Com.* https://www.9news.com/article/news/education/cafeteria-workers-to-try-pay-for-performance-plan/73-334796886

Garner, R. (2012, July 4). Chef wars: Michael Gove asks LEON restaurant founders to review school dinners but Jamie Oliver slams idea. *The Independent.* https://www.independent.co.uk/news/education/education-news/chef-wars-michael-gove-asks-leon-restaurant-founders-review-school-dinners-jamie-oliver-slams-idea-7911927.html

Gee, J. P. (2014). *An introduction to discourse analysis: Theory and method* (4th ed.). Routledge.

Gelles, D. (2020, September 24). Whole Foods founder: 'The whole world is getting fat.' *The New York Times.* https://www.nytimes.com/2020/09/24/business/john-mackey-corner-office-whole-foods.html

Gennetian, L. A., Seshadri, R., Hess, N. D., Winn, A. N., & Goerge, R. M. (2016). Supplemental Nutrition Assistance Program (SNAP) benefit cycles and student disciplinary infractions. *Social Service Review, 90*(3), 403–433.

Gilbert, G., & Walker, D. (Directors). (2005). *Jamie's school dinners* [TV series; DVD]. Freemantle Media.

Gillam, C. (2012, March 25). Scientist who coined "pink slime" reluctant whistleblower. *Reuters.* https://www.reuters.com/article/us-food-slime-scientist/scientist-who-coined-pink-slime-reluctant-whistleblower-idUSBRE82N0AG20120325

Giuda, K. (2012, December 6). An insecure and uninformed political class is stealing our freedoms. *Forbes.* http://www.forbes.com/sites/kellengiuda/2012/12/06/an-insecure-and-uninformed-political-class-is-stealing-our-freedoms

Gorard, S. (2012). Who is eligible for free school meals? Characterising free school meals as a measure of disadvantage in England. *British Educational Research Journal, 38*(6), 1003–1017.

Gordon, N., & Ruffini, K. (2021). Schoolwide free meals and student discipline: Effects of the community eligibility provision. *Education Finance and Policy, 16*(3), 418–442.

Gore, L. (2014, January 9). Just desserts? Bill would require White House meals to meet school food nutrition standards. *AL.Com.* https://www.al.com/breaking/2014/01/just_desserts_bill_would_requi.html

Gramsci, A. (1971). *Selections from the prison notebooks of Antonio Gramsci* (Q. Hoare & G. Nowell-Smith, Eds. & Trans.). International Publishers.

Gray, E. (2010, June 16). Panel suggests ways to improve nutrition. *Wall Street Journal.* https://www.wsj.com/articles/SB10001424052748703280004575309093112074112

Green, E. L. (2010, May 26). City schools serve up supper program. *The Baltimore Sun.*

Greene, J. L. (2012). *Lean finely textured beef: The "pink slime" controversy.* Congressional Research Service. https://nationalaglawcenter.org/wp-content/uploads/assets/crs/R42473.pdf

Gregory, P. R. (2011, November 20). Are one in five American children hungry? *Forbes.* https://www.forbes.com/sites/paulroderickgregory/2011/11/20/are-one-in-five-american-children-hungry/?sh=6209e3caeb26

Griffin, T. (2017, April 1). This mom says her son was stamped on the wrist because he ran out of lunch money. *BuzzFeed News.* https://www.buzzfeednews.com/article/tamerragriffin/lunch-money-stamp#.vyyPQqmxW

Gruenewald, D. A. (2003). The best of both worlds: A critical pedagogy of place. *Educational Researcher, 32*(4), 3–12.

Gunderson, G. W. (2013). *The National School Lunch Program: Background and development.* U. S. Department of Agriculture. http://www.fns.usda.gov/cnd/Lunch/AboutLunch/NSLP-Program%20History.pdf

Gunlock, J. (2011, October 6). Sesame Street tells a fib … about hunger. *National Review.* https://www.nationalreview.com/the-home-front/sesame-street-tells-fib-about-hunger-julie-gunlock/

Gustafson, K. (2012). *Change comes to dinner: How vertical farmers, urban growers, and other innovators are revolutionizing how America eats.* Macmillan.

Gustafson, K. S. (2011). *Cheating welfare: Public assistance and the criminalization of poverty.* New York University Press.

Gustafsson, U. (2004). The privatisation of risk in school meals policies. *Health, Risk & Society, 6*(1), 53–65.

Haberman, M. (2011, November 18). Newt: Fire the janitors, hire kids to clean schools. *Politico.* https://www.politico.com/story/2011/11/newt-fire-the-janitors-hire-kids-to-clean-schools-068729

Hall, S. (1979, January). The great moving right show. *Marxism Today*, 14–20.

Hall, S. (1985). Authoritarian populism: A reply to Jessop et al. *New Left Review, 151*, 115–124.

Handbury, J., & Moshary, S. (2021). *School food policy affects everyone: Retail responses to the National School Lunch Program*. National Bureau of Economic Research.

Hannon, J. (2006). Lessons from Ana. *Rethinking Schools, 20*, 47.

Harvey, D. (2005). *A brief history of neoliberalism*. Oxford University Press.

Harwell, M., & LeBeau, B. (2010). Student eligibility for a free lunch as an SES measure in education research. *Educational Researcher, 39*(2), 120–131.

Haskins, D. (2020, January 31). Vancouver 8-year-old raises $4,015 to pay off school lunch debt. *KGW8 News*. https://www.kgw.com/article/life/heartw arming/8-year-old-raises-4015-to-pay-off-school-lunch-debt/283-83ed4ecc-240b-470d-8577-4ab543caea8d

Haskins, R. (2005). The school lunch lobby. *Education Next, 10*(2).

Hayden-Smith, R. (2007). "Soldiers of the soil": The work of the United States School Garden Army during World War I. *Applied Environmental Education & Communication, 6*(1), 19–29.

Hecht, A. A., Pollack Porter, K. M., & Turner, L. (2020). Impact of The Community Eligibility Provision of the Healthy, Hunger-Free Kids Act on student nutrition, behavior, and academic outcomes: 2011–2019. *American Journal of Public Health, 110*(9), 1405–1410.

Helms, A. D. (2011, January 2). Lunch data debate growing. *Charlotte Observer*. http://www.charlotteobserver.com/2011/01/02/v-print/1949537/lunch-data-debate-growing.html

Hill, M. (2012, September 14). School lunch rules for healthier meals get mixed reviews from students. *Huffington Post*. Internet Archive Wayback Machine. https://web.archive.org/web/20120918213236/, http://www.huffingtonpost.com/2012/09/14/mixed-grades-for-new-heal_n_1883763.html

Hinrichs, P. (2010). The effects of the National School Lunch Program on education and health. *Journal of Policy Analysis and Management, 29*(3), 479–505.

Hoar, W. P. (2010, June 8). Feeding insatiable government appetite won't end obesity. *The New American*. http://www.thenewamerican.com/index.php/usnews/politics/3729-feeding-insatiable-government-appetite-wont-end-obesity

Hochschild, A. R. (1985). *The managed heart: Commercialization of human feeling*. University of California Press.

Hochschild, A. R. (2003). *The second shift*. Penguin Books.

Hojjat, T. A. (2021). *The economics of obesity: Poverty, income inequality, and health*. Springer International.

Hood, J., & Eng, M. (2011, January 26). Chicago approves free breakfasts for all elementary students. *Chicago Tribune.* https://www.chicagotribune.com/news/ct-xpm-2011-01-26-ct-met-mandatory-school-breakfast-012201 10126-story.html

Horan, T. (2012, November 10). Food fight: One size does not fit all. *Abilene Reflector Chronicle.* http://www.abilene-rc.com/printer_friendly/20782173/

Hornby, N. (Director).(2006). *Jamie's return to school dinners* [Television broadcast]. Channel 4.

House Budget Committee Majority Staff. (2014). *The war on poverty: 50 years later: A House Budget Committee report.* Republicans of the House of Representatives Budget Committee. https://republicans-budget.house.gov/upload edfiles/war_on_poverty.pdf

House, S. (2021). Elegy for a school: The lunch ladies were my first role models in social justice. *Gravy, 81.* https://www.southernfoodways.org/elegy-for-a-school/

Hovde, E. (2010, August 22). Is there a better way to get healthy meals in students? *OregonLive.Com.* https://www.oregonlive.com/hovde/2010/08/is_there_a_better_way_to_get_h.html

Inness, S. A. (Ed.). (2001). *Cooking lessons: The politics of gender and food.* Rowman & Littlefield.

Institute of Medicine. (2005). *Dietary reference intakes for water, potassium, sodium, chloride, and sulfate* (p. 10925). National Academies Press.

Institute of Medicine. (2006). *Food marketing to children and youth: Threat or opportunity?* The National Academies Press.

Institute of Medicine. (2010). *School meals: Building blocks for healthy children.* The National Academies Press.

Interagency Working Group on Food Marketed to Children. (2011). *Preliminary proposed nutrition principles to guide industry self-regulatory efforts: Request for comments.* Federal Trade Commission. https://www.ftc.gov/sites/default/files/documents/public_events/food-marketed-children-forum-int eragency-working-group-proposal/110428foodmarketproposedguide.pdf

Jackson, P. W. (1968). *Life in classrooms.* Holt.

Jhally, S. (Director). (2003). *Captive audience: Advertising invades the classroom* [Film]. Media Education Foundation.

Johnson, B. (2011, August 5). Enough to make you lose your appetite. *The Washington Times.* http://www.washingtontimes.com/news/2011/aug/5/eno ugh-to-make-you-lose-your-appetite

Johnson, C. (2014, January 23). Senator Hoeven visits Century Elementary to discuss changes to the National School Lunch Program. *WDAZ News.* http://www.wdaz.com/event/article/id/22089/

Johnson, R. (2012, September 18). Parody video questions national school lunch policy. *KWCH News.* Internet Archive Wayback Machine. https://web.archive.org/web/20120922091707/http://articles.kwch.com/2012-09-18/school-lunches_33932920

Jolly, J. (2021, February 4). Firm in "unacceptable" school meals row to pay for half-term provision. *The Guardian.* https://www.theguardian.com/education/2021/feb/04/firm-in-meagre-free-school-meals-row-to-pay-for-half-term-provision-compass-marcus-rashford

Jordan, M. (2012, July 14). The big war over a small fruit. *Wall Street Journal,* C1.

Jost, J. T., Federico, C. M., & Napier, J. L. (2009). Political ideology: Its structure, functions, and elective affinities. *Annual Review of Psychology, 60*(1), 307–337.

Kalafa, A. (Director). (2007). *Two angry moms* [Film]. A-RAY Productions.

Kang, M. O. (2011). Free for all, organic school lunch programs in South Korea. In S. A. Robert & M. B. Weaver-Hightower (Eds.), *School food politics: The complex ecology of hunger and feeding in schools around the world* (pp. 120–142). Peter Lang.

Karasouli, E., Latchford, G., & Owens, D. (2014). The impact of chronic illness in suicidality: A qualitative exploration. *Health Psychology and Behavioral Medicine, 2*(1), 899–908.

Kasperowicz, P. (2012, September 17). GOP bill would repeal Agriculture Dept. calorie caps on school lunches. *The Hill.* https://thehill.com/blogs/floor-action/house/249849-rep-king-pushes-to-repeal-usdas-calorie-cap-at-school-lunch?fbclid=IwAR2dUjEuo7o6uwg_mcrRyBOu7K_w5cOLMzx0ZFQjyIjkeTCNILXB9cUfR9k

Katz, M. B. (1990). *The undeserving poor: From the war on poverty to the war on welfare.* Pantheon Books.

Kawamoto, D. (2010, November 2). Spud wars: Potato farmers prepare to battle new USDA guidelines. *DailyFinance.* http://www.dailyfinance.com/story/spud-wars-potato-farmers-prepare-to-battle-new-usda-guidelines/19688208/

Kenner, R. (Director). (2008). *Food, Inc* [Film]. Participant Media.

Kerns, K. (2012, February 22). Have Americans become too timid to make simple decisions? *The Laurel Outlook.* http://www.laureloutlook.com/opinion/columns/article_67d49a2a-5d7d-11e1-9090-0019bb2963f4.html

Kerwick, J. (2013). The neoconservative conundrum. *Modern Age*, *55*(1/2), 5–12.

Kessler, G. (2014, March 6). A story too good to check: Paul Ryan and the tale of the brown paper bag. *The Washington Post*. http://www.washingto npost.com/blogs/fact-checker/wp/2014/03/06/a-story-too-good-to-check-paul-ryan-and-the-story-of-the-brown-paper-bag/

Kimmett, C. (2011, September 7). On nutrition, Canada's schools are out to lunch. *The Tyee*. https://thetyee.ca/News/2011/09/07/Canada-School-Lun ches/

Komisar, L. (2011, December 3). How the food industry eats your kid's lunch. *New York Times*. https://www.nytimes.com/2011/12/04/opinion/sunday/sch ool-lunches-and-the-food-industry.html

Kozlowski, K. P., & Lauen, D. L. (2019). Understanding teacher pay for performance: Flawed assumptions and disappointing results. *Teachers College Record*, *121*(2), 1–38.

Kraus-Polk, J., & Hamerschlag, K. (2021). *The state of school lunch in California: Opportunities for improving the health and environmental profile of school food*. Friends of the Earth. https://1bps6437gg8c169i0y1drtgz-wpengine.netdna-ssl.com/wp-content/uploads/2021/03/SchoolFoodRe port_No-Execsummary.pdf

Kumashiro, K. K. (2012). *Bad teacher!* Teachers College Press.

Lalli, G. S. (2020). *Schools, food and social learning*. Routledge.

Lalli, G. S. (2021). A review of the English school meal: 'Progress or a recipe for disaster'? *Cambridge Journal of Education*, *51*(5), 627–639.

Lappé, F. M. (1971). *Diet for a small planet*. Ballantine Books.

Las Vegas Review-Journal editorial board. (2011, December 24). A failed experiment with healthy school meals. *Las Vegas Review-Journal*. https:// www.reviewjournal.com/opinion/editorials/a-failed-experiment-with-hea lthy-school-meals/

Lateef, H., & Androff, D. (2017). "Children can't learn on an empty stomach": The Black Panther party's free breakfast program. *Journal of Sociology and Social Welfare*, *44*(4), 3–17.

Lautenschlager, J. L. (2006). *Food fight! The battle over the American lunch in schools and the workplace*. McFarland.

Leggott, J., & Hochssherf, T. (2010). From the kitchen to 10 Downing Street: Jamie's School Dinners and the politics of reality cooking. In J. A. Taddeo & K. Dvorak (Eds.), *The tube has spoken: Reality TV and history* (pp. 47–64). University Press of Kentucky.

LEON. (2013). *LEON dinner menu.* Accessed 4 Mar 4 2013, from http://leo nrestaurants.co.uk/downloads/dinner_menu.pdf

Levine, S. (2008). *School lunch politics: The surprising history of America's favorite welfare program.* Princeton University Press.

Lindblom, C. E. (1959). The science of "muddling through." *Public Administration Review, 19*(2), 79–88.

Lingard, B., & Douglas, P. (1999). *Men engaging feminisms: Pro-feminism, backlashes, and schooling.* Open University Press.

Linnane, R. (2021, August 25). Every eligible Wisconsin school district is providing all students free meals this year. Except Waukesha. *Milwaukee Journal Sentinel.* https://www.jsonline.com/story/news/education/2021/08/25/waukesha-students-there-really-no-such-thing-free-lunch/5573671001/

Liu, J., Micha, R., Li, Y., & Mozaffarian, D. (2021). Trends in food sources and diet quality among US children and adults, 2003–2018. *JAMA Network Open, 4*(4), e215262.

Loeb, K. L., Craigen, K. E., Goldstein, M. M., Lock, J., & Grange, D. L. (2011). Early treatment for eating disorders. In D. Le Grange & J. Lock (Eds.), *Eating disorders in children and adolescents: A clinical handbook* (pp. 337–361). Guilford Press.

Lomawaima, K. T., & McCarty, T. L. (2006). *To remain an Indian: Lessons in democracy from a century of Native American education.* Teachers College Press.

Ludvigsen, A., & Scott, S. (2009). Real kids don't eat quiche: What food means to children. *Food, Culture & Society, 12*(4), 417–436.

Lundborg, P., Rooth, D.-O., & Alex-Petersen, J. (2021). Long-term effects of childhood nutrition: Evidence from a school lunch reform. *The Review of Economic Studies* [online first].

Lusk, J. (2013). *The food police: A well-fed manifesto about the politics of your plate.* Crown Forum.

Lusk, J. L. (2012). The political ideology of food. *Food Policy, 37*(5), 530–542.

Lyall, M. (2013, January). Are we eating our words about the School Food Plan? *Educatering,* 38–39.

Lyons, R. (2010, September 8). Britain's neverending school-meals saga. *Spiked.* https://www.spiked-online.com/2010/09/08/britains-neverending-school-meals-saga/

MacKendrick, N. (2014). Foodscape. *Contexts, 13*(3), 16–18.

Mader, J. (2010). *Cleveland school gardens.* Arcadia Publishing.

Malkin, M. (2010, February 3). SEIU fat cats behind first lady's anti-obesity campaign. *Real Clear Politics.* https://www.realclearpolitics.com/articles/2010/02/03/seiu_fat_cats_behind_first_ladys_anti-obesity_campaign_1 00144.html

Mattinson, A. (2013, March 22). Headland to lead LEON restaurants' DfE-commissioned school meals campaign. *PR Week*. https://www.prweek.com/article/1175669/headland-lead-leon-restaurants-dfe-commissioned-school-meals-campaign

May, L., Standing, K., Chu, A., Gasper, J., & Riley, J. (2014). *Special nutrition program operations study: State and school food authority policies and practices for school meals programs school year 2011–12.* U.S. Department of Agriculture. https://fns-prod.azureedge.net/sites/default/files/SNOPSYear1.pdf

McChesney, R. W. (1998). Introduction. In N. Chomsky (Ed.), *Profits over people: Neoliberalism and global order* (iBook ed., pp. 6–16). Seven Stories Press.

McGee, K. (2015, April 20). Fried food in school cafeterias: "It's about freedom and liberty," says Ag Commissioner. *KUT 90.5*. http://kut.org/post/fried-food-school-cafeterias-its-about-freedom-and-liberty-says-ag-commissioner

McNulty, I. (2008, September 30). "Rethinking" school lunch. *My New Orleans*. https://www.myneworleans.com/rethinking-school-lunch/

Meadows, M. (2017). *First 100 days: Rules, regulations, and executive orders to examine, revoke, and issue.* https://meadows.house.gov/first-100-days

Media Matters. (2010, December 3). Conservative media rail against efforts to ensure safe and healthy food. *The Indypendent*. https://indypendent.org/2010/12/conservative-media-rail-against-efforts-to-ensure-safe-and-healthy-food/

Michael Gove doesn't give a s*** about school meals, says Jamie Oliver. (2012, November 27). *Evening Standard*. https://www.standard.co.uk/showbiz/celebrity-news/michael-gove-doesn-t-give-a-s-about-school-meals-says-jamie-oliver-8360010.html

Millimet, D. L., Tchernis, R., & Husain, M. (2010). School nutrition programs and the incidence of childhood obesity. *Journal of Human Resources, 45*(3), 640–654.

Mission: Readiness. (2010). *Too fat to fight: Retired military leaders want junk food out of America's schools.* Mission: Readiness. http://cdn.missionreadiness.org/MR_Too_Fat_to_Fight-1.pdf

Mission: Readiness. (2018). *Unhealthy and unprepared: National security depends on promoting healthy lifestyles from an early age.* Council for a Strong America. https://strongnation.s3.amazonaws.com/documents/484/389765e0-2500-49a2-9a67-5c4a090a215b.pdf?1539616379&inline;%20filename=%22Unhealthy%20and%20Unprepared%20report.pdf%22

Mitchell, C. (2020, April 15). As demand for food grows under coronavirus, schools step up. *Education Week*. https://www.edweek.org/leadership/as-demand-for-food-grows-under-coronavirus-schools-step-up/2020/04

Molnar, A., & Boninger, F. (2015). *Sold out: How marketing in school threatens children's well-being and undermines their education.* Rowman & Littlefield.

Molnar, A., & Boninger, F. (2020). The commercial transformation of America's schools. *Phi Delta Kappan, 102*(2), 8–13.

Molnar, A., Boninger, F., & Fogarty, J. (2011). *The educational cost of schoolhouse commercialism—The fourteenth annual report on schoolhouse commercializing trends: 2010–2011.* National Education Policy Center. http://nepc.colorado.edu/publication/schoolhouse-commercialism-2011

Montessori, M. (2004). *The Montessori method: The origins of an educational innovation, including an abridged and annotated edition of Maria Montessori's* The Montessori Method (G. L. Gutek, Ed.). Rowman & Littlefield Publishers.

Montour, L. (2015). *Nizhónígo ííná: Cooking with Navajo traditional foods.* STAR School. https://static.prod01.ue1.p.pcomm.net/greenschoolsalliance/user_content/files/000/002/2804/5fcfd0763beb99d476ad9773cd60506b-star-nizhonigo-iina-recipe-book-editedpb-1.pdf

Mooney, C. (2012). *The Republican brain: The science of why they deny science and reality.* Wiley.

Morgan, K., & Sonnino, R. (2008). *The school food revolution: Public food and the challenge of sustainable development.* Earthscan.

Mull, T. (2017, February 24). Why cutting back 'free' school lunches would be a favor to families. *The Hill.* https://thehill.com/blogs/pundits-blog/education/321021-why-cutting-back-free-school-lunches-would-be-a-favor-to

Murray, E. B. (2018). *Grits: A cultural and culinary journey through the South.* St. Martin's Press.

National Dairy Council. (2015). *Fluid milk in school meal programs.* National Dairy Council. https://www.usdairy.com/getmedia/68cd4cf2-eb2f-4851-a3df-397894994290/school%20milk%20report.pdf.pdf.aspx

National Institutes of Health. (2021a). *Calcium fact sheet for health professionals.* National Institutes of Health. https://ods.od.nih.gov/factsheets/Calcium-HealthProfessional/

National Institutes of Health. (2021b). *Potassium fact sheet for health professionals.* National Institutes of Health. https://ods.od.nih.gov/factsheets/Potassium-HealthProfessional/

National Institutes of Health. (2021c). *Vitamin D fact sheet for health professionals.* National Institutes of Health. https://ods.od.nih.gov/factsheets/VitaminD-HealthProfessional/

Neal, B., & Perry, D. (1991). *Good old grits cookbook: Have grits your way.* Workman.

Nelson, M., Nicholas, J., Riley, K., & Wood, L. (2012). *Seventh annual survey of take-up of school lunches in England*. School Food Trust & Local Area Caterers Association. https://www.researchgate.net/publication/242311950

Nestle, M. (2007). *Food politics: How the food industry influences nutrition and health* (Revised and expanded ed.). University of California Press.

New healthier school lunches will take longer and cost more. (2013). *WSPA News.* http://www.wspa.com/story/21500264/new-healthier-school-lunches-will-take-longer-and-cost-more

Ngo, M. (2021, September 27). No veggies, no buns, few forks: Schools scramble to feed students amid shortages. *New York Times.* https://www.nytimes.com/2021/09/27/us/politics/schools-labor-supply-shortages.html

Nicholas, J., Wood, L., Harper, C., & Nelson, M. (2013). The impact of the food-based and nutrient-based standards on lunchtime food and drink provision and consumption in secondary schools in England. *Public Health Nutrition, 16*(6), 1052–1065.

Nixon, R. M. (1969). *Special message to the Congress recommending a program to end hunger in America.* http://www.presidency.ucsb.edu/ws/?pid=2038

Nocella, A. J., Ducre, K. A., & Lupinacci, J. (Eds.). (2017). *Addressing environmental and food justice toward dismantling the school-to-prison pipeline: Poisoning and imprisoning youth.* Palgrave Macmillan.

Nord, M., Coleman-Jensen, A., Andrews, M., & Carlson, S. (2010). *Household food security in the United States in 2009* (No. 108). U. S. Department of Agriculture. https://www.ers.usda.gov/webdocs/publications/44776/7024_e rr108_1_.pdf?v=5410.2

Norris, C. (2011, September 11). Feds: No child's lunch left behind. *World News Daily.* https://www.wnd.com/2011/09/344081/

O'Neil, C. E., & Nicklas, T. A. (2008). A review of the relationship between 100% fruit juice consumption and weight in children and adolescents. *American Journal of Lifestyle Medicine, 2*(4), 315–354.

O'Neill, B. (2011, August 26). This jihad against junk food is driven by naked snobbery for the lifestyles of the lower orders. *The Daily Telegraph.* http://blogs.telegraph.co.uk/news/brendanoneill2/100102199/this-jihad-against-junk-food-is-driven-by-naked-snobbery-for-the-lifestyles-of-the-lower-ord ers/

Obama, M. (2012). *American grown: The story of the White House kitchen garden and gardens across America.* Crown Publishers.

Office of Senator John Hoeven. (2014). *Hoeven touts permanent flexibility in school lunch program at Century Elementary.* https://www.hoeven.senate.gov/news/news-releases/hoeven-touts-permanent-flexibility-in-school-lunch-pro gram-at-century-elementary

Ogden, C. L., Carroll, M. D., Curtin, L. R., Lamb, M. M., & Flegal, K. M. (2010). Prevalence of high body mass index in U.S. children and adolescents, 2007–2008. *Journal of the American Medical Association, 303*(3), 242–249.

Ogden, J., Reynolds, R., & Smith, A. (2006). Expanding the concept of parental control: A role for overt and covert control in children's snacking behaviour? *Appetite, 47*(1), 100–106.

Ogle, M. (2013). *In meat we trust: An unexpected history of carnivore America* (ebook). Houghton Mifflin Harcourt.

Olusoga, D., & Olusoga, P. (2020, December 22). What Marcus Rashford's campaign for hungry children tells us about the footballer—and Britain. *The Guardian.* https://www.theguardian.com/lifeandstyle/2020/dec/22/what-marcus-rashfords-campaign-for-hungry-children-tells-us-about-the-footballer-and-britain

Osowski, C. P., & Sydner, Y. M. (2020). Traditional or cultural relativist school meals? The construction of religiously sanctioned school meals on social media. In U. Gustafsson, R. O'Connell, A. Draper, & A. Tonner (Eds.), *What is food? Researching a topic with many meanings* (pp. 72–86). Routledge.

Osowski, C. P., Göranzon, H., & Fjellström, C. (2013). Teachers' interaction with children in the school meal situation: The example of pedagogic meals in Sweden. *Journal of Nutrition Education and Behavior, 45*(5), 420–427.

Owens, E. (2014, August 23). Now Michelle Obama has caused America's 'best cafeteria cookie' to be outlawed. *Daily Caller.* https://dailycaller.com/2014/08/23/now-michelle-obama-has-caused-americas-best-cafeteria-cookie-to-be-outlawed/

Paarlberg, R. (2010). *Food politics: What everyone needs to know.* Oxford University Press.

Palin, S. [@SarahPalinUSA]. (2010, November 9). *2 PA school speech; I'll intro kids 2 beauty of laissez-faire via serving them cookies amidst school cookie ban debate* [Tweet]. Twitter. https://twitter.com/sarahpalinusa/status/2054576433795072?lang=en

Park, E., & Graziano, M. (Directors). (2011). *Lunch line* [Film]. Uji Films.

Patel, R. (2007). *Stuffed and starved: Markets, power, and the hidden battle for the world food system.* Portobello Books.

Pham, S. (2010, December 15). Food, obesity, and regulation: Simmering culture war boils over. *ABC News.* http://abcnews.go.com/CleanPrint/cleanprintproxy.aspx?1292599317864

Phillips, N. (2016, May 2). What happened to the School Food Plan? *Schools Week*. https://schoolsweek.co.uk/what-happened-to-the-school-food-plan/

Pike, J., & Kelly, P. (2014). *The moral geographies of children, young people, and food: Beyond* Jamie's School Dinners. Palgrave Macmillan.

Pinke, K. (2013, March 2). Call to action: Sensible School Lunches Act [Blog]. *The Pinke Post*. http://thepinkepost.com/2013/03/call-to-action-sensible-school-lunches-act/

Plant, M. (2020, December 31). Marcus Rashford's inspirational 2020. *Manchester United News*. https://www.manutd.com/en/news/detail/timeline-of-marcus-rashfords-charity-work-and-awards-in-2020

Poe, T. (2014, September 9). *Feds cook up new rules for school bake sales* [Video]. YouTube. https://youtu.be/LycTSl8gsU4

Pollan, M. (2006). *The Omnivore's dilemma: A natural history of four meals*. Penguin Books.

Pollan, M. (2008). *In defense of food: An eater's manifesto*. Penguin Press.

Poole, M. K., Musicus, A. A., & Kenney, E. L. (2020). Alignment of US school lunches with the EAT-Lancet healthy reference diet's standards for planetary health. *Health Affairs, 39*(12), 2144–2152.

Poore, J., & Nemecek, T. (2018). Reducing food's environmental impacts through producers and consumers. *Science, 360*(6392), 987–992.

Popkin, B. (2009). *The world is fat: The fads, trends, policies, and products that are fattening the human race*. Avery.

Popovich, D., McAlhany, A., Adewumi, A. O., & Barnes, M. M. (2009). Scurvy: Forgotten but definitely not gone. *Journal of Pediatric Health Care, 23*(6), 405–415.

Poppendieck, J. (2010). *Free for all: Fixing school food in America*. University of California Press.

Portnoy, H. (2010, December 17). New poll: Americans oppose First Lady's new childhood nutrition law. *The Examiner*. http://www.examiner.com/libertarian-in-national/sesame-street-character-pushes-michelle-obama-s-food-police-law

Portnoy, H. (2011). Michelle Obama's MyPlate food guide a spectacular failure. *HotAir*. Retrieved December 27, 2011, from http://hotair.com/greenroom/archives/2011/12/21/michelle-obamas-myplate-food-guide-a-spectacular-failure/

Powell, D., & Gard, M. (2015). The governmentality of childhood obesity: Coca-Cola, public health and primary schools. *Discourse: Studies in the Cultural Politics of Education, 36*(6), 854–867.

Powell, L. M., Nguyen, B. T., & Han, E. (2012). Energy intake from restaurants: Demographics and socioeconomics, 2003–2008. *American Journal of Preventative Medicine, 43*(5), 498–504.

Preece, R. (2012, July 15). Michael Gove "went on holiday to Moroccan villa with top chef he later commissioned to carry out school meals review." *Daily Mail.* https://www.dailymail.co.uk/news/article-2173810/Michael-Gove-facing-heat-Marrakech-villa-holiday-Leon-chef-asked-improve-school-meals.html

Radke, A. (2012, August 27). New USDA school lunches lack protein power. *Beef Magazine.* https://www.beefmagazine.com/blog/new-usda-school-lunches-lack-protein-power

Ralston, K., Newman, C., Clauson, A., Guthrie, J., & Buzby, J. (2008). *The National School Lunch Program: Background, trends, and issues* (Economic Research Report Number 61). US Department of Agriculture.

Ralston, K., Treen, K., Coleman-Jensen, A., & Guthrie, J. (2017). *Children's food security and USDA child nutrition programs* (Economic Information Bulletin Number 174). US Department of Agriculture. https://www.ers.usda.gov/webdocs/publications/84003/eib-174.pdf?v=1823.3

Ralston. (2011). It takes a garden project: Dewey and Pudup on the politics of school gardening. *Ethics and the Environment, 16*(2), 1.

Rashford, M. (2020, June 15). Open letter to all MPs in Parliament. *The Guardian.* https://www.theguardian.com/football/2020/jun/15/protect-the-vulnerable-marcus-rashfords-emotional-letter-to-mps

Rashford, M. [@MarcusRashford]. (2020, March 19). *Guys, across the UK there are over 32,000 schools. Tomorrow all of these will close. Many of the children attending* [Tweet]. Twitter. https://twitter.com/marcusrashford/status/1240698652475002880?s=21

Rauzon, S., Wang, M., Studer, N., & Crawford, P. (2010). *An evaluation of the School Lunch Initiative: Final report.* https://edibleschoolyard.org/file/865260/download?token=0pl-PJz2

Rawal, S. (2020). *Gather* [Film]. Monument Releasing. http://gather.film

Rector, R. (2007). *How poor are America's poor? Examining the "plague" of poverty in America.* Heritage Foundation. https://www.heritage.org/poverty-and-inequality/report/how-poor-are-americas-poor-examining-the-plague-poverty-america

Rector, R. (2014, September 23). The war on poverty: 50 years of failure. *Heritage Foundation.* https://www.heritage.org/marriage-and-family/commentary/the-war-poverty-50-years-failure

Rice, S. (2013). Three educational problems: The case of eating animals. *Journal of Thought, 48*(2), 112–127.

Richardson, H. (2013, February 15). Horsemeat found in some school dinners. *BBC News.* https://www.bbc.com/news/education-21475337

Riley, N. S. (2017, September 15). In New York, there's no alternative to a free school lunch. *Wall Street Journal.*

Ritchie, M. (2010, October 8). Mind over platter. *Times Educational Supplement.* https://www.tes.com/news/mind-over-platter

Robert, S. A., & Weaver-Hightower, M. B. (Eds.). (2011). *School food politics: The complex ecology of hunger and feeding in schools around the world.* Peter Lang.

Roberts, P. (2008). *The end of food* (iBook ed.). Mariner Books.

Roden, G. (2014, September 11). School lunch revival (No. 6) [Television broadcast]. In *Food Forward.* PBS.

Rogers, D. (2014, May 19). House GOP releases ag budget. *Politico.* https://www.politico.com/story/2014/05/house-gop-agriculture-budget-white-house-106831

Rosenthal, A. (2011, November 16). It's delicious. But is it a vegetable? [Blog]. *New York Times: Taking Note: The Editorial Page Editor's Blog.* https://takingnote.blogs.nytimes.com/2011/11/16/its-delicious-but-is-it-a-vegetable/

Ruetz, A. T., & McKenna, M. L. (2021). Characteristics of Canadian school food programs funded by provinces and territories. *Canadian Food Studies, 8*(3), 70–106.

Ruis, A. R. (2017). *Eating to learn, learning to eat: The origins of school lunch in the United States.* Rutgers University Press.

Rutledge, J. G. (2016). *Feeding the future: School lunch programs as global social policy.* Rutgers University Press.

Sabatier, P. A. (2007). *Theories of the policy process* (2nd ed.). Westview Press.

Samuels, C. A. (2010, December 13). Obama signs long-awaited school lunch bill. *Education Week.* https://www.edweek.org/leadership/obama-signs-long-awaited-school-lunch-bill/2010/12

Sandler, J. (2011). Reframing the politics of urban feeding in U.S. Public schools: Parents, programs, activists, and the state. In S. A. Robert & M. B. Weaver-Hightower (Eds.), *School food politics: The complex ecology of hunger and feeding in schools around the world* (pp. 25–45). Peter Lang.

Schanzenbach, D. W. (2009). Do school lunches contribute to childhood obesity? *Journal of Human Resources, 44*(3), 684–709.

Scheier, L. M. (2005). What is the hunger-obesity paradox? *Journal of the American Dietetic Association, 105*(6), 883–885.

Schencker, L. (2014, January 30). Lunches seized from kids in debt at Salt Lake City elementary. *Salt Lake Tribune.* https://archive.sltrib.com/article.php?id=57468293&itype=CMSID

Schlosser, E. (2001). *Fast food nation: The dark side of the all-American meal.* Houghton Mifflin Company.

School food campaign update. (2012, July 4). JamieOliver.com *Campaigns.* https://www.jamieoliver.com/features/school-food-campaign-latest/

School Food Plan Alliance. (2017, May 23). *The School Food Plan Alliance responds to the manifesto announcement regarding Universal Infant Free School Meals.* Food for Life. https://www.foodforlife.org.uk/whats-happening/news/news-post/the-school-food-plan-alliance-response

School Food Plan Alliance. (2020). *School food checklist for COVID-19.* https://www.unison.org.uk/content/uploads/2020/06/School-Food-Plan-Alliance-checklist-for-COVID-19.pdf

School Food Plan. (2015). *School food standards: A practical guide for schools their cooks and caterers.* http://www.schoolfoodplan.com/wp-content/uploads/2015/01/School-Food-Standards-Guidance-FINAL-V3.pdf

School Food Plan. (2016a). *School Food Plan Alliance.* School Food Plan. http://www.schoolfoodplan.com/sfp-alliance/

School Food Plan. (2016b). *Academy free school sign ups.* http://www.schoolfoodplan.com/wp-content/uploads/2016b/04/Academy-Free-School-sign-ups-31_03_16.pdf

School Food Trust. (2008a). *The impact of primary school breakfast clubs in deprived areas of London.* http://www.childrensfoodtrust.org.uk/assets/research-reports/sft_breakfast_club_findings_dec08.pdf

School Food Trust. (2008a). *A fresh look at the school meal experience.* School Food Trust. http://www.fhf.org.uk/meetings/2008b-07-08_SFT_school_meal_experience.pdf

School Food Trust. (2008b). *A guide to introducing the Government's food-based and nutrient-based standards for school lunches.* School Food Trust.

School Food Trust. (2008c). *The impact of primary school breakfast clubs in deprived areas of London.* http://www.childrensfoodtrust.org.uk/assets/research-reports/sft_breakfast_club_findings_dec08.pdf

School Food Trust. (2009a). *A fresh look at marketing school food.* School Food Trust.

School Food Trust. (2009b). *School lunch and learning behaviour in primary schools: An intervention study.* http://www.schoolfoodtrust.org.uk/partners/reports/school-lunch-and-learning-behaviour-in-primary-schools-an-intervention-study

School Food Trust. (2009c). *Research summary: Primary school food survey 2009*. http://www.schoolfoodtrust.org.uk/UploadDocs/Library/Doc uments/sft_primary_school_food_survey_2009c.pdf

School Food Trust. (2009d). *School lunch and learning behaviour in secondary schools: An intervention study*. http://www.schoolfoodtrust.org.uk/partners/ reports/school-lunch-and-learning-behaviour-in-secondary-schools-an-int ervention-study

School Food Trust. (2012a). *Food and academies: A qualitative study*. School Food Trust. http://www.childrensfoodtrust.org.uk/assets/research-rep orts/Food_and_Academies_-_a_qualitative_study4.pdf

School Food Trust. (2012b). *Food and drink provision in secondary academies in England: A telephone survey*. School Food Trust. http://www.childrensfoo dtrust.org.uk/assets/research-reports/Academies_telephone_survey_May_ 2012b.pdf

School Food Trust. (2012c). *A further analysis of secondary school food provision and consumption, England, 2010–2011*. School Food Trust. http://www.childrensfoodtrust.org.uk/assets/research-reports/Second ary_school_food_study_analysis_acad_vs_other.pdf

School Meals Review Panel. (2005). *Turning the tables: Transforming school food*. Department for Education and Skills.

School Nutrition Association. (2008). *Little big fact book: The essential guide to school nutrition*. School Nutrition Association.

School Nutrition Association. (2009). *School nutrition operations report: The state of school nutrition 2009*. School Nutrition Association.

School Nutrition Association. (2013). *Little big fact book: The essential guide to school nutrition* (2013 ed.). School Nutrition Association.

School Nutrition Association. (2018). *School nutrition operations report: The state of school nutrition 2018: Executive summary*. School Nutrition Associa- tion. https://schoolnutrition.org/uploadedFiles/6_News_Publications_and_ Research/8_SNA_Research/2018-Operations-Report-Exec-Summary.pdf

School Nutrition Association. (2019a). *2019 School nutrition trends report [summary]*. School Nutrition Association. https://schoolnutrition.org/upl oadedFiles/6_News_Publications_and_Research/8_SNA_Research/2019a- school-nutrition-trends-summary.pdf

School Nutrition Association. (2019b). *The power of we! 2018–19 annual report*. https://schoolnutrition.org/uploadedFiles/About_SNA/Ove rview/SNA-2018-19-Annual-Report.pdf

School Nutrition Association. (2020). *Eliminate the reduced-price category (ERP)*. School Nutrition Association. https://schoolnutrition.org/uploadedF iles/Legislation_and_Policy/SNA_Policy_Resources/2020-ERP-Fact.pdf

School Nutrition Association. (2021). School Nutrition *rates and requirements*. https://schoolnutrition.org/uploadedFiles/2._Meetings_and_Events/ SN_Magazine/Pages/SN-Rates-Specs-for-Print-Publications.pdf

School Nutrition Association. (n.d.). *SNA member talking points on unpaid meal charges*. https://schoolnutrition.org/uploadedFiles/Legislation_and_Pol icy/State_and_Local_Legislation_and_Regulations/Unpaid-Meal-Charge-Talking-Points.docx

Schram, S., Soss, J., & Fording, R. C. (Eds.). (2003). *Race and the politics of welfare reform*. University of Michigan Press.

Schwartz, A. E., & Rothbart, M. W. (2020). Let them eat lunch: The impact of universal free meals on student performance. *Journal of Policy Analysis and Management, 39*(2), 376–410.

Schwartz, D. S. (2022). Recovering the lost general welfare clause. *William & Mary Law Review, 63*(3), 857-938.

Scrinis, G. (2013). *Nutritionism: The science and politics of dietary advice* (Kindle ebook). Columbia University Press.

Severns, M., & Parti, T. (2014, March 11). Food fight starting early over school lunch rules. *Politico*. https://www.politico.com/story/2014/03/food-fight-sta rting-early-over-school-lunch-rules-104528

Severson, K. (2010, August 25). A school fight over chocolate milk. *The New York Times*, p. D3.

Shaffer, C. T. (2012, May 13). Hysteria wins, and consumers lose. *Lebanon Daily News*.

Sheffey, A. (2021, August 27). A Wisconsin school district says students can "become spoiled" with free meals and opts out of Biden's free-lunch program. *Business Insider*. https://www.businessinsider.com/waukesha-school-district-says-free-school-meals-spoil-students-2021-8

Shoichet, C. E. (2014, January 31). At Utah school, there really was no such thing as a free lunch. *CNN*. https://www.cnn.com/2014/01/30/us/utah-sch ool-lunches-snatched/index.html

Shoup, M. E. (2017, October 26). School Milk Nutrition Act of 2017 aims to lift declining milk consumption among US students. *DairyReporter*. https://www.dairyreporter.com/Article/2017/10/26/School-Milk-Nutrition-Act-of-2017-aims-to-lift-declining-milk-consumption-among-US-students

Siegel, B. E. (2017, April 30). Shaming children so parents will pay the school lunch bill. *New York Times.* https://www.nytimes.com/2017/04/30/well/family/lunch-shaming-children-parents-school-bills.html

Siegel, B. E. (2019). *Kid food: The challenge of feeding children in a highly processed world.* Oxford University Press.

Sinclair, W. (1981, September 9). Q: When is ketchup a vegetable? A: When tofu is meat. *Washington Post.* https://www.washingtonpost.com/archive/politics/1981/09/09/q-when-is-ketchup-a-vegetable-a-when-tofu-is-meat/7d305f0c-3cc9-480a-a119-e9307dd5ff91/

Singer, J. (2011, April 19). The unwise war against chocolate milk. *Wall Street Journal.* https://online.wsj.com/article/SB10001424052748704004004576270773639365188.html

Smith, B. (Director). (2010). *Jamie Oliver's food revolution* [TV series]. American Broadcasting Corporation (ABC).

Smith, D. (2011, September 11). Why can't lunch just be lunch? *Mystic River Press.* http://www.thewesterlysun.com/mysticriverpress/news/why-cant-lunch...lunch/article_0c6ca5f6-dad8-11e0-bc13-001cc4c002e0.html

Smith, M. D. (2014, May 22). What white privilege looks like when you're poor. *The Nation.* https://www.thenation.com/article/archive/what-white-privilege-looks-when-youre-poor/

Smith, M. L. (2004). *Political spectacle and the fate of American schools.* RoutledgeFalmer.

Smits, D. D. (1994). The Frontier Army and the destruction of the buffalo: 1865–1883. *The Western Historical Quarterly, 25*(3), 312.

Sole-Smith, V. (2021, September 21). Please stop romanticizing your child's lunchbox: Universal free school lunch could save us all, but diet culture is getting in the way [Blog]. *Burnt Toast.* https://virginiasolesmith.substack.com/p/please-stop-romanticizing-your-childs

STAR School. (2019, October 23). *STAR School core values.* STARschool.Org. https://sites.google.com/starschool.org/newsite/about/philosophy/star-core-values

Stewart, K., & Cole, M. (2009). The conceptual separation of food and animals in childhood. *Food, Culture & Society, 12*(4), 457–476.

Stockholm International Peace Research Institute. (2021). *SIPRI military expenditure database 2021.* https://www.sipri.org/databases/milex

Storey, H. C., Pearce, J., Ashfield-Watt, P. A., Wood, L., Baines, E., & Nelson, M. (2011). A randomized controlled trial of the effect of school food and dining room modifications on classroom behaviour in secondary school children. *European Journal of Clinical Nutrition, 65*(1), 32–38.

Stuart, M. (2010, November 7). EPA mandates will sour school lunches. *South Florida Sun-Sentinel*. http://sun-sentinel.com/news/opinion/fl-school-lunch-forum-1107%E2%80%9320101107,0,6609869.story

Suprynowicz, V. (2010, December 10). Choosing 'profusion and servitude' over 'economy and liberty.' *Las Vegas Review-Journal*. http://www.review journal.com/columns-blogs/vin-suprynowicz/choosing-profusion-and-servit ude-over-economy-and-liberty

Taber, D. R., Chriqui, J. F., Powell, L., & Chaloupka, F. J. (2013). Association between state laws governing school meal nutrition content and student weight status: Implications for new USDA school meal standards. *JAMA Pediatrics, 167*(6), 513–519.

Tach, L., & Edin, K. (2017). The social safety net after welfare reform: Recent developments and consequences for household dynamics. *Annual Review of Sociology, 43*(1), 541–561.

Taibbi, M. (2012, August 29). Greed and debt: The true story of Mitt Romney and Bain Capital. *Rolling Stone*. https://www.rollingstone.com/politics/pol itics-news/greed-and-debt-the-true-story-of-mitt-romney-and-bain-capital-183291/

Talbot, M. (2013, August 8). Obesity lessons for liberals and conservatives. *The New Yorker*. https://www.newyorker.com/news/daily-comment/obesity-lessons-for-liberals-and-conservatives

Tanner, M., & Hughes, C. (2013). *The work vs. welfare trade-off: 2013*. Cato Institute. https://www.cato.org/sites/cato.org/files/pubs/pdf/the_work_versus_welfare_trade-off_2013_wp.pdf

Tanumihardjo, S. A., Anderson, C., Kaufer-Horwitz, M., Bode, L., Emenaker, N. J., Haqq, A. M., Satia, J. A., Silver, H. J., & Stadler, D. D. (2007). Poverty, obesity, and malnutrition: An international perspective recognizing the paradox. *Journal of the American Dietetic Association, 107*(11), 1966–1972.

Taras, H. (2005). Nutrition and student performance at school. *Journal of School Health, 75*(6), 199–213.

Tarkalson, M. (2012, December 18). It is my responsibility to feed my children not the government's. *Times-News*. https://magicvalley.com/hold/article_6 4d9b8df-d4c9-5f03-b459-a2f6543c76d8.html

Taylor, K. (2020, August 31). Federal government relaxes rules on feeding low-income students. *New York Times*. https://www.nytimes.com/2020/08/31/us/schools-food-coronavirus.html

Tennant, M. (2010, December 6). House passes school nutrition bill that is no treat. *The New American.* http://www.thenewamerican.com/index.php/usnews/congress/5397-house-passes-school-nutrition-bill-that-is-no-treat

Terkel, A. (2014, January 23). Rep. Jack Kingston proposes that poor students sweep floors in exchange for lunch. *Huffington Post.* https://www.huffpost.com/entry/jack-kingston-school-lunch_n_4467711

Terry-McElrath, Y. M., Turner, L., Sandoval, A., Johnston, L. D., & Chaloupka, F. J. (2014). Commercialism in US elementary and secondary school nutrition environments: Trends from 2007 to 2012. *JAMA Pediatrics, 168*(3), 234.

Theobald, B. (2014, October 14). Ariz. students eat their vegetables at the White House. *AZ Central.* https://www.azcentral.com/story/news/politics/2014/10/15/ariz-students-eat-vegetables-white-house/17288903/

Thompson, C. B. (2011, March). Neoconservatism unmasked. *Cato Unbound: A Journal of Debate.* https://www.cato-unbound.org/2011/03/07/c-bradley-thompson/neoconservatism-unmasked

Timotijevic, L., Barnett, J., & Raats, M. M. (2011). Engagement, representativeness and legitimacy in the development of food and nutrition policy. *Food Policy, 36*(4), 490–498.

Trapp, M. M. (2018). The right to taste: Conceptualizing the nourishing potential of school lunch. *Food and Foodways, 26*(1), 1–22.

Truman, E., Lane, D., & Elliott, C. (2017a). Defining food literacy: A scoping review. *Appetite, 116*, 365–371.

Truman, E., Raine, K., Mrklas, K., Prowse, R., Hoed, R. C. D., Watson-Jarvis, K., Loewen, J., Gorham, M., Ricciardi, C., Tyminski, S., & Elliott, C. (2017b). Promoting children's health: Toward a consensus statement on food literacy. *Canadian Journal of Public Health, 108*(2), e211–e213.

U.S. CattleTrace. (2021). *Meet our staff* [Web Page]. https://www.uscattletrace.org/ourstaff

U.S. Department of Agriculture. (2012). *School Nutrition Dietary Assessment Study-IV* (CN-12-SNDA). U. S. Department of Agriculture.

U.S. Department of Agriculture. (2016). *Strategies for successful implementation of the healthy, hunger-free kids Act: Plate waste.* U.S. Department of Agriculture, Food and Nutrition Service. https://fns-prod.azureedge.net/sites/default/files/ops/HHFKA-PlateWaste.pdf

U.S. Department of Agriculture. (2017). *Ag Secretary Perdue moves to make school meals great again* [Press release]. U. S. Department of Agriculture. https://www.usda.gov/media/press-releases/2017/05/01/ag-secretary-perdue-moves-make-school-meals-great-again

U.S. Department of Agriculture. (2019). *School nutrition and meal cost study: Summary of findings*. U. S. Department of Agriculture. https://fns-prod.azu reedge.net/sites/default/files/resource-files/SNMCS_Summary-Findings.pdf

U.S. Department of Agriculture. (2020). *Dietary guidelines for Americans: 2020 - 2025* (9th ed.). United States Department of Agriculture. https:// www.dietaryguidelines.gov/sites/default/files/2021-03/Dietary_Guidelines_ for_Americans-2020-2025.pdf

U.S. Department of Agriculture. (2021a). *Farm to school census and comprehensive review summary report*. U. S. Department of Agriculture. https://fns-prod.azureedge.net/sites/default/files/resource-files/Farm-to-School-Census-Comprehensive-Review-Summary.pdf

U.S. Department of Agriculture. (2021b). *Federal cost of school food programs*. https://fns-prod.azureedge.net/sites/default/files/resource-files/cncost-10.pdf

U.S. Department of Agriculture. (2021c). *National School Lunch Program: Commodity costs*. U. S. Department of Agriculture. https://fns-prod.azuree dge.net/sites/default/files/resource-files/07slcomm$-9.pdf

U.S. Department of Agriculture, Food and Nutrition Service, Office of Policy Support. (2019). *School nutrition and meal cost study, final report volume 1: School meal program operations and school nutrition environments*. U. S. Department of Agriculture. https://fns-prod.azureedge.net/sites/default/ files/resource-files/SNMCS-Volume1.pdf

U.S. Department of Agriculture & U.S. Department of Health and Human Services. (2010a). *Dietary guidelines for Americans, 2010*. Government Printing Office.

United Nations General Assembly. (1948). *Universal declaration of human rights*. United Nations. https://www.un.org/en/about-us/universal-declar ation-of-human-rights

United Nations General Assembly. (1989). *Convention on the rights of the child*. United Nations. https://www.ohchr.org/EN/ProfessionalInterest/ Pages/CRC.aspx

US House of Representatives. (2010). *Expressing the support of the House of Representatives for the goals and ideals of the National School Lunch Program., no. H. Res. 362, 111th Congress (2010)*. https://www.govinfo.gov/app/det ails/BILLS-111hres362eh/summary

US teacher suspended over chicken nugget spat. (2012, March 7). *News.com.au*. https://www.news.com.au/breaking-news/us-teacher-sus pended-over-chicken-nugget-spat/news-story/87c3c61b804c8ba950d83bfc b8d29c2d

USA Today Staff. (2012, September 25). Students push back on new school lunches. *USA Today.* https://www.usatoday.com/story/news/nation/2012/09/25/kids-school-lunch/1592947/

Vanyo, B. (2014). Regulating school lunch oversteps government's authority. In R. D. Lankford, Jr. (Ed.), *At issue: Should the government regulate what people eat?* Greenhaven Press.

Vileisis, A. (2008). *Kitchen literacy: How we lost knowledge of where food comes from and why we need to get it back.* Island Press.

Vonthron, S., Perrin, C., & Soulard, C.-T. (2020). Foodscape: A scoping review and a research agenda for food security-related studies. *PLOS ONE, 15*(5), e0233218.

Walker, P. (2013, January 30). Fears over school meal standards as children's food charity loses funding. *The Guardian.* https://www.theguardian.com/education/2013/jan/30/fears-school-meal-standards-charity

Wall Street Journal editorial board. (2009, August 1). The fat of the land: A soda pop tax and government health care won't cure obesity. *Wall Street Journal.* https://www.wsj.com/articles/SB10001424052970203609204574316022329001200

Wall Street Journal editorial board. (2011). Not so grrrreat! *Wall Street Journal, 258*(6), A14.

Wall Street Journal editorial board. (2021, April 28). Biden's cradle-to-grave government; his latest $1.8 trillion plan rejects the old social contract of work for benefits. *Wall Street Journal.*

Walljasper, C. (2021, April 14). Biden to cancel Trump's pandemic food aid after high costs, delivery problems. *Reuters.* https://www.reuters.com/article/us-health-coronavirus-food-aid-insight/biden-to-cancel-trumps-pandemic-food-aid-after-high-costs-delivery-problems-idUSKBN2C11CY

Wang, R. (2012, October 12). Kids create parody video to protest school lunches. *Time.* https://newsfeed.time.com/2012/10/01/kids-create-parody-video-to-protest-school-lunches/

Wansink, B. (2007). *Mindless eating: Why we eat more than we think.* Bantam Books.

Waters, A. (2008). *Edible Schoolyard: A universal idea.* Chronicle Books.

Weale, S. (2020, October 21). Marcus Rashford clashes with Tory MPs over free school meals. *The Guardian.* https://www.theguardian.com/education/2020/oct/21/marcus-rashford-clashes-with-tory-mps-over-free-school-meals

Weaver, C. M., & Miller, J. W. (2017). Challenges in conducting clinical nutrition research. *Nutrition Reviews, 75*(7), 491–499.

Weaver-Hightower, M. B. (2008a). An ecology metaphor for educational policy analysis: A call to complexity. *Educational Researcher, 37*(3), 153–167.

Weaver-Hightower, M. B. (2008b). Inventing the "all-American" boy: A case study in the capture of boys' education issues by conservative groups. *Men and Masculinities, 10*(3), 267–295.

Weaver-Hightower, M. B. (2008c). *The politics of policy in boys' education: Getting boys "Right."* Palgrave Macmillan.

Weaver-Hightower, M. B. (2011a). Fixing up lunch ladies, dinner ladies and canteen managers: Cases of school food reform in the United States, England and Australia. In S. A. Robert & M. B. Weaver-Hightower (Eds.), *School food politics: The complex ecology of hunger and feeding in schools around the world* (pp. 46–70). Peter Lang.

Weaver-Hightower, M. B. (2011b). Why educational researchers should take school food seriously. *Educational Researcher, 40*(1), 15–21.

Weaver-Hightower, M. B. (2012, February 1). The case for partisanship in rewriting ESEA. *Education Week*, 22–23.

Weaver-Hightower, M. B., & Robert, S. A. (2011). School food politics. In S. A. Robert & M. B. Weaver-Hightower (Eds.), *School food politics: The complex ecology of hunger and feeding in schools around the world* (pp. 1–22). Peter Lang.

Weinstein, J. N., Geller, A., Negussie, Y., Baciu, A., & National Academies of Sciences, Engineering, and Medicine (Eds.). (2017). *Communities in action: Pathways to health equity.* The National Academies Press.

Weissmann, S. (2019, April 17). A silly lawsuit over school lunches. *Wall Street Journal.*

Welsh, J., & MacRae, R. (1998). Food citizenship and community food security: Lessons from Toronto, Canada. *Canadian Journal of Development Studies, 19*(4), 237–255.

West, M. G. (2011, March 18). Donor of the day: Promoting healthy eating. *Wall Street Journal*, p. A25.

Whitaker, M. (2014, March 12). Paul Ryan blames poverty on lack of work ethic in inner cities. *MSNBC*. https://www.msnbc.com/politicsnation/ryan-generations-men-not-working-msna284561

Wickramasinghe, K. K., Rayner, M., Goldacre, M., Townsend, N., & Scarborough, P. (2016). Contribution of healthy and unhealthy primary school meals to greenhouse gas emissions in England: Linking nutritional data and greenhouse gas emission data of diets. *European Journal of Clinical Nutrition, 70*(10), 1162–1167.

Wilking, C. (2014). *Copycat snacks in schools*. The Public Health Advocacy Institute. https://www.phaionline.org/wp-content/uploads/2014/05/PHAI-Copy-Cat-Snacks-Issue-Brief-FINAL.pdf

Willett, W., Rockström, J., Loken, B., Springmann, M., Lang, T., Vermeulen, S., Garnett, T., Tilman, D., DeClerck, F., Wood, A., Jonell, M., Clark, M., Gordon, L. J., Fanzo, J., Hawkes, C., Zurayk, R., Rivera, J. A., De Vries, W., Majele Sibanda, L., ... Murray, C. J. L. (2019). Food in the Anthropocene: The EAT–Lancet commission on healthy diets from sustainable food systems. *The Lancet, 393*(10170), 447–492.

William J. Clinton Foundation. (2010). *Press release: Beverage industry delivers on commitment to remove regular soft drinks in schools, driving 88% decline in calories*. https://www.clintonfoundation.org/main/news-and-media/press-releases-and-statements/press-release-beverage-industry-delivers-on-commitment-to-remove-regular-soft-dr.html

Williamson, V. (2017, June 8). How much do the poor actually pay in taxes? Probably more than you think. *PBS News Hour*. https://www.pbs.org/newshour/economy/column-much-poor-actually-pay-taxes-probably-think

Wilson, B. (2008). *Swindled: The dark history of food fraud, from poisoned candy to counterfeit coffee*. Princeton University Press.

Wilson, J. J. (2011, October 31). Enjoy Halloween candy despite the food cops. *Washington Examiner*. https://www.washingtonexaminer.com/enjoy-halloween-candy-despite-the-food-cops

Wittaker, F. (2020, March 31). Coronavirus: DfE confirms plans for £15-a-week free school meal vouchers. *Schools Week*. https://schoolsweek.co.uk/coronavirus-dfe-confirms-plans-for-15-a-week-free-school-meal-vouchers/

Woldow, D. (2012, September 25). Cafeteria man Tony Geraci: Hype or hope? *Beyond Chron*. https://beyondchron.org/cafeteria-man-tony-geraci-hype-or-hope/

Wolfgang, B. (2011, May 16). 'Healthier' school lunch at what cost? *The Washington Times*. https://www.washingtontimes.com/news/2011/may/16/healthier-school-lunch-at-what-cost/

Woodward, S. (1978). *It's grits* [Video; originally 16 mm film]. Folkstreams. https://www.folkstreams.net/film-detail.php?id=335

World Food Programme. (2013). *State of school feeding worldwide 2013*. World Food Programme. http://www.wfp.org/content/state-school-feeding-worldwide-2013

World Food Programme. (2020). *State of school feeding worldwide 2020*. World Food Programme. https://docs.wfp.org/api/documents/WFP-0000123923/download/

World Health Organization. (2017, September 28). *Prevalence of overweight among adults, BMI ≥ 25, crude, estimates by country.* World Health Organization. https://apps.who.int/gho/data/node.main.BMI25C?lang=en

Wu, S. (2011). *Fed up with lunch: How one anonymous teacher revealed the truth about school lunches—And how we can change them!* Chronicle Books.

Yee, V. (2012, October 5). No appetite for good-for-you school lunches. *New York Times.* http://www.nytimes.com/2012/10/06/nyregion/healthier-school-lunches-face-student-rejection.html

Zhang, J. (2007, April 26). Proposal would tighten school-food standards. *Wall Street Journal,* D6.

Index

© The Editor(s) (if applicable) and The Author(s), under exclusive
license to Springer Nature Switzerland AG 2022
M. B. Weaver-Hightower, *Unpacking School Lunch*,
https://doi.org/10.1007/978-3-030-97288-2

94, 105, 136, 139, 141, 151,
154, 155, 157, 160, 209
heterarchies 60, 195–197
high fructose corn syrup 106
history of school meals
England 183–84
United States 41–53
Hoeven, John 148, 155–156, 158
holiday hunger (school breaks) 245
horse meat scandal (England) 182
Huelskamp, Tim 139, 157, 158
human rights 86, 223, 234
hunger. *See* food insecurity
hunger-obesity paradox 88
hypocrisy 142, 206

identity 2, 21, 24, 32, 96, 97
immigration 127, 152
incentives 18, 82, 84, 117,
132–133, 237
income verification. *See* eligibility
for free and reduced-price
meals, certification
incrementalism 25, 51, 53, 77, 78,
154, 210
India 37
indirect costs 105
industry-sponsored research 75, 146
information access 80, 83, 120, 180,
194
internal tensions in political
ideologies 60–61, 83, 103–104
international school feeding
programs 35–37
Iowa 157
Italy 36, 37

J

Jamie's School Dinners 165, 171,
184, 187
Jefferson, Thomas 89
Johnson, Boris 163, 188, 198, 245,
246
juice 6

K

Kansas 156, 157
ketchup as a vegetable 50, 154. *See
also* pizza as a vegetable
King, Steve 157, 158
kosher 70, 234

L

labeling 28, 29, 83, 223
lactose intolerance 124
large city districts 216–218
lean finely textured beef. *See* pink
slime
leaving campus for lunch 166, 177,
182
LEON restaurants 176, 178, 179,
199
Let's Move! program 51
lobbying 8, 53, 74, 105, 129, 142,
146, 237
Local Area Caterers' Association 196
local control 57, 90, 94, 134, 139,
148, 195
local food 214, 215, 233, 238
lunch shaming 105, 112, 144,
201–203, 221, 222, 228, 239.
See also stigma

CPSIA information can be obtained
at www.ICGtesting.com
Printed in the USA
BVHW050134140123
656283BV00023BA/412